Turkey

D0947849

The birth of Recep Tayyip Erdoğan's 'New Turkey' is a textbook example of the rise of the 'illiberal democracies' that authoritarian governments all around the world are creating through the erosion of civil rights and press freedoms, the separation of powers and the independence of the judicial system. Yet each country has done this in its own particular way – and each has found its own distinctive form of resistance. Turkey was always a complex country, long before the rise of its new Ottomanist sultan; established as a nation state just a hundred years ago from the ashes of a multi-ethnic, multi-religious empire, the republic still has to deal with the artificially secular and homogenous identity imposed by the 'father' of the nation, Kemal Atatürk, who visited unspeakable suffering upon anyone unwilling to conform to his definition of Turkishness. The conflict between the Kemalist legacy and Erdoğan's political Islam is just one of the many unresolved contradictions in a divided country that has gone through one crisis after another over the past decade, from narrowly avoiding a coup to a series of terrorist attacks and wars both within and beyond its borders. By one means or another, Erdoğan's cynical and corrupt government has always succeeded in overcoming the difficulties it has created for itself, thanks in part to a fierce repression of dissent and the use of the state's resources for its own ends – one striking example being the development of infrastructure projects based not only on an economic case but also less noble motives such as the erasure of history, as has happened to the ancient Kurdish city of Hasankeyf, now flooded by the backed-up waters of the Tigris from a dam further downstream. But there is also hope for a different Turkey, one that gains strength from its own diversity, keeping alive the spirit of 2013's Gezi Park demonstrations, the most exciting protest movement in the country's history. Resistance takes many forms, often individual, but is everywhere: women rising up against men who love them 'to death', minorities trying to take back control of their culture through dialogue with the Turkish majority, cartoonists defying censorship, rappers giving voice to a generation silenced by government-promoted consumerism and even football fans setting aside their rivalries – even if only for a moment – to join in the fight against the common enemy.

1

Contents

The photographs in this issue were taken by **Nicola Zolin**, a photojournalist and writer based in Venice, Athens and Istanbul. His work aims to investigate the social and environmental transformations on the frontiers between Europe, the Middle East and Asia, while asking questions about the way people around the world compete for natural resources and the meaning that each population assigns to freedom, from young people to utopians to migrants in search of a better life. He is the author of a book, *I passeggeri della terra* (Alpine Studio, 2016), and his articles and features have been published in the likes of *Stern*, *6Mois*, *Politico*, *Al Jazeera*, *Vice*, *Der Spiegel*, *La Repubblica*, *Le Parisien*, *Corriere della Sera*, *El Mundo*, *De Standaard*, *Aftenposten*, *Internazionale*, *Süddeutsche Zeitung*, *The Caravan*, *La Croix* and *Left*. His projects have been nominated for prizes including the Bayeux Calvados-Normandy Award for war correspondents (2019), the Festival of Ethical Photography Award (2016, 2018) and the Tokyo Foto Awards (2018).

Turkey in Numbers

EUROPEAN MEDIA LITERACY INDEX

The index measures citizens' ability to access the media and critically evaluate its different aspects in European countries.

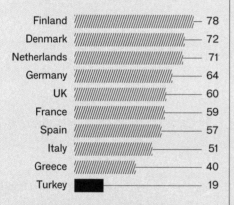

Finland	78
Denmark	72
Netherlands	71
Germany	64
UK	60
France	59
Spain	57
Italy	51
Greece	40
Turkey	19

SOURCE: OPEN SOCIETY INSTITUTE SOFIA

WORKING HARD

Percentage of people who work more than 60 hours in their main job each week; global ranking.

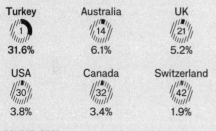

Turkey	Australia	UK
1	14	21
31.6%	6.1%	5.2%

USA	Canada	Switzerland
30	32	42
3.8%	3.4%	1.9%

SOURCE: OECD

ISTANBUL VS. LONDON

—— Istanbul ---- London

Million people

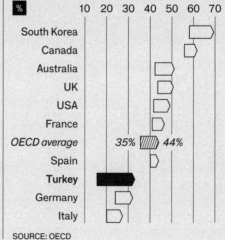

18				
14				
10				
6				
2				
1950	1970	1990	2010	2030

SOURCE: MACROTRENDS

HIGHER EDUCATION

Percentage of people between 25 and 34 undertaking higher education, 2008 → 2018.

%	10 20 30 40 50 60 70
South Korea	
Canada	
Australia	
UK	
USA	
France	
OECD average	35% ⟶ 44%
Spain	
Turkey	
Germany	
Italy	

SOURCE: OECD

MILITARY MIGHT

The Turkish Army has the second-highest number of active troops in NATO.

 = 50,000 troops

1 USA
1,348,400

2 Turkey
355,200

3 France
202,700

4 Germany
178,600

5 Italy
174,500

6 UK
146,650

SOURCE: WIKIPEDIA

TIME FOR TEA

Consumption per capita

1
**Turkey
(3.16 kg)**

2
Republic
of Ireland
(2.19 kg)

3
UK
(1.94 kg)

4
Russia
(1.34 kg)

5
Morocco
(1.22 kg)

SOURCE: WIKIPEDIA

HAZELNUTS

515

thousand tonnes
produced
in Turkey in 2018.
Ferrero buys
a third of Turkey's
output to make
Nutella.

SOURCE: FAO AND NYT

REFUGEES

4.1

million refugees
living in Turkey
in 2020. Since 2014
Turkey has taken
in more refugees
than any other
country.

SOURCE: UNHCR

CENSORSHIP

Number of legal
requests for removal
of content from
Twitter over six
months (January–
June 2019).

Turkey
— 6,073

Japan
— 5,144

Russia
— 3,810

South Korea
— 1,670

India
— 504

SOURCE: TWITTER

ALLIES?

Percentage of public in favour of NATO or otherwise.

○ Unfavourable ● Favourable   ⋮⋮ NATO members' average

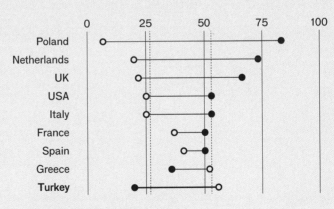

SOURCE: PEW RESEARCH CENTER

The National Obsession: *Rakı* and *Çay*

KALEYDOSKOP
Translated by Alan Thawley

During the Global Alcohol Policy Symposium held by the World Health Organization in Istanbul in April 2013, the then prime minister, Recep Tayyip Erdoğan, stated that, 'Our national drink is *ayran* not *rakı*,' contrasting the drink made from yoghurt, water and salt with the spirit distilled from grapes and flavoured with aniseed. His claim led to weeks of irreverently ironic commentary in newspapers and on social media that might well still be going on today had not the Gezi Park protests broken out a month later.

Known as 'lion's milk' and the 'national liquor', Turkish *rakı* is a relative of Greek *ouzo* and French *pastis* but not to be confused with the Balkan fruit brandy *rakija*. According to the journalist and food expert Mehmet Yaşın it is 'the most important element of Turkish culture'. Drinking *rakı* involves any number of rules and rituals that are tacitly shared and scrupulously respected. You would not, for example, drink *rakı* alone at the bar – in fact, many cocktail bars and pubs do not even serve it – and, if you were to do so, it would be because you want to draw attention to yourself, because you are particularly desperate or because you're a foreigner. *Rakı* is drunk in company, at a leisurely pace, accompanied by food – not a full meal, rather *rakı* is imbibed with a series of small dishes, meze, which are mainly, but not exclusively, cold and might include vegetables in olive oil, fresh cheese, marinated fish, sauces, fruit … This is because the food accompanies the drink rather than vice versa, so you need dishes that will not spoil if left on the table for a few hours.

Meze culture has echoes of Greek and Armenian cuisine – not surprising, given that many of the taverns in which *rakı* was drunk, known as *meyhaneler*, literally wine houses, were run by the empire's non-Muslims, the perfect *meyhaneci*. The rules of the *rakı masası*, or *rakı* table, cover not just hygiene and cuisine but also codes of conduct. Ideally the table is not too crowded, although the number of guests can grow over the course of an evening, with the conversation revolving around anecdotes and personal experiences, politics, literature and, when the company isn't mixed, sex. Even though there was no law explicitly prohibiting women from entering a meyhane, there was talk of a *kadın tabusu*, a taboo on women, and women were not allowed into traditional meyhanes until the early years of the republic. Things began to change in Greek-owned establishments in the late 1940s, and from the 1950s women from the Turkish intellectual elite became regular visitors. However, it wasn't until the 1970s that women's presence in meyhanes became socially accepted more generally, at which point they took on their current incarnation as 'restaurants with alcohol'.

Music also plays a role at the *rakı masası*. In a 2019 encyclopaedia devoted to the music of the meyhane, the author Murat Meriç explains how the music changed depending on the political climate and the period: rock, pop, arabesk, folk music and alaturka (traditional Ottoman classical music, the oldest accompaniment to *rakı*). The *Rakı Ansiklopedisi* ('Encyclopaedia of Rakı', 2011), which features contributions from dozens of writers and journalists, devotes a whole section to arabesk, which is defined as follows: 'A musical genre combining elements of traditional Turkish music, Arabic, Indian and Western pop and classical music. Perceived as a social phenomenon since it emerged in the 1960s, it became the natural accompaniment to wine and *rakı*.'

Raki was once the drink of choice for all classes of society, thanks to its affordability compared with imported liquors, but over the last decade the price has risen disproportionally, putting it out of the reach of many, particularly younger people, among whom meyhane culture is less popular than it was for previous generations. The luxury tax, which is applied twice a year, went up by 600 per cent between 2009 and 2019, and almost 75 per cent of the cost of a seventy centilitre 'big bottle' is made up of taxes of one kind or another. The trend in consumption has been inversely proportional: down from forty-five million litres annually in 2012 to thirty-eight million in 2019. But there is also another factor in the mix: making

KALEYDOSKOP — *Turchia, cultura e società* ('Turkey, Culture and Society') is an Italian online magazine and cultural association providing news and promoting a deeper understanding of contemporary Turkey. The magazine's subject areas range from cinema to literature and photography to satire. In addition, Kaleydoskop organises events in Italy and Turkey. Founded in 2017, it is run by a team consisting of Lea Nocera, Valentina Marcella, Carlotta De Sanctis and Giulia Ansaldo. The regular features in this issue of *The Passenger* have been curated by Kaleydoskop.

rakı at home has become increasingly popular among those unable to give it up. These home-brews are rarely made using a proper distillation process, however, and in most cases simply involve flavouring ethanol with aniseed and sugar. This practice became so widespread that in a bid to combat it the government passed a law in late 2017 making it mandatory for any ethanol sold to the public to have denatonium benzoate added, which gives the alcohol an unpleasant taste.

While the public ritual of *raki* drinking is heavily codified, the way it is consumed can be personalised, becoming a badge of distinction and individuality. Single, double, neat, with water on the side, with water in the glass, with one or two ice cubes, in a narrow, tall *rakı* glass, in a squat, tulip-shaped tea glass ...

It is often advised, following the second or third *rakı*, to take a break with a glass of hot tea before continuing. Which leads us on to another essential element in Turkish culinary and social culture, tea, *çay*, which is also shrouded in numerous rules and rituals for preparation and production: tea bag or loose leaf, weak or strong, Turkish or smuggled?

The tea industry in Turkey was a state monopoly until 1984 and is still mainly produced by Çaykur, a state-run enterprise that accounts for almost half the country's production, with forty-six processing plants and a packing plant in the Black Sea Region between Rize, Trabzon, Giresun and Artvin. But there has always been a huge trade in *kaçak çay*, smuggled tea. When the market was opened up to private companies and imports in 1984, *kaçak çay* – traditionally Ceylon tea transported from Sri Lanka by mule train through Iran, Iraq and Syria – became legal. This tea had long been prized for its large leaves that infuse quickly and deliver a strong, zesty taste, producing a pleasingly dark-coloured drink. Today it remains the most popular and most widely consumed tea in the east

and southeast of the country, where people still call it *kaçak* even though it is no longer contraband.

Despite the fact that imported tea has now been legally available for almost forty years, the smuggling routes have remained open; with estimated annual imports of more than forty thousand tonnes, *kaçak çay* accounts for a significant proportion of the 250,000 tonnes of tea consumed annually in the country. The branding that identifies Ceylon tea produced in Sri Lanka, a lion in profile brandishing a sword, has been pirated and used on illegally imported tea – from Iran in particular, which is now the main producer and supplier for the smuggled product in Turkey – as well as illicitly produced domestic tea. The practice has become so widespread that in August 2019 the Sri Lankan Ministry of Agriculture formally complained about the improper use of the logo in Turkey.

For obvious economic reasons the authorities have tried to crack down on the consumption of *kaçak çay*, from customs confiscations – an average of two thousand tonnes a year – to periodic pronouncements on the alleged health risks caused by the unregulated use of pesticides by producers and even alarmist stories claiming that smuggled tea is dyed with pigs' blood to give it that rich, deep colour. To try to counter the trade in illegal imports, in 2014 Çaykur even made an (unsuccessful) attempt to come up with a product with the same taste characteristics as the *kaçak* variety.

For the nationalist palate *kaçak çay* is a poor match for Turkish cuisine, something that has been discussed in newspaper articles on the subject, but in the southeast – that is, in the majority-Kurdish areas of the country – boycotting the state manufacturer is also part of the struggle for identity, and the almost exclusive consumption of *kaçak çay* is not just to do with taste or geography but also politics.

The Icon:
Bülent Ersoy, 'The Diva'

KALEYDOSKOP

Translated by Alan Thawley

Thick black hair, eyes ringed with eyeliner, a small nose, a full mouth and an eccentric taste in clothes: Bülent Ersoy – known since her gender-reassignment surgery by her nickname 'Diva' – is a musical icon, described by the journalist Pınar Öğünç as a 'singer of traditional Turkish music, alaturka, with an exceptional voice, an unrivalled ability to interpret and a personality to match'.

Born Bülent Erkoç in the city of Malatya in 1952, the Diva has left an indelible mark on the history of music in Turkey. She grew up with her family in Istanbul and says she began studying music at the age of three, taking lessons at the conservatoire from important composers such as Rıdvan Aytan. Her public debut came in 1970, and she recorded her first album a year later before turning twenty. Throughout the 1970s she performed in meyhanes and *gazinos*, venues licensed for alcohol consumption and offering live music, where she met some of the great names of traditional Turkish classical singing such as Müzeyyen Senar and Zeki Müren. She became one of the famous faces at Istanbul's prestigious Maksim Gazinosu as well as starring in numerous films towards the end of the 1970s and into the 1980s, appearances that document how she was gradually transforming physically. In August 1980, a month before the military coup in Turkey, in response to the audience's ovation during a concert at the Izmir International Fair, she revealed her breasts, a shocking act for the time and following which the public prosecutor opened an investigation. After insulting the judge sent to notify her at home, Ersoy was arrested and given an eleven-month sentence, forty-five days of which she spent in prison. In 1981, during the period of martial law, the police in Istanbul banned a concert she was due to give in June of that year, and, soon after, all transvestite and transsexual artists were prohibited from performing. The ban remained in place for eight years.

The decision had been taken two months after the artist underwent gender-reassignment surgery in London in April 1981, a story that received exceptional media coverage in Turkey – the newspapers at the time even reported the cost of the operation, such was the level of interest. High-circulation satirical magazines like *Gırgır* published numerous

'Sefam Olsun', a paean to hedonism and sexual freedom.

Ersoy has inspired countless headlines through her involvement in various scandals and legal issues, one of which led to a two-month prison term for assaulting a journalist in 1982. This time she was sent to a women's prison. In 1989, during a concert in Adana, she was shot and wounded (resulting in her losing a kidney) by a fan for refusing to sing 'Cırpınırdı Karadeniz', a well-known Black Sea ballad popular with ultra-nationalists.

Bülent Ersoy is an icon who sports eccentric hairstyles and uses a complex vocabulary that includes numerous Ottoman words. Even her interpretation of nationalism is singular, oscillating between conservative and liberal views – and her evident closeness to Recep Tayyip Erdoğan has recently put her in the media's firing line, in particular on 26 June 2016, the day the LGBTQ-rights march was banned for the second year running, when the Diva was photographed at an *iftar* (evening meal during Ramadan) event hosted by Erdoğan for performers. The media took the opportunity to remind people of the declarations she had made immediately following the 1980 coup praising General Kenan Evren for having put a stop to the daily street violence between left and right – although she later distanced herself from those same views and criticised the law banning trans artists from performing. From champion and pioneer in the battle for LGBTQ rights in Turkey to a conservative figure with close ties to the wielders of power, from an extraordinary career comprising more than fifty albums to countless incidents reported in the press, her experience as an artist and a human being makes the Diva an embodiment of some of the key stages in Turkish history over the past five decades.

cartoons on the subject of transvestism and transsexuality, without explicitly naming the Diva but helping to raise public awareness of the matter. The media also ran the story that, having left Turkey as a woman and returning as a man, she was unable to obtain a woman's pink ID card – those issued to men are blue. It was not until 1988, when the government of Turgut Özal passed a law recognising the legal right of a person to change gender, that this was resolved, the same year that the ban on performances by transsexual artists was lifted. During the 1980s and '90s – which included a period spent in exile, largely in Germany and Australia – her fame spread beyond national borders, and Ersoy became the first Turkish artist to perform at such legendary music venues as the London Palladium (1980), New York's Madison Square Garden (1983) and at the Olympia in Paris (1997). A celebrated performer of traditional Turkish music, when her career was at its peak in the 1980s and '90s she also dabbled in more commercial genres, including arabesk, pop and fantazi, following the fashion at the time, with songs that became cult hits on the LGBTQ scene, such as 1993's

THE
BIG DIG

The Ottoman-era Nusretiye Mosque,
which is situated beside the Bosphorus
in the Tophane district of Istanbul

Urban planners in Istanbul have a problem: too much history and too many agendas. Which chapter of the past should they showcase? Turkey's pre-Islamic origins, as promoted by Atatürk, or the Ottoman glories so dear to President Erdoğan's heart?

ELIF BATUMAN

15

When it came to choosing the exact location of the first tunnel spanning the Bosphorus – the narrow strait that divides the European and Asian sides of Istanbul and links the Black Sea with the Sea of Marmara – one of the principal considerations was how to avoid encountering any archaeological marvels. The tunnel was for a new high-speed train called Marmaray (a combination of 'Marmara' and *ray*, the Turkish word for 'rail') connecting to Istanbul's metro system. Of particular concern was the placement of the main station on the European shore, on the site of ancient Byzantium and Constantinople: everything within the ancient city walls has been designated both by UNESCO and by the Turkish government as a historical site, and all digging must be supervised by the Istanbul Archaeological Museum. The location that was eventually chosen, in the working-class district of Yenikapı, had conveniently spent much of antiquity underwater. In Byzantine times, it was a harbour.

'What's going to turn up in a harbour?' one official explained, when I asked about the decision. 'Seabed and sand fill. Architectural structures aren't going to turn up.'

In fact, a tiny Byzantine church did turn up in Yenikapı, under the foundations of some razed apartment buildings. But the real problem was the large number of Byzantine shipwrecks that began to surface soon after the excavation began in 2004. Dating from the 5th to the 11th centuries, the shipwrecks illustrated a previously murky chapter in the history of shipbuilding and were exceptionally well preserved, having apparently been buried in sand during a series of natural disasters.

In accordance with Turkish law, control of the site shifted to the museum and use of mechanical tools was suspended. From 2005 to 2013 workers with shovels and wheelbarrows extracted a total of thirty-seven shipwrecks. When the excavation reached what had been the bottom of the sea, the archaeologists announced that they could finally cede part of the site to the engineers, after one last survey of the seabed – just a formality, really, to make sure they hadn't missed anything. That's when they found the remains of a Neolithic dwelling, dating from around 6000 BCE. It was previously unknown that anyone had lived on the site of the old city before around 1300 BCE. The excavators, attempting to avoid traces of Istanbul's human history, had ended up finding an extra five thousand years of it. It took five years to excavate the Neolithic layer, which yielded up graves, huts, cultivated farmland, wooden tools and some two thousand human footprints, miraculously preserved in a layer of silt-covered mud. In the Stone Age, the water level of the Bosphorus was far lower than it is now; there's a chance that the people who left

ELIF BATUMAN is an American writer and journalist with Turkish roots. Since 2010 she has written on a wide range of subjects for *The New Yorker*, from Epictetus to dung beetles, from a women's theatre group in a Turkish village to families for rent in Japan – an article for which she won a US National Magazine Award. Her first novel, *The Idiot* (Penguin USA, 2018/Jonathan Cape UK, 2017), was shortlisted for the 2018 Pulitzer Prize. She was a finalist in the National Book Critics Circle Award in 2010 for her non-fiction collection *The Possessed: Adventures with Russian Books and the People Who Read Them* (Farrar, Straus and Giroux USA, 2010/Granta UK, 2011). She holds a doctorate in comparative literature from Stanford University.

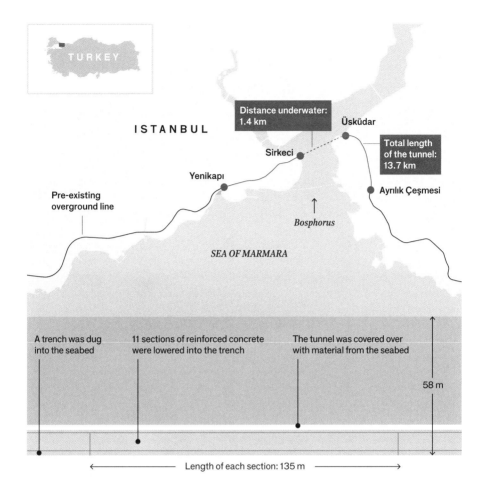

TURKEY

ISTANBUL

Distance underwater:
1.4 km

Üsküdar

Total length
of the tunnel:
13.7 km

Sirkeci

Yenikapı

Ayrılık Çeşmesi

Pre-existing
overground line

Bosphorus

SEA OF MARMARA

A trench was dug
into the seabed

11 sections of reinforced concrete
were lowered into the trench

The tunnel was covered over
with material from the seabed

58 m

←———— Length of each section: 135 m ————→

those prints might have been able to *walk* from Anatolia to Europe.

Exciting as these discoveries were for archaeologists, they did not delight the prime minister, Recep Tayyip Erdoğan, who had been championing the tunnel since he was mayor of Istanbul, in the 1990s. (He has been president since 2014.) Istanbul is one of the world's fastest-growing cities, with a population of more than fourteen million – up from less than a million in 1950 – and, according to a recent study, it has the worst traffic in the world. In 2013, at least two million people crossed the Bosphorus daily, by bridge or ferry; the number of motor-vehicle crossings rose 1,180 per cent between 1988 and 2012. The tunnel was long overdue.

In 2011, Erdoğan celebrated his fifty-seventh birthday inside the still unfinished tunnel and blamed the construction delays on the archaeological discoveries: 'Oh, some archaeological crockery turned up – oh, some finding turned up,' he told the press. 'That's how they put obstacles in our path. Are these things really more important than the human?' (In this, as in subsequent remarks on the subject,

'Archaeology is a destructive science. The site has to be recorded scrupulously, because the excavation will annihilate it.'

Erdoğan called the Yenikapı findings 'çanak çömlek': a dismissive term for tableware, generally translated as 'pots and pans'.) He vowed that there would be no more delays: the train would begin running on 29 October 2013 – the ninetieth anniversary of the Republic of Turkey.

Marmaray did open on 29 October. You can now cross the Bosphorus in four minutes. The connecting metro service at Yenikapı began in 2014. One report estimated that it would save Istanbul's commuters twenty-five million hours a year. An engineer once described the Yenikapı station to me as a knot tying together different kinds of rail transport. It's equally a knot tying together different kinds of time: millennia and minutes, eras and hours. The restoration of the ships, employing a technology first used on Viking galleys, takes anything from five to twenty years. Ufuk Kocabaş, the Istanbul University marine archaeologist who started working on the ships in 2005, at the age of thirty-five, and is now in charge of their preservation, doesn't expect to see the job completed in his lifetime. A museum and an archaeological park are under construction to showcase the findings, and, in an apt figure for the seemingly endless nature of the Yenikapı project, it seems likely that their construction will turn up even more shipwrecks.

*

When I first visited the Yenikapı excavation site, in July 2013, the Marmaray station was already nearly completed – a concrete colossus topped by a flat, glass-enclosed rotunda – but the metro station was still an archaeological dig. The total site was 58,000 square metres, about the size of eight football fields. Workers on the Marmaray side wore fluorescent hard hats with matching vests. On the metro side they wore faded caps or white shirts tied around their heads, against the blazing sun. They were constructing an edifice of their own, as striking, in its way, as the station: a fortress of plastic milk crates, ten crates high, stretching farther than the eye could see, packed with broken amphorae, horse bones, anchors, ceramic lamps, hewn limestone, mining refuse – anything that had been left there, accidentally or on purpose, by human hands. It was as if you were watching, in real time, the ancient harbour being replaced by a modern station.

To one side stood an armada of long objects wrapped in white plastic resembling monstrously elongated pianos. They turned out to be escalators awaiting installation. The shipwrecks were likewise hidden from view, in long white plastic tents, where sprinklers kept them damp twenty-four hours a day. Wood can absorb eight times its mass in water. If allowed to dry naturally, it cracks and warps beyond recognition.

'This work is like surgery – you can't leave the patient unattended,' Ufuk Kocabaş said when we visited the tents together. He had been directing a team there since 2007. During most of the excavation, there were between six hundred and a thousand workers on-site, plus about eighty archaeologists and other experts. The ships really did resemble surgical subjects, their rib cages opened up as each was measured, recorded and documented by graduate students. Archaeology, Kocabaş explained, is a destructive science. The site has to be recorded scrupulously, because the excavation will annihilate it. The Yenikapı team used a drone-like electric helicopter to shoot video from above, while a motorised camera on a scaffold took thousands of photographs and stitched them together into high-resolution images. Students traced a full-size outline of each ship on clear acetate.

Two kinds of vessel were found at Yenikapı: long, light scouting ships and shorter, heavier cargo ships, five of which had their original cargo. One ship, double-bottomed and lined with thick tiles, might have been used to carry marble from Marmara Island. Kocabaş speculates that the ships found with cargo sank suddenly, during storms or floods, which prevented the crew or the owners from retrieving their lost goods. These disasters would also have sealed the ships' remains in a layer of sand, protecting them from air and from naval shipworm, a shipwreck-eating species of salt-water mollusc.

Kocabaş was particularly excited about the ship known as YK12, which was recovered along with both a large cargo of amphorae and the captain's personal belongings: a mess kit, a brazier and a large basket of cherry pips. The cherry pips indicated that the ship sank during the relatively brief cherry season – perhaps during one of the summer storms common in the Marmara Region. Most of the ships with cargo date from the 9th to the 11th centuries. There were also fragments of empty cargo ships distributed throughout the harbour. The ships had likely been scuttled and forgotten centuries earlier.

After on-site documentation, the ships were transported to a specially constructed laboratory in the twisted back streets of Yenikapı. In several black rectangular pools, up to thirty metres long, dismembered ship pieces glimmered like eels. Nearby, some workers were easing a waterlogged beam on to a custom-built wooden bracket so that they could move it somewhere else. (Ancient shipwrecks have the soft, friable texture of feta cheese, so you can't just pick them up and carry them.) Dark, slightly twisted, the ancient beam glistened in the sun. Steam rose from the surface, contributing to a faint manure-like smell that hung in the air.

'This is a beautiful piece,' Kocabaş said. 'It's what we call the chin – it's a connector between the stern and the keel. The way it's dovetailed is very interesting – here it's going to lock together. It's a marvellous technology.'

Inside the laboratory a doctoral student was studying a brontosaurus-size rib from ship YK27, one of several ships built using techniques from different historical periods. Ships like YK27 have shed light on a transition in the history of shipbuilding, from the time-consuming shell-based (outside-in) mode of construction, favoured in antiquity, to the more efficient skeleton-based (inside-out) mode that prevailed during the Middle Ages.

'In technology, as in other areas of life, progress often comes about almost by accident, isn't immediately recognised and only later acquires the appearance of a purposeful step.'

This shift was originally believed to have taken place around CE 1000. The Yenikapı ships suggest that key elements of skeleton-based construction were already known by the 7th century – long before the shell-based construction was abandoned. In other words, the better technology supplanted the older one only after centuries of experimentation, hybridisation and regional variation. In technology, as in other areas of life, progress often comes about almost by accident, isn't immediately recognised and only later acquires the appearance of a purposeful step.

*

In addition to the ships, tens of thousands of museum-worthy objects turned up in the harbour: a 4th-century marble Apollo, an ivory carving of the Virgin Mary, a 19th-century emerald necklace that someone had dropped in the harbour. There were beautiful miniature ships – exactly like the shipwrecks but smaller and less wrecked. There was a device that Kocabaş described as 'a Byzantine tablet computer': a seven-inch wooden notebook with five removable wax pages that could be written on and erased again. The 'tablet' had an 'app' at the bottom: a sliding compartment concealing a tiny assay balance.

In Yenikapı, I visited the makeshift lab where all of these objects are processed by the Istanbul Archaeological Museum. In one trailer, a group of conservators, all women, were restoring small wooden objects. Reaching into plastic water-filled boxes, they fished out dripping marvels: spoons, tiny spools and pulleys, combs. There was a Byzantine child's sandal sole, and many larger adult soles, gleaming, black, worn out in just the places one's shoes do get worn out. One smallish sole was engraved with birds and bore a Greek inscription: 'Wear it in good health, lady'.

In a shed nearby, a noisy filtration machine was chugging its way through approximately two thousand sacks of Byzantine and Neolithic dirt. Water gushed and cycled through the machine, pushing the dirt through a filter.

'What turns up in there?' I asked the worker in charge of the machine.

'There could be seeds,' he said.

'What else, besides seeds?'

'So far, nothing but seeds.' He showed me a number of 8,000-year-old seeds, sorted, labelled and set aside for the archaeobotanists.

The most space in the lab was taken up by thousands of milk crates, which were stacked to the roof in the yard and in the hallways. Their contents spilled out on to tables, where some had been neatly arranged into rows: hundreds of lamps, vessels and plates in terracotta and ceramic, many with human or animal faces, with big, startled Byzantine eyes. The museum staff had to process fifteen boxes a day, cleaning, recording, cataloguing and sorting the contents into three groups: display quality, study quality and uninteresting. The first two groups

Photographs published in *Geçmişe Açılan Kapı: Yenikapı Batıkları* ('A Door Opens on the Past: The Ships of Yenikapı'; Ege Yayınları, 2015) by Ufuk Kocabaş, showing archaeological work in progress in the Yenikapı district of Istanbul. The excavations uncovered numerous Byzantine shipwrecks, the remains of an 8,000-year-old forest, Neolithic footprints, tombs, human skeletons arranged in the foetal position and more human remains in urns.

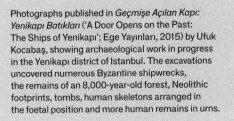

The megacity of fifteen million people that is Istanbul is thought to be home to 130,000 stray dogs and 125,000 stray cats, and, like the human population, the animals also receive essential services from the authorities: refuges, regular food, sterilisation and veterinary checks. In Istanbul alone there are six public clinics for stray animals. Cats, in particular, seem to love Istanbul – curled up on chairs at open-air bars or searching for fresh fish between the feet of the fishermen lined up on the Galata Bridge – and the feeling is mutual among the city's inhabitants, who put out bowls of water and leftovers from their dinners in the evenings, let them into the foyers of their apartment blocks when it gets cold and take them to the vet when they are ill or injured. It is said that cats arrived in Byzantium on Egyptian boats and were welcomed with open arms as rat-catchers – and Istanbul remains a coastal city with no rats to be seen. Religion helps, as cats are ritually pure animals in Islam – many Hadith tell of Mohammed's love for felines. So, to this day, cats are the stars of the city. The Turkish film director Ceyda Torun even devoted a documentary to them, *Kedi* (2016), which followed seven cats around the city's streets, collecting the thoughts of the people who were drawn to them. The @catsofIstanbul are also social media sensations, with tens of thousands of followers ... and they are simply adorable.

would be sent to the museum; the third would be put into sacks and reburied. Contemporary Turkish coins would also be put in the sacks, as a message to future archaeologists that the materials had been reburied in the 21st century.

Leaving the lab, I passed a colossal embankment of sacks, which I had previously mistaken for a sandbag barricade. Inside, thousands of uninteresting Byzantine artefacts awaited their reburial.

*

At the veterinary faculty of Istanbul University, on a remote suburban campus out past the airport, there is a small research centre devoted to the animal remains uncovered at Yenikapı. Vedat Onar, the archaeozoologist responsible for the centre, took me on a tour this spring. We entered through a padlocked iron gate, passed the word 'osteoarchaeology' spelled out in bones and eventually came to a narrow hallway lined, from floor to ceiling, with three hundred Byzantine horse skulls. No other archaeological site has yielded so many Byzantine horse skulls. A few complete horse skeletons had also been found. I saw one in a photograph, laid out on the ground among the mussel shells. It looked like a constellation.

Byzantine horses were crossbred for height and strength, in the Roman fashion. They started carrying heavy loads at the age of two, and were controlled by iron bits, which eroded their upper palates, wearing clean through the bone, and eventually making a large hole that connected the mouth and the nose cavity.

'This great stress on the mouth passed to the whole body,' Onar explained. Though most of the recovered horses had been younger than ten when they died, they were already beset by skeletal disease: 'foot problems, vertebral-column deformities, spondylitis, terrible spinal problems – they couldn't turn right or left'. Once the horses could no longer work, they were slaughtered and flayed. When the skins, horsehair and meat had been taken, the bones were dumped into the harbour. The Byzantines, unlike the Romans, ate horses.

Byzantine written sources had mentioned nobles eating bears and donkeys, but nobody had known whether the stories were true. At Yenikapı, donkey and bear bones were found with unmistakable marks of butchery. Ostrich bones were found, but only the legs. 'That's where all the meat is,' Onar explained, pointing at his own leg. People might have eaten the ostrich legs during ship journeys from North Africa. Butchered elephant bones were found, presumably from the circus at the hippodrome. Onar suspects that the thrifty Byzantines had fed the elephants, upon their retirement, to the lions.

From the elephant bones we passed to the skulls of dancing bears. The cubs' skulls showed compression fractures, from having been hit during training. The adult skulls had marks on the muzzles, from having been bound shut. Dancing bears had been a popular Byzantine entertainment. Empress Theodora's father was a bear trainer.

We came to a wall covered with hundreds of Byzantine dog skulls. Onar's partiality to dogs immediately became apparent. As a student, he had researched the dog burials of Urartu, an Iron Age civilisation in the Caucasus, where people had been buried in mass graves with large numbers of dogs so that they could all spend the afterlife together. The Byzantines, he said, had stray dogs, watchdogs and pet dogs (a sign of social status). When I mentioned that I had a cat, he showed me a small number of cat skulls, and assured me that cats were treated better in the Byzantine Empire than in western Europe. Gently, as if consoling me for something, he said, 'I can tell you this: those cats had no problems that were caused by human hands.' In general, he said, you could tell a lot about a society by the way it treated its animals. I asked what conclusions he had drawn about the Byzantines. 'We found a dog with a broken foot, and its foot was set,' he said. 'It was treated. The dog didn't die from that injury. So even the lame dog was fed.'

*

In April 2013, Erdoğan drew a telling comparison between the findings at Yenikapı and a controversial new shopping centre that he was proposing to build in Gezi Park, near Istanbul's Taksim Square. The shopping centre was to be housed in a replica of an Ottoman barracks that had been destroyed in 1940. At a press conference, a month before the Gezi plan sparked nationwide anti-government protests, Erdoğan asked why Yenikapı's Byzantine findings were more worthy of preservation than the Ottoman barracks. 'Three or five pots and pans turned up from the bottom of the sea, a spoon turned up, and these have to be preserved,' he said. 'But the barracks, which could save Taksim Square, it's a perfectly good building, architecturally and aesthetically, and this you won't preserve. If that's not ideology, what is?'

He was right: archaeology is ideology, especially in modern Turkey. Mustafa Kemal, who founded the republic, in 1923, once wrote in a cable to his prime minister: 'More students should be trained in archaeology.' The Ottoman Empire – an entity that at its peak encompassed the Balkans and much of the Caucasus, North Africa and the Middle East – had recently been dismantled by the Allied Powers, after the catastrophic defeat of the First

'Kemal understood that, if Turkish-speaking Muslims were going to retain any land in the former Ottoman Empire, they would have to come up with a unifying mythology of Turkishness.'

World War. Woodrow Wilson's Fourteen Points, asserting the principle of self-determination, was one of many signs that the age of multi-ethnic empires, such as the Ottoman and the Austro-Hungarian, was giving way to an age of ethnic nation-states. Kemal understood that, if Turkish-speaking Muslims were going to retain any land in the former Ottoman Empire, they would have to come up with a unifying mythology of Turkishness, based on the western-European ideals of ethnic nationalism, positivism and secularism. Adopting the surname Atatürk (Father Turk), he quickly set about inventing a new national identity. Of course, it couldn't *seem* invented; that's where archaeology came in.

In 1930, Atatürk appointed a committee to establish an ethnohistorical basis for a Turkish state in Anatolia. In 1931, the Society for the Examination of Turkish History published a radical four-volume history of Turkey, propounding the so-called 'Turkish-history thesis'. The thesis held that the Turks were descended from an ancient people who lived around an inland sea in Central Asia, where they basically started civilisation all by themselves. At the end of the Ice Age, the sea dried up, propelling waves of Turks to China, India, Mesopotamia, Greece and Italy, where they intermingled with the native populations and spread their knowledge of metalworking and of domesticated animals. In 5000 BCE a core group of Turks settled in Anatolia: their second homeland.

In a recent article, the historian Clive Foss enumerated other colourful tenets of the theory. In Mesopotamia, 'Sumerian Turks' drained swamps and developed a written language; Turkish Thracians founded Troy. Turkish Lydians migrated to Italy, became Etruscans and so more or less established Rome. The Minoans of Crete, having come from Anatolia, were basically Turks. The Buddha was a Turk; so was the 3rd-century Roman emperor Maximinus.

The theory solved any number of problems. It countered the Allied Powers' characterisation of the Turks as civilisation-resistant occupiers of other people's lands. ('No other race has brought such devastations and massacres, such lasting derangements, into the life of other nations,' a British naval-intelligence publication of the time stated.) By emphasising a pre-Islamic past, it kept the national identity separate both from the disgraced Ottoman Empire and from the Muslim caliphate. By making the Turks out to be the ancestors of Western civilisation, it allowed the nation to modernise without losing face: to 'Westernise' was simply to rediscover a lost patrimony. Perhaps most important, by positing a genetic relationship between the modern Turks and the prehistoric Anatolians, it protected the new republic from territorial claims by the Greeks, the Italians, the Armenians and the Kurds.

By the logic of the Turkish-history thesis, all prehistoric Anatolian civilisations of unknown origin were determined

THE PASSENGER   Elif Batuman

to be Turkish. Discovering their relics became a matter of national importance, and the emphasis of archaeology shifted from the Classical and Hellenistic ruins of the Aegean Region to the Neolithic, Hittite, Phrygian and Iron Age sites of Central Anatolia. Some excavations were led by German archaeologists who had fled the Third Reich, and whom Atatürk had invited to Turkish universities. Vast Hittite tombs were excavated. The capital had moved from the Ottomans' beloved Istanbul to Ankara, in the middle of the Anatolian steppe – within driving distance of the Hittite capital of Hattusha. New state banks were called Sümerbank (Sumerian Bank) and Etibank (Hittite Bank). Artefacts from all over Asia Minor were sent to the Museum of Anatolian Civilizations in Ankara, where, as a child, I spent many hours gazing at eyeless ceramic deer and emaciated bronze stags, developing a love of Hittites, that was not totally unrelated to the snack cakes produced by the Eti (Hittite) biscuit company.

Erdoğan, perhaps the most charismatic Turkish leader since Atatürk, rose to power by specifically appealing to those whom the Kemalist narrative excluded, or seemed to exclude: the emerging pious Muslim middle class, working-class Muslims and Kurds. This approach meant that Erdoğan had to distance himself from Kemalism, without appearing to do so. (Insulting Atatürk is still punishable under Turkish law.) Where Atatürk was ashamed of the Ottomans, Erdoğan championed them. Where Atatürk expanded Ankara's Anatolian museum, Erdoğan inaugurated a Panorama 1453 Historical Museum in Istanbul, which features a 360-degree painting of the Ottoman conquest of Constantinople. At the opening ceremony of the Marmaray station, at Yenikapı, Erdoğan quoted Mehmet the Conqueror

CATHEDRAL, MOSQUE, MUSEUM, MOSQUE

Built on the orders of the Eastern Roman Emperor Justinian I, the Church of Hagia Sophia was completed in CE 537. With its huge dome, it remained, for almost a thousand years, the largest cathedral in the world. When the Ottoman Turks conquered Constantinople in 1453 Mehmed II ordered that the building be repurposed as a mosque, and it became the template for many mosques built during the Classical Age of the empire. Then came Atatürk and his rejection of Turkey's Ottoman past, and Hagia Sophia reopened in 1935 as a museum and, arguably, the most representative symbol of the new secular country. Calls to reconvert the museum (which attracted 3.7 million visitors in 2019) into a mosque started to gain traction in the early 2010s, although Erdoğan himself was sceptical, saying that it could set a dangerous precedent for mosques in Christian countries to be closed. In July 2020, however, he signed a decree annulling Hagia Sophia's museum status and allowing it once again to be a place of Muslim prayer, prompting protests in the Christian world – especially in Orthodox countries – and widespread rebuke. The writer Orhan Pamuk said, 'There are millions of secular Turks like me who are crying against this, but their voices are not heard.' The decision, which is profoundly symbolic but in practice doesn't really affect the building much (all mosques in Turkey are open to visitors), was deemed by many to be a distraction from the country's economic woes following the COVID-19 pandemic, although it was supported by a majority of the population including, possibly for electoral calculations, Istanbul's opposition mayor Ekrem İmamoğlu.

Mustafa Kemal Atatürk

Nicknames: Father of the Turks, Pasha (General), Gazi (Victorious), Tek Adam (the Only Man).

Role: Founder of the Republic of Turkey.

Born in: Salonica, Ottoman Empire, now Thessaloniki, Greece, in 1881, the third child of a middle-class Turkish-speaking family. His exact date of birth is uncertain, but official accounts put it as 19 May, thus coinciding with the first day of the Turkish War of Independence (1919–23).

Education: He attended military schools from an early age, graduating with the rank of staff captain. Arrested for his anti-monarchist activities, he was sent to serve in Damascus. In 1907 he founded Motherland and Liberty, the first secret nationalist organisation in the Ottoman Army. He went on to join the Young Turks.

Military career: He received numerous distinctions for his service during the First World War, in particular at the Battle of Gallipoli (1915–16). Following the defeat and break-up of the empire, he led the Turkish National Movement, establishing a provisional government in Ankara and defeating the Allied forces in what became known as the War of Independence.

Offices held: Between 1920 and 1921 he was speaker of the Turkish Grand National Assembly in Ankara as well as prime minister. In 1923 he founded the Republic of Turkey. Voted president of the republic three times (1927, 1931 and 1935), he was opposed to the idea of a presidency for life. He nevertheless imposed a single-party regime and, after foiling a plot against him, led a political career characterised by a high level of authoritarianism.

Political project: A fervent supporter of secularism, he abolished the caliphate in 1924. He began a programme of modernisation reforms that also marked a break with the Ottoman Empire. He moved the capital to Ankara, a city symbolising the new republic, and introduced the Latin alphabet. He promoted Westernisation, encouraged the population to wear European-style clothing and hats and introduced the Gregorian calendar. He nationalised various sectors in order to rebuild the economy.

Private life: He married Latife Uşaki – who accompanied him on his travels around the country – but they were divorced after two years. He had no children of his own but adopted eight, seven of whom were girls, including the historian and sociologist Afet İnan – a theorist and promoter of Kemalist history – and Sabiha Gökçen, the world's first female fighter pilot, who now has an airport named after her in Istanbul.

Sport and free time: He liked listening to European classical music, reading, dancing the waltz and playing backgammon and billiards. He enjoyed swimming in the Bosphorus, adored horses and owned a dog. He spent a lot of time outdoors and at his model farms.

Favourite drink: He was a heavy *rakı* drinker, having been fond of beer as a younger man.

Favourite number: Six, like the arrows symbolising Kemalism: republicanism, nationalism, populism, statism, secularism and reformism.

Recep Tayyip Erdoğan

Nicknames: Reis (Boss), Baba (Father), Sultan.

Role: President of the republic since 2014, undisputed political leader since 2002, the year of his first general-election win.

Born in: Istanbul, in the working-class district of Kasımpaşa, on 26 February 1954, the third son of a practising Muslim family from the Black Sea city of Rize.

Education: He attended religious schools and graduated in economics, although the authenticity of his diploma is disputed.

Political career: While at high school he became active in the National Students' Union, at the age of twenty-two becoming president of a youth section of the National Salvation Party (MSP), the Islamist party led by Necmettin Erbakan. In the 1980s he followed Erbakan to his new nationalist Islamist organisation, the Welfare Party (RP), in which he became a leading figure.

Offices held: In 1994 he was elected mayor of Istanbul in what was the first win for an Islamist party in Turkey. In 1998 he was sentenced to ten months in prison and banned from politics for five years for incitement of hatred and violence. In 2001 he founded the Justice and Development Party (AKP) with Abdullah Gül. He became prime minister in 2003 and was re-elected in 2007 and 2011. In 2014 he was voted president of the republic in the country's first direct presidential elections. Following a constitutional referendum he was re-elected in 2018.

Political project: Profoundly inspired by conservative religious values, he promotes regulations that favour the visibility of religious symbols in public as well as greater space for Islam in the education system. He is a proponent of the reintroduction of the Ottoman language in high schools and promotes the country's imperial past. Economically he pursues free-market policies, including privatisation and strong support for the private sector as well as foreign investment.

Private life: Married to Emine Gülbaran, who is also active in an Islamist political association, he has four children, all of them in business, with various roles in pro-government organisations involved in youth issues, partnership and support for women and families. They were all involved in the corruption scandal that broke in 2013.

Sport and free time: Once a semi-professional footballer, he has promoted the construction of sports facilities and has ties with a football club, İstanbul Başakşehir FK, now owned by the Ministry of Youth and Sports. He is a fan of Turkish classical music and not averse to pop music.

Favourite drink: He likes carrot juice and maintains that *ayran* – made with water, yoghurt and salt – is the only true national drink.

Favourite number: Four, often displayed as a hand sign at rallies, standing for the four pillars of his political project: one people, one nation, one motherland, one flag.

in Ottoman Turkish, a language drastically modernised under Atatürk. He described the tunnel as the realisation of a '150-year-old dream', referring to the first plans for a Bosphorus tunnel, which were drawn up in 1860, under Sultan Abdülmecid I. (The plan, by the French engineer Simon Préault, called for a submerged floating tunnel.)

Erdoğan just isn't interested in archaeology – that's not where he's looking for legitimacy. If he's going to dig a hole in the ground, it's going to be to develop natural resources or expand public transit, not to find old pots. The old pots thus become objects of political contention. In 2010, a lawyer associated with the Kemalist party the CHP – the rival of Erdoğan's party, the AKP – launched an investigation into the sacks of archaeological material that were being reburied at Yenikapı, and eventually filed a criminal complaint declaring their reburial unlawful. (The Archaeological Museum later confirmed that it had buried sacks of scientifically uninteresting materials and the matter was dropped.) This legal motion didn't make a lot of practical sense, but it had a certain symbolic logic: if the government was trying to keep something in the ground, dissenters wanted it brought to light.

*

On a side-street near Karaköy, behind a 16th-century mosque below the Atatürk Bridge, and abutted by a Genoese rampart, are the Istanbul metro supervision offices of Yüksel Construction. I met there with Esat Tansev, a project director responsible for the Yenikapı–Taksim metro-line extension, the site where the largest number of ships were found. Tansev's office was spacious and well lit, but the air felt dense – with sunlight, cigarette smoke, the rumble of the AC unit and the ceaseless trilling

of a canary named Coşkun ('enthusiastic, overflowing, ebullient'). Tansev became involved with the project in November 1998, when Yüksel and three other Turkish firms were awarded the contract, for 150 million US dollars. The construction was supposed to take two and a half years. Instead, it took fifteen. One of the other companies ran out of money and backed out of the contract.

Tansev told me that it had been known from Byzantine maps that Yenikapı was the site of a harbour, and that archaeological discoveries had been expected – not in the tunnel itself, which runs two hundred metres underground, but in the stations. 'Sooner or later, a tunnel has to come up,' he said. 'When it reaches the surface of the earth, there are historical encounters.'

When asked what he had learned in almost two decades of such encounters, Tansev said that he had been most impressed by what a big difference it made whether you uncovered something Byzantine or Roman. Either would mess up your project, but Byzantine artefacts could eventually be moved. 'Roman things can't be touched,' he said. 'With Byzantium, you can find a way around it. But when it comes to Rome – condolences.'

He went on, 'At the beginning, we all felt some mutual antipathy with Professor Ufuk and the Archaeology Museum. But after a few months we all saw it wasn't the thing to do. Now we all have all kinds of friendships.' Tansev also came to feel a kind of collegial warmth towards his Byzantine forebears, who had faced the same problems as engineers today but with fewer technical resources. He had wondered how they put a pier in the ground without industrial concrete, and had been interested to learn that they made mortar out of lime.

Still, Tansev had been relieved when

Between 2014 and 2019 Turks were called to the ballot box on a surprising number of occasions, given the country's gradual descent into authoritarianism. It began in March 2014 with local elections and a corruption scandal that forced a number of ministers in Erdoğan's government to resign, but the AKP still won a clear victory over the Kemalist opposition, the CHP. Then, in August the first direct presidential elections in Turkish history were held: Erdoğan won in the first round, but the pro-Kurdish HDP's candidate Selahattin Demirtaş also did well. In the June 2015 general election the AKP lost its majority, partly thanks to the HDP, which exceeded the 10 per cent electoral threshold, but also thanks to the success of the right-wing, nationalist MHP. As president, Erdoğan blocked the formation of a coalition government, pushing for fresh elections and suspending the peace process with the Kurdish separatists in an attempt to regain nationalist votes, and his tactics worked: the AKP won a landslide victory. Then, in 2016 there were terrorist attacks and a failed coup d'état but no elections. Demirtaş was arrested for allegedly engaging in propaganda for the PKK. In April 2017 it was the turn of the constitutional referendum to switch from a parliamentary to a presidential system. The 'yes' camp won, supported by the president and the MHP, with which the AKP formed an alliance for the new presidential elections, which were brought forward to June 2018. Erdoğan won again, while Demirtaş took 8 per cent from his prison cell. But, just when everything seemed settled, along came the 2019 local elections: the opposition parties formed an alliance and, with external support from the HDP, managed to win control of Istanbul, Ankara and other major cities.

the excavation reached the seafloor, and felt only mild discomfiture when the archaeologists asked to perform a further five-square-metre test excavation: what could they possibly find under the seafloor? When the archaeologists called him fifteen days later to say that they had found Neolithic traces, Tansev thought they were joking. 'What are the chances?' he marvelled. 'In a 100,000-square-metre area, you excavate twenty-five square metres, and then you find something! It's unheard of! Well, then they explained it to me. Under the seabed, there's a dark, hard, oily clay. Past that, there's tar. Under that, what they found was some kind of cultivated topsoil. There were seeds planted in it.'

The dig continued. 'They expanded the area, and this time they found graves, they found those footprints, they found a jug,' Tansev said. 'They found plants and insects, they found every kind of thing. They dug and found, dug and found. In that way, three years passed.'

The Neolithic footprints, Tansev recalled, hadn't looked like much at first. 'Whoever discovered them deserves praise,' he said. 'Of course, now when you go to the museum they're footprints, clear as day. I said to myself, "Five thousand feet walked here, maybe twenty thousand – are we going to collect all of them?"'

He showed me a group photograph taken in August 2006 – forty-odd engineers, officials, architects and students, dressed variously in suits and hard hats, waving happily at the camera from the tunnel of the Şişhane metro station. None of them knew about the immaculately preserved 8,000-year-old footprints that were going to cause them so many problems.

I was unable to find Tansev in the photograph. When he pointed himself out, I felt a pang. He looked so young.

I visited Tansev with my friend Sibel Horada, a conceptual artist whose work often involves urban development and the historical legacy of non-Turkish Istanbul. I first met Sibel in 2012, when Istanbul's matzo factory was being converted into an art space. (Jewish community leaders had found that it was cheaper to import all Istanbul's matzo from Israel.) For the opening exhibit, Sibel ran squares of thick white paper through the factory's machine, so that they came out imprinted like matzo. She called the papers 'ghost matzo'.

Sibel had been fascinated by Yenikapı for years – particularly by the mountains of plastic crates, and the fate of their contents. Tansev seemed genuinely baffled by her determination to know the exact number of crates removed from the site.

'The essence of all your work is in those crates,' Sibel told him. 'It's not in a few cleaned-up ships in the museum. The real thing is in the boxes.' For Sibel, the most characteristic finding from Yenikapı was precisely 'the surplus'. 'When one piece is found,' she said, 'it teaches you something. When thousands of pieces are found, it's something else. At a certain point, you have the knowledge already, and the rest is a surplus.' You don't have to be a conceptual artist to see in the surplus an irresistible metaphor for certain historical questions in Istanbul: once you start digging, so much stuff comes out that there's nowhere to put it, and, eventually, you have to just bury it back in the ground.

Tansev seemed moved. He made a few phone calls, and wrote a number on a slip of paper: 83,562 – the number of boxes his workers had removed from the site.

Sibel introduced me to her friend Hayri Fehmi Yılmaz, an art historian who worked as a consultant on the metro construction. As with Tansev, his most vivid recollections involved the Neolithic phase. The Neolithic period is when the first nomadic hunter-gatherers began living in settlements and practising agriculture. In a process that started in the Fertile Crescent around 10,000 BCE and slowly moved west towards Europe, the human condition underwent changes that we still can't begin to imagine – in everything from social organisation to physiology. Each new site may hold another clue to what happened.

At first, officials had proposed that the entire Neolithic layer be dumped somewhere for the archaeologists to sort through: the whole layer had been a bog, so everything must be mixed up in there anyway. The archaeologists objected that this wasn't the case, and that hand excavation was required. One senior official went to Yenikapı and said that all he saw was mud, so why not excavate it with mechanical shovels? Just then, the archaeologists discovered the remains of an 8,000-year-old forest – nearly sixty trees with their roots spread out – followed by the graves, with human skeletons laid out in foetal-like position between wooden covers, and other human remains in urns. They found three different burial techniques from the same historical period.

When the officials saw the graves, they backed down, and the excavation proceeded by hand. It was then that archaeologists found the hut, the pots, the tools and the footprints. Some of the prints had been left by bare feet, others by wooden slippers. 'We had to laugh when we saw them,' Hayri said. 'They're the same wooden slippers we still wear at baths and in mosques.'

Hayri talked about the rules of excavation and the difficulties of getting a construction permit in the old city. Hayri himself has for many years abstained from expanding the basement of his house;

Above: An illuminated billboard at the entrance to Sirkeci Marmaray station, showing a train running under the Bosphorus and a photograph of President Erdoğan, with the caption: 'The dream came true. Marmaray is 5 years old.'

because he lives in a historic district, this relatively small home-improvement project could fall under the purview of the Istanbul Archaeological Museum. He made it sound like something out of Kafka. 'Archaeologists would have to do an excavation in my house,' he said. 'Who knows how long it would take?'

'Aren't you curious what's under there?' I asked.

'No,' he replied promptly. He said that Istanbul homeowners were generally more curious about archaeological findings under their neighbours' houses than under their own.

*

Two years after I saw the ships being excavated, I returned to Istanbul University to see their preservation. Kocabaş showed me two once-identical blocks of Byzantine wood: one dried in the sun, and the other preserved by the freeze-drying process used on the ships. The sun-dried wood had shrunk to a blackish twisted jerky-like strip. The freeze-dried wood was an airy, lightweight, bone-coloured block, restored to its original size and shape.

Before freeze-drying, each piece of wood must be saturated in a 45 per cent solution of polyethylene glycol, a waxy compound that replaces the water inside the cell walls, preventing shrinking or warping. Because the waterlogged wood is too delicate to be dumped straight into a 45 per cent solution, the concentration has to be increased by 5 per cent increments every month or two. Getting all the pieces of a ship to the full concentration can take years. During the actual freeze-drying, which takes from one to four months, the remaining water in the wood freezes solid, and then, under very low pressure, sublimates to a gas, bypassing the liquid phase.

I looked through the round window of the lab's freeze-drying machine. In

Above: The Boğaziçi Köprüsü ('Bridge over the Bosphorus'), known as 15 Temmuz Şehitler Köprüsü ('15 July Martyrs Bridge') since the 2016 coup; it connects Ortaköy on the European side with Beylerbeyi on the Asian side.

the gloom inside, distributed among six shelves, pieces of Byzantine ship were entering a new phase of existence. Nearby, in forty-ton tanks, some other pieces were marinating in the solution. The level was up to 35 per cent; Kocabaş hoped to reach full strength by the end of the year. He seemed more tired than he had two years earlier. He talked about missing the sea, and about how his son had just turned fourteen; he had been four when the ships were discovered.

I went to the Marmaray station. The crates had vanished. The building itself looked flat, glassy, unremarkable. Most of the impressive concrete structure I had seen earlier was now underground.

Although the shipwreck museum and the archaeological park have yet to materialise, there is now a sixty-five-acre 'meeting space' alongside the station. Built mostly by dumping a large amount of infill into the Sea of Marmara, the concrete protuberance quickly became known on social media as 'the tumour', and has been used almost exclusively for pro-AKP gatherings. The AKP held its first rally there before Erdoğan ran for president, in 2014, after he had exhausted his party's term limit as prime minister. Newspaper estimates of attendance ranged from hundreds of thousands to more than a million. Erdoğan himself said it was two million.

In 2015, an AKP rally called the Feast of Conquest was held at Yenikapı to mark the 562nd anniversary of the Ottoman conquest of Constantinople – one week before the June general elections. In the presence of 562 historically costumed Ottoman

'If fifteen houses are built on top of one another, which one is the most important? Whose voices should be heard – those of the living or those of the dead?'

military personnel, Erdoğan read from a chapter of the Koran known as the 'Conquest sura', and spoke of the upcoming election as a future 'conquest', re-enacting the triumph of Mehmet the Conqueror.

The following week, the AKP lost its absolute majority for the first time in thirteen years, and a new party, the HDP, passed the 10 per cent threshold required to win seats in parliament. The HDP is a spin-off of pro-Kurdish and leftist movements that gained momentum from the Gezi protests. Led by a Kurdish human-rights lawyer, it actively solicited female and LGBTQ candidates. The party slogan, 'Great Humanity', comes from a poem by Nâzım Hikmet, whom many consider the greatest 20th-century Turkish poet, though he spent most of his career in prison or in exile because of his Marxist views. 'Great Humanity' isn't Hikmet's most subtle work, but there is a certain power in the sweeping panorama and the concrete detail, and in the way that each sentence ends unexpectedly, tripping up against itself:

> The great humanity is the
> deck-passenger on the ship
> third class in the train
> on foot on the highway
> the great humanity.

On the escalator at Yenikapı the great humanity wore a tired expression and was often staring at its cell phone. It stepped on your foot, the great humanity. We descended to a cavernous rotunda with a skylight and pillars. High above the turnstiles, a fresco showed two stylised Byzantine slipper soles, resembling exclamation points.

I found myself remembering Erdoğan's exasperation: 'Are these things really more important than the human?' I remembered, too, how Kocabaş had told me that, of all the discoveries at Yenikapı, he was most moved by the Neolithic footprints: because they 'directly evoke the man', they tell us something that none of the other objects, even the shipwrecks, can. 'They represent the human without mediation,' he said. Back in the Stone Age, far fewer things mediated between humans and the world. There were no nations, no third class.

Few find a seat on Marmaray: each carriage accommodates five standing passengers for every seated passenger. Like Neolithic man, I crossed the Bosphorus upright, 'on foot on the highway'. I went to Asia and back again. I got off at the first European stop: Sirkeci Station, the old terminus of the Orient Express, where the Marmaray platform is connected to the surface of the earth by a twenty-storey escalator – the longest in Turkey. Strange questions may pass through your mind as you travel on this escalator. If fifteen houses are built on top of one another, which one is the most important? Whose voices should be heard – those of the living or those of the dead? How can we all fit in this world, and how do we get where we're going? (2015) ✒

Don't Call Them Soap Operas

Turkish TV series like *Magnificent Century* are rivalling US programmes in international popularity and taking the Middle East, Asia and Latin America by storm. What are the reasons for their global success?

FATIMA BHUTTO

Left and pages 39, 46: Extras from the *dizi Payitaht Abdülhamid* (*The Last Emperor*) on set in İzmit. The show tells the story of Sultan Abdul Hamid II, who ruled over a declining Ottoman Empire from 1876 until the 1909 military uprising led by the Young Turks.

'The first agreement we should make is: don't call them soap operas,' Dr Arzu Öztürkmen, who teaches oral history at Boğaziçi University in Istanbul, scolds me. 'We are very much against this.' What Turkey produces for television are not soap operas, or *telenovelas*, or period dramas: they are *dizi*. They are a 'genre in progress', declares Öztürkmen, with unique narratives, use of space and musical scores. And they are very, very popular.

Thanks to international sales and global viewership, Turkey is second only to the USA in worldwide TV distribution, finding huge audiences in Russia, China, Korea and Latin America. At present Chile is the largest consumer of *dizi* in terms of the number of shows sold, while Mexico then Argentina pay the most to buy them.

Dizi are sweeping epics, with each episode usually running to two hours or longer. Advertising time is cheap in Turkey, and the state broadcasting watchdog mandates that every twenty minutes of content be broken up by seven minutes of commercials. Every *dizi* has its own original soundtrack and can have up to fifty major characters. They tend to be filmed on location in the heart of historic Istanbul, using studios only when they must.

Dizi storylines, which have covered everything from gang rape to scheming Ottoman queens, are 'Dickens and the Brontë sisters', I am told by Eset, a young Istanbul screenwriter and filmmaker. 'We tell at least two versions of the Cinderella story per year on Turkish TV. Sometimes Cinderella is a 35-year-old single woman with a child; sometimes she's a 22-year-old starving actress.' Eset, who worked on perhaps the most famous *dizi*, *Magnificent Century*, recounts the narrative themes to which *dizi* are usually loyal:

- You can't put a gun in your hero's hand.
- The centre of any drama is the family.
- An outsider will always journey into a socio-economic setting that is the polar opposite of their own – moving from a village to the city, for example.
- The heart-throb has had his heart broken and is tragically closed to love.
- Nothing beats a love triangle.

Dizi are built, Eset insists, on the altar of 'communal yearning', both for the audience and the characters. 'We want to see the good guy with the good girl, but, dammit, life is bad and there are bad characters around.'

According to İzzet Pinto, the founder of the Istanbul-based Global Agency, which bills itself as the 'world's leading independent TV-content distributor for global markets', the upwards course of *dizi* imperialism began with 2006's *Binbir*

FATIMA BHUTTO is a Pakistani writer originally from Kabul who grew up between Syria and Pakistan. She has written seven works of fiction and non-fiction, including *Songs of Blood and Sword: A Daughter's Memoir* (Nation Books USA, 2010/Jonathan Cape UK, 2010) on the life and assassination of her father Murtaza Bhutto, the Pakistani politician and son of the former president and prime minister Zulfikar Ali Bhutto. Her debut novel, *The Shadow of the Crescent Moon* (Penguin, 2015) won the Prix de la Romancière in France, and her most recent work of fiction is *The Runaways* (Verso USA, 2020/Viking UK, 2019). She wrote a regular column for *Jang* – Pakistan's leading Urdu newspaper – and her articles have appeared in the *New Statesman*, the *Daily Beast*, the *Guardian* and *The Caravan*. *New Kings of the World*, from which this article is taken, was published by Columbia Global Reports in 2019.

> 'The international success of *dizi* is just one sign of the way new forms of mass culture from the east – from Bollywood to K-pop – are challenging the dominance of American pop culture in the 21st century.'

Gece ('1001 Nights'). At the time, another Turkish show, *Gümüş* ('Silver'), was already a hit in the Middle East, but it was *Binbir Gece* that became a truly global success. Wherever it was sold – in almost eighty countries – it was a ratings smash.

The show featured a blue-eyed Turkish dreamboat, Halit Ergenç, who would go on to star in the lead role of *Magnificent Century*. Based on the life of Suleiman the Magnificent, the tenth Ottoman sultan, *Magnificent Century* told the story of the sultan's love affair with a concubine named Hürrem, whom he married, in a major break with tradition. A largely unknown historical figure, Hürrem is believed to have been an Orthodox Christian from modern-day Ukraine.

When it first aired in Turkey in 2011 *Magnificent Century* claimed one-third of the country's TV audience. The foreign press called it an 'Ottoman-era *Sex and the City*' and compared it with a real-life *Game of Thrones*. It had multiple historical consultants and a production team of 130, with twenty-five people working on costumes alone.

Magnificent Century was so popular in the Middle East that Arab tourism to Istanbul skyrocketed. Turkey's minister of culture and tourism even stopped charging certain Arab countries broadcasting fees. Global Agency estimates that, even without counting its most recent buyers in Latin America, *Magnificent Century* has been seen by more than five hundred million people worldwide. It was the first *dizi* bought by Japan. Since 2002 about 150 Turkish *dizi* have been sold to more than a hundred countries, including Algeria, Morocco and Bulgaria. It was *Magnificent Century* that blazed the trail for others to follow.

The international success of such *dizi* is just one sign of the way new forms of mass culture from the east – from Bollywood to K-pop – are challenging the dominance of American pop culture in the 21st century. Ergenç feels that the runaway success of the *dizi* is partly down to the fact that American TV is entertaining but not moving. 'They don't touch the feelings that make us human,' he tells me, nursing a cold cup of coffee, when we meet in Istanbul. Turkey's gaze was once keenly turned to the West, studying its films and television for clues about how to behave in a modern, fast-paced world, but today American shows offer little guidance.

'I was thinking of one American TV series – let's not say its name. The philosophy of the series was being lonely. Being, um ...' – he searches for the polite word – 'multi-partner at the same time and searching for happiness. And all the people who were watching those series were very excited about it.' I can only guess he is referring to *Sex and the City*, but Ergenç doesn't say. 'That's a tiring thing, isn't it? Being alone, changing partners quickly and searching for happiness, and each time you search for it, it's a failure. But it was in a very fancy world, so people were very interested. They're spending and

Turkish cinema currently produces a few dozen films a year; this is an improvement on the crisis that followed the 1980 coup, but the overall numbers do not equate to a real film industry – in stark contrast to the rude health of Turkish television. However, between the early 1960s and late 1970s the country enjoyed a golden age of film with annual figures for movie production topping three hundred. The epicentre of 'Hollywood on the Bosphorus' was Yeşilçam, a street in Istanbul's Beyoğlu district. It was home to many of the city's cinemas (the last, the Emek Sineması, was demolished in 2013) as well as most of the studios. With an average audience of three thousand per screening, Turkish cinema was a mass cultural phenomenon; visits to the cinema gave structure to people's days, and subject matter was led by public – particularly women's – taste. Such was the demand that studios would put out a film a week, despite the shortage of film stock, the lack of resources and even a dearth of ideas. As a result, and given the loose adherence to copyright law in Turkey at the time, it was easier to copy and/or reuse footage from Hollywood hits, resulting in the likes of *Dünyayı Kurtaran Adam* ('The Man Who Saved the World' – *Star Wars*), *Badi* (*ET*), *Kara Şimşek* ('Black Lightning' – *Rocky*) or *Vahsi Kan* ('Wild Blood' – *Rambo*). The most popular genre, however, was the romantic drama, even though in 1979 there was talk of a not so romantic sex boom (*seks furyası*): of 193 productions that year, 131 were erotic. Following the coup, production stopped for three years, and many films ended up being destroyed. It was only thanks to the home-video market and the Turkish expatriate community in Germany that they survived.

spending – spending their time, spending their love, spending everything.'

The *dizi* that became global behemoths were powered by narratives that pitted traditional values and principles against the emotional and spiritual corruption of the modern world. *Fatmagül'ün Suçu Ne?* ('What Is Fatmagül's Fault?') centred on the gang rape of a young girl named Fatmagül and her battle for justice. It was a huge hit in Argentina, and in Spain its prime-time slot drew close to a million viewers per episode. *Fatmagül* is soon to get a full Spanish *telenovela* remake, adapted to a daily, half-hour afternoon format. The show addresses a woman's place in society while subjecting her to myriad problems, from forced marriage to tense family relations to the suffocating power of the rich. But Fatmagül perseveres. She educates herself and defeats every hardship as she fights for and receives justice on all fronts: civil justice through the nation's courts, divine justice through the punishment of her violators – and, of course, the justice of true love.

Although *dizi* have dealt with abuse, rape and honour killings, by and large Turkish men are portrayed as more romantic than Romeo. 'They show people what they want to see,' Pinar Çelikel, an Istanbul fashion editor tells me. 'It's not real.' Yet Eset argued that *Fatmagül* was groundbreaking in its approach to women's issues. Previously, agents of change and the heroes of *dizi* stories were always men, but 'Fatmagül didn't accept women's place as being subjugated, almost invisible'.

It was such a persuasive vehicle for soft power that in 2012 Eset was hired by a 'Republican American think tank' to write a *dizi* telling the 'good American story' of a woman in the Middle East out to enact positive change, 'a woman who softens America's image'. Eset declines to say which

think tank commissioned him, except to hint that a former Bush administration undersecretary was involved with the institute. 'I wrote it,' Eset shrugs as he rolls a cigarette, 'but they weren't able to sell it.'

*

I am standing in the drizzle in a bleak car park on the Asian side of Istanbul in front of a white van. A man named Ferhat hands me a Glock 19 pistol. It is the same model Turkish soldiers use, he says, as he swings open the van doors. Inside, there is a rocket-launcher lying on the floor and about sixty other weapons hanging on racks. Ferhat, who is ex-military, pulls out a 'bad guy rifle' – an AK-47 – and a sniper rifle. Men in military uniform prowl across the car park. All around us there are street signs in Arabic and extras in cheap suits.

We are on the set of *Söz* ('The Oath'), a show made by Tims Productions, the company behind *Magnificent Century*. They are filming Episode 38. A demolition expert saunters by, chatting to a man in a balaclava while an actor rehearses a scene, holding a rifle in each hand. *Söz* is a military *dizi* – a new sub-genre that is sweeping the nation. Although it is too early to have a sense of its global effect, *Söz* has already received remake offers from far-away markets including Mexico. Tims has always had an international outlook, I am told. They tried to cast Hollywood stars in *Magnificent Century* and were reportedly close to signing Demi Moore to play a European princess until her divorce from Ashton Kutcher got in the way.

Each of the five major television channels in Turkey has one of these 'soldier-glorifying' shows, Eset the screenwriter tells me later, and all the shows are 'zeitgeist relevant'. The baddies are either 'internal enemies' or foreign villains. *Söz* takes place in a Turkey beset by violence and existential threats. Soldiers are everywhere, blazing through the wreckage of suicide bombings at shopping malls and hunting terrorists who are hard at work kidnapping pregnant women. In the first episode, after an attack on a mall, a soldier promises they will not rest until 'we drain this swamp' – an eerily familiar refrain.

After more than a hundred hours of watching *dizi*, *Söz* was the first one in which I saw a woman wearing a hijab. The father of modern Turkey, Mustafa Kemal, later renamed Atatürk, famously declared that he wished 'all religions [were] at the bottom of the sea'. He removed Islam as the state religion from the constitution and banned the fez, which he described as emblematic of 'hatred of progress and civilisation'. The veil – which Atatürk lambasted as a 'spectacle that makes the nation an object of ridicule' – did not fare much better. By the 1980s women in all public institutions, including universities, were banned from covering their heads.

Five minutes on the streets of Istanbul presents multiple encounters with women in headscarves, yet they are nowhere to be seen on screen. 'They tried it,' Eset says, 'but even the conservative folks don't like to see conservative women on TV. You can't get them to kiss, to stand up to their fathers, to run away, to do very much at all that would be considered drama.'

Women in hijabs are almost never shown in television adverts, the journalist and novelist Ece Temelkuran tells me. Her diagnosis was clear: 'This country is torn between these two pieces of cloth – flag and headscarf.'

Back on the *Söz* set, as we move upstairs to a cold office building to watch a man pick up a phone for an hour while the demolition guys shoot glass windows in the corridor, I tell Selin Arat – director of international operations at Tims and my guide for the day – that I watched an episode of *Söz* the previous night. Every time I looked down at my notebook, I explain, by the time I looked up again, everyone in the scene seemed to have been murdered. Who are the terrorists supposed to be? Arat, a delicate, strawberry-blonde woman in a business suit, laughs. 'It would be life threatening if we knew who they were,' she jokes.

Whoever the terrorists are, *Söz* is a hit. 'It's the first Turkish show that has surpassed one million subscribers on YouTube,' Arat notes proudly. Selling *Söz* outside Turkey may prove tougher, though. 'We do want this show to be global,' says Timur Savcı, the founder of

Tims Productions, 'but right now not many countries are really interested in watching Turkish soldiers be glorified.' He pauses and smiles. 'The US always makes shows and, at the end, they say "God bless America". Well, God bless Turkey!'

*

Savcı sits at his desk in the Levent district of Istanbul, as five TVs, all tuned to different channels, illuminate his spacious office. He sets the tone for the *dizi* industry at large, and today he is preparing an English adaptation of *Magnificent Century*. He is not the least bit interested in taking American shows and remaking them in Turkish. 'We are just making originals. It's better!' he says with a big laugh.

Dizi have yet to penetrate the English-speaking world. That could be because audiences in the USA and UK don't like to watch subtitled shows, Savcı muses, 'or it could be the fact that this is about an Islamic state at the end of the day'. I ask if that is something Tims would tone down in the English version of *Magnificent Century*? Savcı, a jaunty, jovial man, shakes his head. 'It's important to remember that at the time the Ottoman Empire was the superpower of the world. What the US is to the world now is what the Ottoman Empire was. If people look at it from this perspective, they would understand it more, but if they don't know this, they would feel threatened.'

Turks have been watching quality US TV since the 1970s. Turkish actors, such as Mert Fırat, told me they learned their chops from the likes of *Dallas* and *Dynasty*. That was where they learned to emote and to perform the melodrama that *dizi* require. But there was something lacking, something fundamental missing from those early guides to how to be rich and powerful in the modern world.

EVERY TURK IS BORN A SOLDIER

In a country founded by a victorious general who came to power after his defence of the motherland's borders, it is perhaps not surprising that the army is a source of great national pride. Military service (a twelve-month compulsory period for all men, which can be reduced to six months for graduates) is a fundamental right of passage, one of the five stages of manhood, along with circumcision, work, marriage and fatherhood. Traditionally, families do not give their consent for a daughter to marry a man who has not done his military service, and companies will not employ him. Conscientious objection is illegal – a popular slogan proudly proclaims that 'every Turk is born a soldier' – and it is a crime to 'insult the spirit of the armed forces'. The fact that since 1984 hundreds of thousands of conscripts have been sent to fight against Kurdish separatists (and more than six thousand have died) does not discourage the new recruits, and patriotism and martyrdom remain deeply ingrained. In one notorious episode Erdoğan expressed a wish that a six-year-old girl would become a martyr and be wrapped in the Turkish flag. 'You're ready for anything, aren't you?' he asked her, drying her tears. The reputation of the army, which has always been the guardian of Turkey's secular ideology, was tarnished by the failed coup of 2016, but, despite the purges that followed (around 40 per cent of generals and admirals were removed), the army, the second-largest in NATO, retains, in Turkish eyes, a reputation for invincibility.

'Turkish actors told me they learned their chops from the likes of *Dallas* and *Dynasty*. That was where they learned to emote and to perform the melodrama that *dizi* require.'

Kıvanç Tatlıtuğ, the star of the hit *dizi Gümüş*, among others, doesn't feel it is necessarily a question of values or conservatism but empathy. By email, he told me why he thinks audiences around the world are turning to *dizi* over Western productions. 'Most of these audiences feel that their everyday stories are "underexplored" by Hollywood and Europe,' Tatlıtuğ wrote. 'This is ultimately a matter of diversity in storytelling. I understand the appeal of a story like *Breaking Bad* or *Game of Thrones*, these are both amazing TV shows. However, some people may also feel disenfranchised from these Hollywood themes and may want to watch a story they can empathise with.'

'Disappearing family values are not concerns for the West,' Eset says. 'For the past four years or so, 40 per cent of the most-watched Turkish shows have been remakes of Korean dramas,' he continues, pointing out that the Koreans have been swifter than the Turks at penetrating the Latin American market. 'Korea is also a country that gives great importance to family, but, in the West, the romantic notion of those good old family values is gone.'

At the time of our meeting Eset is working with a Turkish-American production house, Karga 7, which has global ambitions for their shows. 'When I talk to people about Turkish TV series,' he tells me, 'mainly they are taken by this romantic notion of family where everyone is trying to cherish one another. The dangers are external, and socio-economic class plays a great role in the love story of the poor boy loving a rich girl or vice versa. Normally a story like this in the West would be treated through an individual's journey, where there is more sex, there is more violence, there are drugs.' Turkish TV has less of that. He points out that the couple in *Fatmagül* don't kiss until about Episode 58.

*

In August 2017 in Beirut, I speak to Fadi Ismail, the general manager of the Middle East Broadcasting Center's subsidiary O3 Productions and the person responsible for bringing Turkish television to the Middle East. 'To brag a bit,' Ismail corrects me with a laugh, 'I'm the one who opened Turkish culture through TV to the whole world.' MBC is the biggest broadcaster in the Middle East and North Africa, home to almost four hundred million people. MBC has a news channel, a children's channel, a women's channel, a Bollywood channel and a 24-hour drama channel on which it broadcasts Egyptian soaps, Korean dramas and Latin American *telenovelas*.

In 2007 Ismail went to a buyer's cinema festival in Turkey and chanced upon a tiny kiosk showing a local television series. 'I stopped and watched it, not

Right: An actor walks across the set of *Payitaht Abdülhamid*.

understanding anything,' he remembers, 'but immediately I could visualise it as Arabic content. I replaced it in my mind with Arabic audio, and everything else looked culturally, socially – even the food, the clothes – everything for me looked like us, and I thought: "Eureka!"'

Ismail bought a Turkish series for his channel. He doesn't remember the name of that first show, because they had already hit on the formula of giving everything – the title, the characters – new Arabic names. 'Every one of these titles had "love" in it, so I stopped differentiating. Love Something, Blue Love, Long Love, Short Love, Killing Love.' *Gümüş* – renamed *Noor* for the Middle East market – was the first big hit.

Although the Egyptians had traditionally been known for their cinema they also dominated TV across the region until Syria took over in the 1990s. Syrian actors were renowned for their dramatic and comedic skills. Their directors were artists. Talented scriptwriters produced shows of quality with substantial state help. The government poured money into the television industry, providing auteurs with cameras, equipment, state subsidies and permission to film in Syria's historic sites. But then the war broke out and the country's bright promise flickered. It was at this moment, Ismail says, that the Turks were ready to move in.

As Syrian dramas had already become a 'pan-Arab phenomenon', MBC decided to dub all the Turkish dramas they bought into the Syrian Arabic dialect. 'That is one of the reasons for their huge success,' Ismail concludes. 'We dubbed the Turkish dramas with the most prevalent and established drama accent: Syrian.' Before Turkish dramas flooded Middle Eastern screens, people in Lebanon watched Mexican and Brazilian *telenovelas*. Although they were popular, they eventually ran out of steam for two reasons. The first was language. *Telenovelas* were dubbed into Fusha, a standardised literary Arabic that is understood from Iraq to Sudan and is used in newspapers, magazines and newscasts. Free from local accents and slang particular to each country, it is a formal, classical Arabic. The second was a question of values. 'The Mexicans really did not resemble us at all,' says Imane Mezher, the format distribution and licensing coordinator of iMagic, a Beirut-based TV production company. iMagic makes *Arabs Got Talent* and the Middle East version of *The X Factor* and experiments with new formats such as the *World Bellydance Championship* and an Islamically approved *Extreme Makeover* in which contestants don't alter God's design out of vanity but have reconstructive surgery for life-threatening issues.

Mezher shakes her head at the memory of the *telenovelas*. 'You have a daughter and you don't know who her father is, you don't know who the mother is. The stories were moral free. At the end of the day, like it or not, we like things to be a little more conservative. The Turks are amazing at that. They are the real mix: the European freedom that everyone longs for and, at the same time, the problems are conservative, the same we face. The people have the same names as us, the same stories as us, and people love that.'

*

However, since 2018 the international reach of Turkish TV has been significantly curtailed. At 1 a.m. Saudi Arabian time on 2 March that year, MBC took *dizi* off the air. Six were pulled, at a cost to MBC of $25 million. 'There is a decision to remove all Turkish drama from several TV outlets in the region,' the channel's spokesman said. 'I can't confirm who took the decision.'

'It is impossible to separate politics, both internal and geopolitical, from *dizi*'s upwards momentum. Erdoğan himself was famously antagonistic towards *Magnificent Century*, finding it too risqué and not sufficiently versed in true Ottoman history.'

Since 2015 Saudi Arabia's crown prince, Mohammed bin Salman, had been in negotiations to buy MBC but found the $3 billion asking price too high. In November 2017 MBS, as he is known, arrested most of MBC's board and shareholders as part of what was billed as an anti-corruption sweep. After an 83-day stay in a luxury jail MBC's founder, Waleed bin Ibrahim Al Ibrahim, a Saudi businessman whose sister was married to a former king, was released. His company now had a secret new majority owner, whose first order of business was to cancel all of MBC's *dizi* programming.

Before that time the Middle East and North Africa accounted for the largest international consumption of *dizi*. *Magnificent Century* was advertised alongside *Game of Thrones* and *Oprah* in Dubai, while Ece Yörenç – *Fatmagül*'s scriptwriter – was asked by Saudi Arabia to write TV series for its local channels, and rumours circulated of princes and politicians enquiring after show plotlines during state visits to Turkey. It is possible that this kind of Turkish soft power irked MBS. And it is certain that he was infuriated by Turkey's brazen flouting of his 2017 blockade of Qatar. Thus, in March 2018 MBS accused Turkey's president, Recep Tayyip Erdoğan, of trying to build a new 'Ottoman caliphate', included Turkey in what he bizarrely called a 'triangle of evil' and swiftly erased *dizi* from Middle Eastern TV.

It is impossible to separate politics, both internal and geopolitical, from *dizi*'s upwards momentum. Erdoğan himself was famously antagonistic towards *Magnificent Century*, finding it too risqué and not sufficiently versed in true Ottoman history. His government withdrew permission for its producers to film in historical sites such as Topkapı Palace, and Turkish Airlines pulled it from its in-flight entertainment systems in order to avoid government ire. A deputy from Erdoğan's AKP party even went so far as to submit a parliamentary petition to legally ban the show.

Although *Magnificent Century* has never been used by the state to project Turkish soft power to the world, other *dizi* have. Two more recent productions for TRT, Turkish state television, have the government's wholehearted endorsement, if not their guidance. The first, *Diriliş: Ertuğrul* ('Resurrection: Ertuğrul'), begins at the start of Ottoman glory, with Ertuğrul Ghazi, the father of Sultan Osman, the founder of the empire. The *dizi*'s tagline is 'A Nation's Awakening', and for five seasons viewers have watched Ertuğrul battle Crusaders, Mongols, Christian Byzantines and more. It has the honour of being the most popular show to air on state TV. 'Until the lions start writing their own stories,' Erdoğan said of *Ertuğrul*, 'their hunters will always be the heroes.'

Another show, *Payitaht Abdülhamid* (*The Last Emperor*), bookends the Ottoman obsession: it is based on the last powerful

THE PASSENGER   Fatima Bhutto

Magnificent Century is part of a trend – which has grown in tandem with Erdoğan's power – that goes by the name of Ottomania. It can be seen not only in the propagandist attempts to reclaim the historical memory of the Ottoman Empire but also in daily life, from books of Ottoman recipes to the uniforms of Turkish Airlines flight attendants. This new obsession fits well with Erdoğan's ideology of a New Turkey and the neo-Ottoman foreign policy of the past twenty years, which aims to promote greater engagement with areas once under the empire's control (the Balkans, the Middle East and North Africa), in contrast to Kemalist ideology, which has always looked west towards NATO and EU membership. In addition to the country's problematic energy situation (Turkey lies at the centre of flows of gas and oil but does not have its own resources), this is further complicated by two concepts: pan-Islamism (but only Sunni Islam) and pan-Turkism, the protection of Turkish minorities (in Cyprus, for example) and solidarity with Turkic populations in Central Asia. The term neo-Ottomanism actually originated in Greece following the Turkish military intervention in Cyprus in 1974, but the main architect of the policy, summed up in the famous refrain 'zero problems with the neighbours', was Ahmet Davutoğlu, foreign minister between 2009 and 2014. But his departure and Erdoğan's drift towards autocracy have removed any meaning from the slogan, leading to conflicts, some of them armed, with neighbouring states (Syria) and others (Libya, Russia and NATO itself) as well as its closest neighbours of all: the Kurds.

Ottoman sultan, Abdul Hamid II. It first aired in 2017, drawing in big numbers – every Friday one in ten television watchers tuned in as the sultan staved off rebellions by the Young Turks (who would eventually unseat him) and scheming European powers. Both supporters and detractors of the *dizi* pointed out that its portrayal of the sultan was modelled incredibly closely on Erdoğan. Followers of the Turkish president saw symbiosis between the two proud leaders who were unafraid to confront the West and who dreamed of making Turkey central to pan-Muslim unity. Critics pointed out the two men's paranoid reliance on intelligence services and an oppressive grip on power.

By 2023 the Turkish government hopes *dizi* will pull in $1 billion from exports. In his Istanbul glass office, İzzet Pinto, the founder of *dizi* distributor Global Agency, told me that $500 million is a more realistic target given the loss of the Middle East market. But he foresees that remake rights, expansion in Latin America and the opening of western Europe – notably Italy and Spain – will help offset those losses.

Over at Tims, Selin Arat predicts that Turkish series have reached a stable level of popularity. Demand might not grow much more, but there is a global hunger for what Turkish TV can offer. Arat concedes that the Saudi stance against *dizi* is a setback, but, he says, 'It won't be the end of the Turkish *dizi* invasion.'

This article is an adapted excerpt from Fatima Bhutto's book *New Kings of the World: Dispatches from Bollywood, Dizi, and K-Pop*, published in 2019 by Columbia Global Reports.

Turkey's Thirty-Year Coup

A series of images are projected on to a smashed-up car at Istanbul's 15 July Memorial Museum, located a few metres from the first bridge over the Bosphorus, a symbolic location for the 2016 coup.

Was an exiled Islamic preacher behind the attempted military coup of 2016? Dexter Filkins probes the secrets and mysteries of the Gülen movement, which spent decades infiltrating Turkish bureaucracy to undermine the secular state before clashing with former ally President Erdoğan.

DEXTER FILKINS

49

At nine o'clock on the night of 15 July 2016 General Hulusi Akar, the chief of the Turkish Army's general staff, heard a knock on his office door in Ankara, the nation's capital. It was one of his subordinates, General Mehmet Dişli, and he was there to report that a military coup had begun. 'We will get everybody,' Dişli said. 'Battalions and brigades are on their way. You will soon see.'

Akar was aghast. 'What the hell are you saying?' he asked.

In other cities, officers involved in the coup had ordered their units to detain senior military leaders, block major roads and seize crucial institutions like Istanbul Atatürk Airport. Two dozen F-16 fighters took to the air. According to statements from some of the officers involved, the plotters asked Akar to join them. When he refused, they handcuffed him and flew him by helicopter to an airbase where other generals were being held; at one point one of the rebels pointed a gun at Akar and threatened to shoot.

After midnight a news anchor for Turkish Radio and Television was forced to read a statement by the plotters, who called themselves the Peace at Home Committee, a reference to one of the country's founding ideals. Without mentioning the president, Recep Tayyip Erdoğan, by name, the statement said that his government had destroyed the country's institutions, engaged in corruption, supported terrorism and ignored human rights: 'The secular and democratic rule of law has been virtually eliminated.'

For a time the rebels seemed to have the upper hand. Provincial governors and community leaders surrendered or joined in, along with police squads. In a series of text messages discovered after the coup, a Major Murat Çelebioğlu told his group: 'The deputies of the Istanbul police chief have been called, informed, and the vast majority have complied.'

A Colonel Uzan Şahin replied: 'Tell our police friends: I kiss their eyes.'

But the plot seemed haphazard. A helicopter team sent to locate Erdoğan in Marmaris, the resort town where he was vacationing, failed to capture the president, despite a shootout with guards at his hotel. The rebels took control of only one television station and left cellular-phone networks untouched. Erdoğan was able to record a video message, played on CNN Türk, in which he called on Turkish citizens to 'take to the streets'. They did, in huge numbers. Faced with overwhelming

DEXTER FILKINS is a journalist and war reporter. He was a Pulitzer Prize finalist in 2002 for his despatches from Afghanistan and won the prize in 2009 with a team of colleagues from *The New York Times* for their war reporting. He has also published a highly successful book on the conflicts in Iraq and Afghanistan, *The Forever War* (Knopf USA, 2008/Vintage UK, 2009), winner of the US National Book Critics Circle Award in 2008. After years on the front line for *The New York Times* he now writes for *The New Yorker*.

> 'To many outside observers, Erdoğan's accusation sounded like something out of an airport thriller: a secret cabal burrowing into a modern state and awaiting orders from its elderly leader on a hilltop half a world away.'

popular resistance, the troops had to decide between shooting large groups of demonstrators and giving up. By morning the uprising had been broken.

Erdoğan declared a national emergency and, in the weeks that followed, made a series of appearances to remind the nation of the cost of the coup. Some of the plotters had brutally shot demonstrators and comrades who opposed them. One rebel major, faced with resistance, had texted his soldiers: 'Crush them, burn them, no compromise.' More than 260 people were killed and thousands wounded. The F-16s had bombed the parliament building, blasting holes in the façade and scattering chunks of concrete in the hallways.

In Erdoğan's telling, the coup was not a legitimate sign of civic unrest. In fact, it did not even originate in Turkey; the rebels 'were being told what to do from Pennsylvania'. For Turks, the coded message was clear: Erdoğan meant that the mastermind of the coup was Fethullah Gülen, a 78-year-old cleric who had been living in exile for two decades in the Poconos, between Allentown and Scranton, Pennsylvania.

Gülen, a dour, balding proselytiser with a scratchy voice, had fled Turkey in 1999, fearing arrest by the country's military rulers. From afar, though, he had served as a spiritual guide for millions and overseen a worldwide network of charter schools, known for offering scholarships to the poor. Gülen's sermons and writings emphasised reconciling Islam with contemporary science and promoted

charity; his movement is called Hizmet, or Service. For many in the West it represented a hopeful trend in Islam. Gülen met Pope John Paul II and the leaders of major Jewish organisations and was fêted by President Bill Clinton, who saluted his 'ideas of tolerance and interfaith dialogue'.

To many outside observers, Erdoğan's accusation sounded like something out of an airport thriller: a secret cabal burrowing into a modern state and awaiting orders from its elderly leader on a hilltop half a world away. For Erdoğan, though, it was a statement of political reality. Gülen, once a crucial ally, had become the leader of a shadow state, determined to bring down the administration. In the following weeks Erdoğan's forces detained tens of thousands of people who he claimed were loyal to Gülen. In outraged statements to the United States government he demanded that Gülen be extradited so that he could be made to face justice in a Turkish court.

*

Ever since Gülen retreated to the Pennsylvania countryside he has been a recluse, flooding Turkey with audio and video recordings but refusing to appear in public. When I first asked to talk with him in 2014 I wasn't hopeful. At the movement's Manhattan office, the Alliance for Shared Values, the executive director, Alp Aslandoğan, told me repeatedly that an interview might never happen. 'His health is very fragile,' he said. Even if Gülen agreed to speak, it was possible that after a few questions he would be too tired to continue.

The following July, after a year of refusals, I was abruptly summoned to the compound. Getting out of the car, I felt as if I'd arrived in the Anatolian countryside: the two main buildings were in the Ottoman style, with high windows and obliquely slanted roofs; women wore the stylish fitted headscarves popular among Turkey's middle class; everyone was speaking Turkish. Aslandoğan greeted me and led me to an ornate conference room furnished with couches that all faced a throne-like chair, which was reserved for me.

After a few minutes Gülen entered. He was dressed in a black suit, the kind you might find at Target or Marshalls; his head was bowed, and he moved with a hesitant shuffle, more resembling a pensioner awakening from his afternoon nap than the patriarch of a global organisation. He had a large, pale head, an expansive nose and eyes freighted by enormous sacks. The only trace of vanity was a wisp of grey moustache. Gülen greeted me with an indifferent nod; after seventeen years in the USA he speaks almost no English. He led me into a hallway to show me his living quarters: two tiny rooms, with a mattress on the floor, a prayer mat, a desk and bookshelves and a treadmill.

There was no chitchat, and Gülen didn't smile. When I asked about his relationship with Erdoğan, he told me, through an interpreter, that Erdoğan had never willingly shared power with anyone. 'Apparently, he always had this vision of being the single most powerful person,' he said. Erdoğan and his followers were all alike. 'In the beginning of their political careers they put up a façade of a more democratic party and leadership. And they appeared to be people of faith. And therefore we did not want to

second-guess their motives. We believed their rhetoric.'

He spoke elliptically, something he is famous for. 'You can't understand him,' a Turkish intelligence official warned me. When I asked whether his movement had an interest in politics, Gülen told me he had so many followers that some were bound to end up in important positions, but that hardly amounted to a conspiracy. 'No citizen or social group can be completely isolated from politics, because policy decisions and actions affect their lives,' he added. 'Such a role for civil-society groups is normal and welcome in democratic societies – and it doesn't make Hizmet a political movement.' We talked a little more, but, as his aides had predicted, Gülen seemed to tire. After about forty-five minutes Aslandoğan signalled that the interview had come to an end.

*

I had found a better embodiment of Gülen's ideas in Turkey: Mustafa Aksoy, a businessman I met in 2011 in the café of an Istanbul hotel. (Following the coup and the subsequent crackdown, Aksoy asked to be identified by a pseudonym to protect his family in Turkey.) Like many followers of Gülen, he was clean shaven, wore a Western business suit and projected an almost aggressively cheerful appearance. He was a very successful man: he owned a construction firm, a hotel-services company and a housewares factory, which together employed about six hundred people. For three years Aksoy had lived in Europe. He spoke fluent English and was married to a Scandinavian woman; his work had taken him to every corner of the world.

Aksoy told me that he became associated with the Gülenist movement in 1993, when he accompanied a group of businessmen on a trip to Turkmenistan, one of

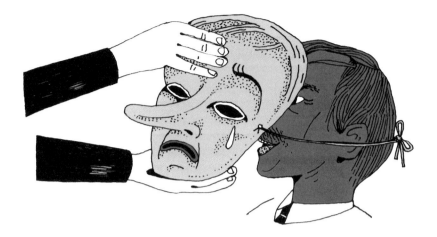

the Turkic-speaking countries of Central Asia. While there, he was given a tour of a secondary school that had been built by Gülen's followers. The school stirred Aksoy's patriotic pride; it was named for a former Turkish president, a Turkish flag flew at graduation and a large photo showed the Turkish and Turkmen presidents shaking hands. 'It was the best school in the country,' Aksoy said. 'All the parents were trying to get their kids into it.'

Through the schools, Aksoy got involved in the Gülen movement, donating money as he travelled throughout Africa, Central Asia and Southeast Asia. 'It became like a hobby for me – whenever I go somewhere, I just go and visit the Gülen school,' he said. The schools served as a sort of beachhead for Turkish interests. 'Even in California, in the Hispanic area, I see schools that are totally Turkish. When I arrived in Tanzania, there were two schools there but no embassy. Now there is an embassy and many businesses.'

Aksoy said the schools formed a loose network. 'They're communicating with each other, and they're keeping up standards. There's a continuous flow of information.' But, like Gülen, he insisted that the movement had no secret agenda. He said the complaints about the Gülenists tended to come from people who were nostalgic for Turkey's old secular order, an era that he regarded as dead. 'The people who lost power cannot see the real changes,' he said. 'Things are changing so fast in Turkey, and they need to blame someone.'

*

From the beginning the Turkish Republic was designed as a secular state. It was founded in 1923 by Mustafa Kemal, better known as Atatürk, a fierce nationalist who believed that religion and politics needed to be kept strictly apart. Once in power, he abolished the Islamic caliphate, which had existed for thirteen hundred years, and put the country's clerics on the state payroll to make sure they didn't step out of line. As a result, for most of the 20th century Turkey's pious majority was governed by a small secular elite. The Turkish military, perhaps the country's strongest institution, saw itself as the guardian of Atatürk's secular state; several times in the 1970s and '80s, Islamist parties rose to prominence only to be shut down and banned. Displays of religious fervour were seen as undesirable, even dangerous.

In 2001 the Justice and Development Party – known by its Turkish initials AKP – was founded by a group of men led by Tayyip Erdoğan. A dynamic former mayor of Istanbul, Erdoğan had recently emerged from prison; he had been jailed by the country's military leaders after giving a speech that included the lines: 'The mosques are our barracks ... and the believers our soldiers.' The next year he announced his candidacy for prime minister. In campaign speeches he proclaimed himself an Islamist, a voice for pious Turks, but he also promised to keep Islam out of politics.

The AKP swept into power in national elections, and Erdoğan began remaking Turkey. He overhauled the judicial system, liberalised the economy and eased relations with long-suppressed minorities like the Alevis and the Kurds. The GDP doubled. In the West, Erdoğan was seen as a bridge to the Islamic world – the leader of a prosperous, democratic and stable Muslim country.

In the same years, Gülen was making his own accommodation with Turkey's secular establishment. Gülen, a preacher in the coastal city of Izmir, may have been

A Brief History of Modern Turkey

1923

At the end of the War of Independence, following the attempt to carve up Ottoman territory by the European powers, Mustafa Kemal, later known as Atatürk, founds the Republic of Turkey.

1925–34

Reforms to modernise the country: abolition of the article of the constitution identifying Islam as the state religion; adoption of the new civil code, which includes the abolition of polygamy and compulsory civil marriage; introduction of the Latin alphabet; guidance on dress; extension of the vote to women.

1938

Death of Mustafa Kemal Atatürk. He is succeeded as president by İsmet İnönü, who decides to remain neutral during the Second World War.

1950s

Following the first elections under a multi-party system in 1950, a government is formed by Adnan Menderes's new Democratic Party (DP), which is not connected to the traditional military and bureaucratic elite. Between 1948 and 1952 Turkey joins the OECD, the Council of Europe and NATO.

1955

Taking as a pretext an explosion at the house where Atatürk was born in the Greek city of Thessaloniki, property owned by Istanbul's Greek community – but also that belonging to the Armenian and Jewish communities – is attacked and destroyed. The pogrom, for which government responsibility has been proven, was yet another act aimed at removing the Greek minority from the country ahead of the expulsions of the 1960s.

27 May 1960

First military coup. Work begins on writing a new constitution, which is approved in 1961.

employed by the state, but he charted his own spiritual path; for inspiration he looked to the theologian Said Nursi, who emphasised the compatibility of Islam with reason and scientific enquiry. While many Islamists espouse anti-Western, anti-capitalist and anti-Semitic views, Gülen's sermons were pro-business, pro-science, and – virtually unheard of in the Muslim world – conciliatory towards Israel.

In 1971, after a military coup, the new regime arrested Gülen on charges of con-spiring to overthrow the secular order, and he served seven months in prison. After that he became a model Islamist of the secular establishment, meeting often with the country's leaders and publicly expressing his support. 'I have said time and again that the republican order and secularism, when executed perfectly, are blessings from God,' he once declared on Turkish television. Such proclamations earned Gülen the ire of Islamist leaders, but they seemed to buy him a measure of protection from secular authorities.

To Western audiences, Gülen's appeal could be mysterious. He speaks in Koran-ically inflected Turkish, and his theology can seem like a blend of bumper-sticker slogans about love, peace, tolerance and interfaith dialogue. 'His charisma comes from his emotion,' one former follower

1968–9
Demonstrations held by the student movement. Protests against the arrival of the US Navy's Sixth Fleet. Radicalisation of the movement leads to the onset of an armed struggle.

12 March 1971
Second military coup. Government resignations and restrictions on personal freedoms, from university autonomy to the independence of the media.

1977
During the 1 May demonstration in Istanbul's Taksim Square, police fire on the crowd, resulting in thirty-four deaths. The operation takes place in a decade rocked by the armed struggle between the radical left and right.

12 September 1980
Third military coup, led by General Kenan Evren. The constitution is suspended and all political parties and organisations are disbanded. This is followed by a period of severe repression, with numerous cases of torture and summary arrests. The civilian government, led by Turgut Özal, is restored in 1983, a year after a new constitution is approved.

1992
Beginning of the forced clearance and burning of thousands of Kurdish villages in the southeast of the country, as clashes with PKK armed guerrillas worsen.

1993
Sivas massacre: a group of radical nationalists and Islamists start a fire during an Alevi cultural event, claiming thirty-seven victims, including many well-known intellectuals and artists.

1996
The customs union with the EU comes into force, following an association agreement signed with the European Economic Community in 1964.

explained. 'He cries, he reacts quickly and unpredictably, he shows all of his emotions. For Westerners, this might be difficult to understand. But for Muslims it can be magical.'

When Erdoğan took office, Gülen estimated that he had as many as three million followers in Turkey, part of a rising class of entrepreneurial, moderately religious Turks who were challenging the secular elite and taking places within the country's bureaucracy. As Gülen preached in favour of business, his followers had set up a network of test-preparation centres, which readied young people to take entrance exams for college, military academies and the civil service. The centres were said to be highly lucrative, and successful adherents donated money to Gülen's programmes. Gradually, his followers built an empire, reportedly worth billions of dollars, that included newspapers, television stations, businesses and professional associations. The Gülenist schools spread; there are now two thousand of them in 160 countries, including at least 120 in the United States.

In the early years of Erdoğan's tenure, he and Gülen shared an interest in finding a place for Islam in public life, but they collaborated only sporadically. Then, in the spring of 2007 Erdoğan and the military had a dramatic confrontation. After he attempted to nominate an Islamist confidant as president, the office of the chief of the general staff posted a memorandum on its website. 'It should not be forgotten that the Turkish armed forces are a side in this debate and are a staunch defender of secularism,' it said. 'They will display their convictions and act openly and clearly whenever necessary.'

Instead of backing down, Erdoğan denounced the military, called for an election and won decisively. Still, he was terrified that the generals, backed by the secular establishment, would come after him again. 'The Gülenists saw an opportunity,'

Ibrahim Kalın, an Erdoğan aide, told me. 'We were newcomers. When our party came to power, the only thing it had was the support of the people. Our party did not have any access to state institutions – no judiciary, no security forces.' Gülen, with his supporters in the bureaucracy, was an appealing ally. He and Erdoğan began to work together more closely.

Erdoğan thrived in the years that followed, but rumours spread about the price that he had paid for his alliance with Gülen. In late 2011 I drove to the outskirts of Ankara to visit Orhan Gazi Ertekin, a judge in the secular tradition; at his office, a portrait of Atatürk hung on the wall and Nina

tourism and promoting knowledge about the country abroad.

2013
Protests break out in late May to defend Gezi Park in Taksim Square, Istanbul, which is earmarked for redevelopment. They are followed by the occupation of the park and demonstrations across the country against Erdoğan's government, growing into the largest mass protests ever seen in modern-day Turkey.

2015
For the first time a progressive left-wing party with a large Kurdish base, the Peoples' Democratic Party (HDP), led by Selahattin Demirtaş and Figen Yüksekdağ, enters parliament. Over the following months the country is rocked by a series of terrorist attacks, including the Suruç massacre, in which thirty-one people lose their lives, and the Ankara massacre during a peace demonstration, which is the worst attack in Turkish history, resulting in 109 deaths.

15 July 2016
Attempted military coup. The AKP government's line is that it was instigated by the Islamic preacher Fethullah Gülen, resident in the USA. The government imposes a state of emergency that lasts for two years. As well as hundreds of arrests, thousands of people are subject to purges across all public offices. There is talk of reintroducing the death penalty, which was abolished in 2004, and numerous newspapers and press agencies are closed. Many people leave the country.

2017
Transition from a parliamentary system to the presidential system. Erdoğan is elected president of the republic.

2019
Local elections: Erdoğan's AKP loses control of the country's most important municipalities, including Istanbul – which is won by Ekrem İmamoğlu – Ankara and Izmir. At the beginning of October the Turkish Army enters northern Syria.

Simone was playing on the stereo. Ertekin told me that he had recently attended a convention to elect the Supreme Council of Judges and Prosecutors, which picks jurists for appointments across the country. 'I had arrived with some candidates in mind, and I came prepared to make deals and coalitions,' he said. At the conference, though, he began to believe that a group of fellow judges, all Gülenists, were conspiring to exclude others. 'In the beginning I had only the vaguest idea of what was happening,' he said. 'They were using a secret language.' After the vote, Ertekin saw that several new council members were followers of Gülen. 'The Gülenists had decided who they were going to choose, and they had no need to cooperate.'

Ertekin told me that Gülen controlled the justice system. 'Erdoğan can accomplish what he wants in the judiciary only by going through Gülen,' he said. 'The Gülenists determine the outcome of every important political and economic trial.' He was increasingly worried but felt that it was dangerous to speak up. 'There is no public domain in which free and open

criticism of the Gülenists can take place,' he said.

I wasn't sure how seriously to take Ertekin's claim. The secular tradition in Turkey was on the wane, and it seemed possible that he was spinning a conspiracy theory to explain its decline. But as I travelled around Turkey I heard more stories of this kind – tales of people who raised questions about the schools or about Gülenist infiltration of the police corps and were arrested and sent to prison. In private, people spoke of a secretive cabal, hidden within the state, that was steadily growing in power.

*

In 1973 Ahmet Keleş, a high-school freshman in the central Turkish city of Kırıkkale, first heard a tape recording of a sermon by Gülen. Keleş was awestruck; Gülen spoke so passionately about the Holy Prophet that as he listened he started to cry. Keleş was from a poor family – his father ran a small store selling table decorations – and for the first time he came alive to his faith. 'Gülen was making people ask themselves, what is

THE PASSENGER   Dexter Filkins

> 'One former Gülen insider estimated that by the early 1990s 40 per cent of the police in Central Anatolia were followers of Gülen and about 20 per cent of the judges and prosecutors.'

your mission as a Muslim?' That summer Keleş travelled to Izmir to meet Gülen, who invited him to attend his summer camp free of charge. Keleş did and returned for the next two summers. After he graduated from high school Gülen asked him to run one of his 'lighthouses' – student dormitories that doubled as religious discussion centres.

Many Gülenists – perhaps most of them – practise their leader's ecumenical ideas earnestly. But as Keleş was pulled into the movement he came to understand that it had a clandestine goal. 'The only way to protect Islam was to infiltrate the state with our followers and seize all the institutions of government,' he explained. 'The legal way to do it was by election, by parliament – but you couldn't do it that way, because the military would step in. The only way to do it was the illegal way – to infiltrate the state and change the institutions from within.'

Keleş, who has since left the movement, said that while Gülen presented himself as a humble, self-denying cleric, in private he was entirely different: vain, megalomaniacal, demanding total obedience. The organisation was hierarchical, divided into seven levels, with Gülen at the top. Keleş joined 'level three' – a senior leadership assembly. 'Level two' conducted covert operations, which he said he was never informed of. (Aslandoğan, the manager of Gülen's Manhattan office, says that this characterisation is misleading.)

In meetings of the leadership assembly, Gülen described his plans as divinely ordained. 'He would tell us, "I met with the Prophet last night, and he told me to do the following things,"' Keleş said. 'Everyone believed him.' Indeed, Gülen's followers came to see his teachings as an entirely new faith. 'He started with Islam, but he created his own theology. We thought Fethullah Gülen was the Messiah.' Other former Gülenists told me much the same thing. 'On the surface he projects this idea that he is not interested in money or women or power, that he only wants to be close to God,' Said Alpsoy, a follower for seventeen years who left the movement in 2003, said. 'The goal is power – to penetrate the state and change it from within. But they will never talk about power. They will deny it.'

In a taped sermon from the late 1990s, Gülen exhorted his followers to burrow into the state and wait for the right moment to rise up. 'Create an image like you are men of law,' he told them. 'This will allow you to rise to more vital, more important places.' In the meantime, he urged patience and flexibility. 'Until we have the power and authority in all of Turkey's constitutional institutions, every step is premature,' he said. But, ultimately, he promised, their work would provide 'the guarantee of our Islamic future'.

Keleş told me that the chief targets of infiltration were the police and the judiciary. In infiltrated police departments, each Gülenist officer had a code name, and each unit was overseen by an outside 'imam', regarded by the officers as a higher authority than the police chief. By the early 1990s, Keleş said, he had become the movement's 'imam' in Central Anatolia, overseeing fifteen cities. By then, he estimated, 40 per cent of the police in the region were followers and about 20 per cent of the judges and prosecutors. 'We controlled the hiring of the police and the entrance exams, and we didn't let anyone in who wasn't a Gülenist,' he said.

Keleş told me that at first he rarely questioned Gülen, even when he started to speak of world domination. 'My father's only goal was to have his son working as a labourer,' he said. 'And here was this man with a plan to manage the world.' Today Keleş is astonished by how credulous he was; he attributes it in part to Gülen's charisma. 'The line between crazy and genius is very thin – with him, it was the same thing,' he said. 'His knowledge, his theological views, his organisational skill – he is a genius. We were all crazy at that time.'

Inside the movement, Keleş and Alpsoy said, people often lost themselves in fantastical rituals. In one, a group of men gathered in a room would grab a comrade, pin his legs and arms and remove his socks and shoes, often against his will. 'They would hold him down, and everyone would kiss his feet,' Alpsoy said. 'This I witnessed hundreds of times.' In the Islamic world, feet and shoes are symbols of filth; in many places it is considered offensive to cross your legs and show the bottoms of your feet. The foot-kissing ritual, Alpsoy said, was a way of demonstrating pure affection. 'If you kiss a person's feet, then you must really love him.' Alpsoy could never bring himself to kiss anyone's feet, he said, 'but they did it to me three or four times'.

Keleş recalled that the ritual sometimes took other forms. 'To show love for someone, people would fill his shoe with water and drink from it.' (Aslandoğan says that he has no knowledge of such rituals.) Alpsoy said that once a man appeared at a service with a shoe that he said had been

worn by Gülen. 'People were so excited – they stripped the leather from the shoe and boiled it for a long time. Then they cut the leather into pieces and ate it.' Members often fought over scraps of food that Gülen had left on his plate. A Turkish intelligence official told me that one Gülenist received a package from her husband, who was living on the compound in Pennsylvania: inside was a piece of bread that Gülen had gnawed on and left behind. 'Gülen knew about all these things,' Keleş said, 'but he would just laugh.'

It took years for Keleş to leave the movement. The turning point came in 1997, when Gülen publicly attacked Necmettin Erbakan, Turkey's first Islamist prime minister, directing his followers in the media to undercut him. Under pressure from the military, Erbakan stepped down later that same year. 'Erbakan and Gülen said they wanted the same things – an Islamic state – and yet Gülen destroyed him,' Keleş said. 'Power was more important to him than religion.' Not long after that Keleş wrote a letter to Gülen, enumerating the ways in which he had drifted from Islam in the pursuit of power. Gülen expelled him from the movement. Keleş said that it was only after he left that he realised how cut off he had been. 'I woke up to the real world,' he said.

*

In 2005, according to a cable written by Stuart Smith, an American diplomat, three senior members of the Turkish

Right and pages 62–4:
Photographs at Istanbul's 15 July Memorial Museum taken during the attempted coup in 2016.

National Police visited the US consulate in Istanbul seeking a favour for Gülen. Three years earlier Gülen, living in exile in the Poconos, had applied for permanent residence, claiming that he was an 'exceptional individual' who deserved special consideration. The US declined his application on the grounds that he was not an especially remarkable person and that he had exaggerated his credentials as a scholar. The policemen at the consulate were pressing an appeal. Smith was sceptical. In his cable, published by WikiLeaks, he noted Gülen's 'sharply radical past as a fiery Islamist preacher' and the 'cult-like obedience and conformity that he and the layers of his movement insist on in his global network of schools, his media outlets, and his business associations'. If anyone was being persecuted, he suggested, it was Gülen's critics. 'Given the Gülenists' penetration of the National Police (TNP) and many media outlets, and their record of going after anyone who criticizes Gülen, others who are skeptical about Gülen's intentions feel intimidated from expressing their views.'

Despite such official American assessments, Gülen won his appeal, in part because influential friends wrote letters in his support. They included George Fidas, a former director of outreach for the CIA; Morton Abramowitz, a former American ambassador; and, perhaps most notably, Graham Fuller, a former senior CIA official.

In Turkey, though, the connection has fed theories that Gülen was supported in his early years by the CIA. Some prominent Turks have said that the assistance continued at least into the 1990s, when the Muslim-majority states of the former Soviet Union declared independence and Gülen's network began to establish itself there. In 2010 Osman Nuri Gündeş, a former senior intelligence official, wrote in a memoir that Gülen's schools in Uzbekistan and Kyrgyzstan had sheltered as many as 130 CIA agents posing as English teachers.

Within the country, the military saw Gülenists as a considerable threat. Gareth Jenkins, a fellow at the Central Asia-Caucasus Institute in Istanbul, said that during the 1990s the armed forces expelled hundreds of officers on suspicion of harbouring links to Gülen. In a cable released by WikiLeaks, an American diplomat wrote that secular officers devised a test: they invited fellow soldiers and their wives to pool parties, reasoning that women who declined to appear in public wearing swimsuits must be restricted by their religion. According to the diplomat, the Gülenist wives became aware of the tactic and came up with a counter-measure: they started wearing bikinis more revealing than their hosts'. When military inspectors began searching officers' homes, the Gülenists stocked their refrigerators with decoy bottles of alcohol and planted empties in the trash.

Gülen's followers recognised that they needed greater numbers in the military. A former AKP member named Emin Şirin told me that in the fall of 1999 he visited the compound in Pennsylvania, and Gülen told him that a 'golden generation' of acolytes was working its way into Turkey's institutions. If a more tolerant general was appointed to lead the military, he said, it would 'bring me peace'. He mentioned General Hilmi Özkok as a desirable candidate. In 2002 Özkok was named chief of the army, and the vigilance within the military relaxed.

*

As Erdoğan started a new term in 2007, the growing momentum towards political Islam in Turkey brought him and Gülen closer. Gülen had divided the country into seven districts, each with a regional chief, who regularly travelled to Pennsylvania to consult on initiatives. Erdoğan, too, sent high-placed representatives to Gülen's compound – 'not every month, but when he needed support for something', Jenkins told me. Gülen was sometimes referred to as the second-most powerful man in the country.

The strengthening alliance helped Erdoğan to confront his rivals in the secular elite and the military. In 2007 police arrested the first of hundreds of people whom the government accused of forming a secret organisation devoted to keeping Islamist aspirations in check. Turks called this network *derin devlet*, the deep state, and it was said to have links across the military, media, academia and law enforcement. Turks have long disputed the exact size and nature of the deep state, but few doubt that something like it once existed. According to scholars and former officials, it was a network of police, soldiers and informants, begun during the Cold War to control domestic dissent and keep democratically elected governments off balance. It is believed to be responsible for many assassinations – of Islamists, leftists and, especially, Kurdish activists.

When the arrests began, police claimed they had finally penetrated the deep state: a secret organisation called Ergenekon, named for a mythological place in Central Asia that is sometimes invoked by ultra-nationalists. Shortly thereafter they began a second investigation, aimed at the most senior generals in the Turkish military, who, they claimed, were fomenting a plot called Sledgehammer to overthrow Erdoğan's government. The cases spread to include not just former military and police officers but also academics, journalists, aid workers – the core of the opposition to the new Islamic order.

According to Turkish and Western

THE DEEP STATE

In contrast to the situation in many other countries, the existence of a parallel state in Turkey is accepted by pretty much everyone and has been known about since the 1970s, when it was confirmed by Prime Minister Bülent Ecevit (who survived an assassination attempt) and the public prosecutor, Doğan Öz (who was killed for his revelations). Turkey was one of the first NATO countries to harbour subversive paramilitary structures belonging to the stay-behind network of organisations and Operation Gladio (the umbrella term for these organisations across Europe). These groups were linked to the CIA, and they popped up throughout western Europe tasked with preventing the rise of left-wing movements and overturning any potential left-wing victory through violent struggle. In Turkey, the activities of this clandestine organisation, in addition to stemming the spread of communism, included pogroms against Greeks, Armenians and Jews in 1955 (which even targeted the ethnic-Greek football hero Lefter Küçükandonyadis) and the murder of trade unionists (the Taksim Square massacre of 1977), Alevis (the Maraş massacre of 1978), journalists, intellectuals and countless Kurds as well as the fight against Islamism (radicalised Islam being unpopular with the military). It was a chance event in 1996 that unmasked some of the scheming undertaken by the deep state (a term coined in Turkey) and led to an unprecedented scandal: a car was involved in a traffic accident, and sitting inside, next to the heroin trafficker and suspected terrorist Abdullah Çatlı, were Hüseyin Kocadağ, a police officer with a past in the Counter-Guerrilla organisation (the Turkish branch of Operation Gladio), and the sole survivor, Sedat Bucak, a controversial Kurdish politician who was being paid by the government to assist in the fight against Kurdish separatists.

officials, both investigations were headed by Gülenists in the police and the judiciary. For years *Zaman*, the country's largest newspaper, and Samanyolu TV, both run by Gülen loyalists, cheered on the investigations and demonised anyone who questioned the evidence. Erdoğan supported the investigations with equal enthusiasm, saying that they were necessary to remove the shadow of the military from public life. 'How and why could anyone try to stop this?' he said in a speech to his party in 2009. 'The crimes in these charges violate our constitution and laws. Let the justice system do its job.'

As diplomats and independent journalists began to review the prosecutions, it became clear that both contained fabricated evidence. In my own investigation into the two cases, I found several instances of unmistakable forgery. The evidence in Sledgehammer was built largely on a series of computer disks, which ostensibly contained blueprints for a wide-ranging military coup. But, while prosecutors alleged that the plan had been drawn up in 2003, it was written mostly in a version of Microsoft Office that wasn't released until 2007. Similarly, many specifics of the plans – licence-plate-numbers of cars to be seized, a hospital to be occupied – referred to things that did not exist in 2003.

Some six hundred people were convicted in the Ergenekon and Sledgehammer trials, including scores of senior generals in the Turkish military and several prominent journalists. About two hundred were sentenced to long prison terms, many in cases presided over by judges thought to be loyal to Gülen. After the trials, Turkey's secular elite was completely vitiated. That left Erdoğan and Gülen as the two strongest forces in the country, and they soon began to turn on each other. The judiciary, emboldened by Ergenekon and Sledgehammer, pursued the investigations ever closer to Erdoğan. In the early months of 2012 police issued a subpoena to Hakan Fidan – the chief of national intelligence and a confidant of the prime minister – and arrested İlker Başbuğ, the country's highest military officer. 'They felt that they could arrest *anyone*,' Gareth Jenkins said. Erdoğan responded in a way that seemed calculated to hobble the Gülenists: he started closing down their schools – a crucial source of income – and working to restrain the police. 'For Erdoğan, that was a declaration of war,' Jenkins said.

*

On the evening of 1 January 2013 a cargo jet from Accra, Ghana, bound for Sabiha Gökçen International Airport in Istanbul, was diverted because of fog to Istanbul Atatürk Airport. When the plane landed, customs officials found that a shipment labelled 'mineral samples' actually contained more than 1,360 kilograms of gold bars. The gold belonged to Reza Zarrab – a 29-year-old Turkish-Iranian businessman who counted among his friends some of Turkey's most powerful politicians – and it was ultimately destined for Tehran. Turkish investigators, listening in on Zarrab's phone, determined that he was transporting extraordinary amounts of gold to Iran as part of a far-reaching scheme to help the Iranian regime evade economic sanctions. At the peak of the operation, Zarrab said later, he was moving nine hundred kilograms of gold a day.

It seemed at first as if the case had limited implications within Turkey. 'We didn't expect this little investigation to give way to a bigger one,' Nazmi Ardıç, the chief of the Istanbul police department's organised-crime unit, told me. Then, investigators say, they heard wiretapped conversations suggesting that Zarrab was bribing officials in Erdoğan's government. Within days, Ardıç said, police and prosecutors determined that Zarrab had paid millions of dollars to at least four Turkish cabinet ministers. According to documents filed in US District Court in Manhattan, the minister for the economy, Zafer Çağlayan, accepted more than $45 million in cash, gems and luxury goods. When police entered the home of Süleyman Aslan – the CEO of Halk Bank, which Zarrab used to launder money – they found shoeboxes stuffed with $4.5 million in cash.

The bribery allegations electrified Turkey. Zarrab, the centre of the investigation, seemed made for tabloid news. A brash young trader with a pouf of dark hair, he was married to one of the country's biggest pop stars, Ebru Gündeş, famous for such songs as 'Fugitive' and 'I Dropped My Anchor in Solitude'. He was also friendly with Erdoğan: he'd stood with him at public functions and donated $4.6 million to a charity run by his wife Emine. The allegations came at a time when Erdoğan was increasingly embattled and also increasingly aggressive. In the spring of 2013 police had broken up a peaceful demonstration in Istanbul's Gezi Park, igniting protests in which millions of people took part. Erdoğan turned the police loose; eleven people died and more than eight thousand were injured. That year more than a hundred journalists were fired after criticising Erdoğan.

On 17 December 2013 police arrested Zarrab and eighty-eight others, including forty-three government officials. Although they did not arrest any of Erdoğan's ministers, they detained the sons of three of them, claiming that they were conduits for bribes. Erdoğan's son Bilal also came under suspicion after a wiretap captured what was alleged to be a conversation between him and his father. Erdoğan has insisted that the tape was doctored, but it circulated widely on social media, and Turks claimed to recognise his voice.

Tayyip Erdoğan: Eighteen people's homes are being searched right now with this big corruption operation ... So I'm saying, whatever you have at home, take it out. OK?

Bilal: Dad, what could I even have at home? There's your money in the safe.

Tayyip: Yes, that's what I'm saying.

A little while later the two apparently spoke again.

Tayyip: Did you get rid of all of it, or ... ?

Bilal: No, not all of it, Dad. So, there's something like €30 million left that we haven't been able to liquidate.

Western officials told me that they regarded the investigation as a Gülenist attempt to topple Erdoğan's government – but that the evidence seemed credible. As the investigation gathered force, four of Erdoğan's ministers resigned. One of them, Erdoğan Bayraktar, called on Erdoğan to quit, saying, 'The prime minister, too, has to resign.'

Instead, Erdoğan struck back. He denounced the investigation as a 'judicial coup' and enacted a wholesale reorganisation of the country's criminal-justice system, forcing out thousands of police, prosecutors and judges linked to the Zarrab case. Ardıç, the police chief who headed the investigation, was removed from the case and later imprisoned. Ultimately, the bribery charges were dropped.

In speeches, Erdoğan began lashing out at his former ally, speaking of a 'parallel structure' that sought to rule Turkey. 'O Great Teacher, if you haven't done anything wrong, don't stay in Pennsylvania,' he told a rally in February 2014. 'If Turkey is your motherland, come back to Turkey, come back to your motherland. If you want to get involved in politics, go ahead and go

JOURNALISTS IN PRISON

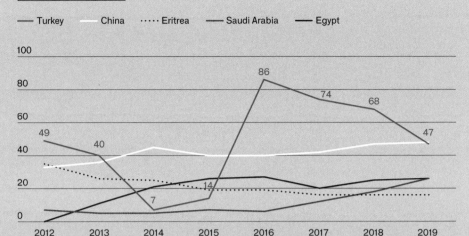

Turkey — China — Eritrea — Saudi Arabia — Egypt

100 · 80 · 60 · 40 · 20 · 0

49 · 40 · 7 · 14 · 86 · 74 · 68 · 47

2012 · 2013 · 2014 · 2015 · 2016 · 2017 · 2018 · 2019

SOURCE: COMMITTEE TO PROTECT JOURNALISTS

POST-COUP PURGES

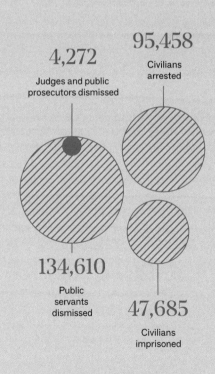

4,272
Judges and public
prosecutors dismissed

95,458
Civilians
arrested

134,610
Public
servants
dismissed

47,685
Civilians
imprisoned

SOURCE: TURKEY PURGE

Teachers, health workers, judges and public prosecutors make up 40% of all public servants dismissed following the failed coup of 15 July 2016.

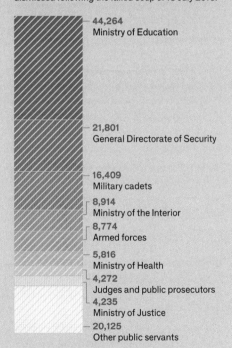

44,264
Ministry of Education

21,801
General Directorate of Security

16,409
Military cadets

8,914
Ministry of the Interior

8,774
Armed forces

5,816
Ministry of Health

4,272
Judges and public prosecutors

4,235
Ministry of Justice

20,125
Other public servants

into the public squares and make politics. But don't mess with this country, don't steal its peace ... The parallel structure is involved in grand treason.'

*

After the bribery case collapsed, Erdoğan pursued the Gülenists relentlessly. Thousands of public employees who were suspected of having ties to Gülen were pushed out, and government agents raided Gülenist businesses. Senior leaders in the movement began to flee the country.

On Christmas Day 2015 Turkish intelligence breached an encrypted messaging app called ByLock – an apparently homemade network with 200,000 users. According to Turkish officials, it was set up not long after Erdoğan began purging suspected Gülenists from the government. When the network was discovered, the server, in Lithuania, quickly closed down, and its users switched to Eagle, another encrypted messaging app. 'They went underground,' a Turkish government aide told me. The intelligence officials say that they were able to decrypt the exchanges, and one told me, 'Every conversation was about the Gülen community.' By checking the ByLock users' names against government records, they found that at least forty thousand were civil employees, mostly from the judiciary and the police department. In May 2016, two months before the coup, the government began suspending them. In July the intelligence department notified the military that it had also identified six hundred officers of the Turkish Army, many of them highly ranked, among the ByLock users. Military officials began planning to expel them at a meeting of senior generals that was scheduled for early the next month. 'We think the coup happened in July because they needed to move before they were expelled,'

Ibrahim Kalın, the Erdoğan aide, told me.

The details of the failed coup are murky and often contradictory, but it seems clear that the attempt was organised in haste. Several detained soldiers said that it was supposed to begin six hours later, at 3 a.m., then was rushed for reasons that are unclear. As the officers scrambled to take control, no leader came forward. In some cases, troops who'd received orders from rebel commanders apparently didn't realise that they were taking part in an operation to overthrow the government and refused to go along when they did. Indeed, it seems that the plotters staked their operation on capturing or killing Erdoğan and persuading General Akar to join them. 'If those things had happened the coup would have succeeded,' Kalın said. But none of the most senior generals of the Turkish armed forces could be persuaded to join, which may have left the plotters without a military leader. By 4 a.m. the coup plotters were running for their lives.

'Has the operation been cancelled, Murat?' one officer asked in a text message.

'Yes, Commander,' Major Çelebioğlu replied. When another officer asked whether to mount an escape, the major replied: 'Stay alive, Commander. The choice is yours.'

After the coup, several statements, purportedly from the plotters, were released to the press. The statements were impossible to verify. None of the men who confessed has spoken publicly, and most of their statements appear to have been heavily expurgated. Photographs have circulated of officers who confessed; in several cases, they have wounds on their faces, suggesting that they were beaten.

Two Western diplomats who spoke on the condition of anonymity told me that they found the government's accusations against Gülen's movement compelling if not entirely convincing. One said, 'Undoubtedly, Gülenists played a credible role in it. But there were also anti-Erdoğan military opportunists mixed in.' Many people in the armed forces, and in Turkish civil society, were enraged by Erdoğan's growing authoritarianism. Brigadier General Gökhan Sönmezateş, one of the plotters who went to Marmaris to capture Erdoğan, said in a confession, 'I am absolutely not a Gülenist.' But when one of the plotters called on a secure line to recruit him, he thought that things in the country were bad enough that he agreed to go along. Some former American officials said it was likely that Gülenists played the leading role. After the purges of the preceding decade, they argued, no other group in the army was large enough or cohesive enough.

Erdoğan's government has given the US tens of thousands of pages of documents, tracking the Gülenists' history in Turkey. According to American officials, little or none of it is relevant to the question of Gülen's direct involvement in the coup. General Akar, the chief of the general staff, said in a statement that while he was being held captive one of the senior plotters said, 'If you wish, we can put you in touch with our opinion leader, Fethullah Gülen.' One of the Western diplomats, who has followed Akar throughout his career, told me, 'Akar has been, since he took the position, a guy defined by integrity.'

The most compelling account came from Lieutenant Colonel Levent Türkkan, one of the officers who took Akar captive. In his confession he identified seventeen colleagues as Gülenists, including Erdoğan's personal military aide, Colonel Ali Yazıcı. (Aslandoğan disputes Türkkan's testimony but says that he can't speak to specific claims.)

In 2011 Türkkan was promoted and became an aide to General Necdet Özel, the chief of the Turkish Army. 'I started carrying out assignments given by the sect,' he said. For four years he planted a small 'listening device' in Özel's office every day and removed it every night. 'The battery lasted one day,' he said. 'I would take the full device to my "sect brother" once a week and get an empty one from him.' The night before the coup, Türkkan said, a fellow Gülenist, a colonel, asked him to step outside for a cigarette. Once they were alone, he described a plan. 'The president, the prime minister, the ministers, the chief of general staff, other chiefs of staff and generals would be picked up one by one. Everything would be done quietly.' Türkkan's assignment was to help find Akar and 'pacify' him. Disturbed, Türkkan went to see his 'brother' in the Gülen movement, who lived in a house behind a nearby gas

Pages 72–3: A woman prepares to enter Istanbul's 15 July Memorial Museum, located a few metres from the first bridge over the Bosphorus.

THE PASSENGER   Dexter Filkins

station. He wasn't there, but several others were, and they confirmed the operation.

Türkkan suffered following the coup. In a photograph released with his testimony he is wrapped in a hospital gown with his face visibly battered and his rib cage and hands swaddled in bandages. In his confession he expressed bitter remorse. 'When I learned from the TV that the parliament was being bombed and civilians were being killed, I started regretting it,' he said. 'What was being done was like a massacre. This was done in the name of a movement that I thought worked for the will of God.'

*

Three weeks after the coup Erdoğan, addressing a group of local officials in Ankara, apologised for having once been Gülen's ally. 'We helped this organisation with good will,' Erdoğan said. He added that he had trusted Gülen because of his apparent reverence for education and his organisation's aid work. 'I feel sad that I failed to reveal the true face of this traitorous organisation long before.'

For Erdoğan, though, retribution has always come more easily than apologies. The state of emergency that he declared after the coup gave him dictatorial powers, which he used to carry out a far-reaching crackdown that began with Gülenists but grew to encompass almost anyone who might pose a threat to his expanded authority. The figures are stupefying: forty thousand people detained and huge numbers of others forced from their jobs, including twenty-one thousand police officers, three thousand judges and prosecutors, twenty-one thousand public-school workers, fifteen hundred university deans and fifteen hundred employees of the Ministry of Finance. Six thousand soldiers were detained. The government also closed a thousand Gülen-affiliated schools and

İMAM HATİP ISLAMIC SCHOOLS

Alongside the Gülen private schools, Turkey also offers state-funded religious education, which was originally intended only to train imams and *hatip* (preachers). After Atatürk had closed all the madrasas, a form of Islamic education was reintroduced in the 1950s for those who wanted to go on to study theology. These schools have become increasingly important and widespread, especially since the AKP has been in power. In its controversial 2012 school reform (which included measures to exclude Darwinian evolution from syllabuses and to set up a prayer room in every school), the government made things easier for religious schools by giving them comparable status to other high schools and transforming seven hundred middle schools into *imam hatip*, triggering protests from many parents. From 4,200 in 1961, student numbers grew to 229,000 in 1985 and 511,000 in 1997, after which there was a fall following reforms demanded by the military, who forced Prime Minister Erbakan to resign, but under Erdoğan, himself a former *imam hatip* pupil, there has been a surge in enrolments to almost 1.5 million. In these schools, classes are single sex, girls wear veils and the main foreign language is Arabic, enabling large numbers of people to decipher the Koran. Even though Arabic is spoken by neither the imam nor the congregation, it is the language of prayer and readings in many mosques, particularly in the provinces – as the more orthodox do not accept translations of religious texts, believing the only true version to be that dictated to Mohammed by the Archangel Gabriel in Arabic.

> 'For Erdoğan, retribution has always come more easily than apologies. The state of emergency that he declared after the coup gave him dictatorial powers, which he used to carry out a far-reaching crackdown.'

suspended twenty-one thousand teachers.

It's difficult to know whether those targeted were hard-core followers of Gülen, or sympathisers, or not related to the movement at all. Public criticism of Erdoğan was almost entirely squelched, either by the outpouring of national support that followed the coup or by the fear of being imprisoned. Erdoğan closed more than 130 media outlets and detained at least forty-three journalists, and the purge continued for months. 'The Gülenist cult is a criminal organisation, and a big one,' Kalın, the president's aide, told me. 'You know, over eleven thousand people participated in the coup, according to our current estimates. We're going after anyone with any connection with this Gülenist cult, here and there, in the judiciary, the private sector, the newspapers and other places.'

The irony of the attempted coup is that Erdoğan emerged stronger than ever. The popular uprising that stopped the plot was led in many cases by people who disliked Erdoğan only marginally less than they disliked the prospect of a military regime. But the result was to set up Erdoğan and his party to rule, with nearly absolute authority, for as long as he wants. 'Even before the coup attempt, we had concerns that the government and the president were approaching politics and governance in ways that were designed to lock in a competitive advantage – to ensure you would have perpetual one-party rule,' the second Western diplomat said.

*

The day after the coup Gülen emerged from seclusion. He spoke to reporters who had gathered at his compound and denied any involvement. As he watched his followers being arrested en masse – and as he became a national pariah – an edge crept into his voice. He told his followers that Erdoğan had staged the coup and that no one outside Turkey believed that Gülen was responsible. In a sermon recorded a few days later, he said, 'Let a bunch of idiots think they have succeeded, let them celebrate, let them declare their ridiculous situation a celebration, but the world is making fun of this situation, and that is how it is going to go down in the history books. Be patient,' he told his followers. 'Victory will come.'

Gülen is old and ailing; it seems unlikely that he will be able to keep up the fight for much longer. Listening to his sermon, I thought back to my meeting with him in 2015. Even then his movement was being dismantled, his followers on the run. I asked how he thought he would be remembered, and he gave me an answer the like of which I've never heard from another leader in politics or religion. 'It may sound strange to you, but I wish to be forgotten when I die,' he said. 'I wish my grave not to be known. I wish to die in solitude, with nobody actually becoming aware of my death and hence nobody conducting my funeral prayer. I wish that nobody remember me.' ✒

Business à la Turca

Alev Scott paints a portrait of the Turkish economy, which is driven by an innate entrepreneurial spirit and the great dream of instant wealth but forced to operate in a political climate that is prone to instability.

ALEV SCOTT

A waxwork of Turkish businessman Rahmi Mustafa Koç, who was included in the 2016 *Forbes* list of the world's thousand richest people; he has been chairman of Koç Holding – Turkey's largest industrial conglomerate – for many years.

After the California Gold Rush of 1849 a new American Dream emerged. As opposed to the old, Puritanical ethos that had inspired people to accumulate a modest fortune year by year, the new aim has been described by the historian H.W. Brands as 'the dream of instant wealth, won in a twinkling by audacity and good luck'.

There has been no equivalent gold rush in Turkey, but there are infinite business opportunities and people hungry and audacious enough to seize them in an economy infamously prone to highs and lows. The years 2010 to 2020 were particularly dramatic; in 2012 the number of Turkish-lira millionaires in the country rose from seven thousand to more than fifty thousand. In 2018, when the lira collapsed, losing 45 per cent of its value against the dollar, the number of billionaires fell from thirty-five to twenty-two. Over roughly the same six-year period unemployment rose from 8 to 14 per cent.

Meanwhile, risk-averse Turks have honoured a long tradition of hoarding gold under their mattresses to get them through hard times; every few years the government embarks on a campaign to persuade them to trust in banks instead. National income from tourism and foreign investment rises and falls with terrorist attacks, coups or attempted coups roughly every decade and a wildly unpredictable exchange rate. Domestic and personal stability in Turkey is variable, to say the least, which perhaps explains the stubbornly held dream of instant wealth, won in a twinkling by audacity and good luck, kept alive in the perennially entrepreneurial spirit of the nation.

When big dreamers succeed, their success is all-embracing, attended by huge celebrity – perhaps the best example of a rags-to-riches transformation is İbrahim Tatlıses ('Abraham Sweet Voice'), a Kurdish arabesk pop singer and alleged mafia king who created a massive business empire from nothing. He is a hyperbolic example of the potential of Turkish entrepreneurship: a former construction worker with very little education and boundless ambition who came from a minority background, made shrewd decisions and manipulated his music celebrity to create a one-man business conglomerate. 'Ibo' is a national icon, loved for his unapologetically sentimental music and revered for his wealth and influence, which has also made him serious enemies – in 2011 he survived being shot in the head, having been the victim of two earlier assassination attempts during his career.

Aside from selling millions of albums

ALEV SCOTT, a former Istanbul correspondent for various publications, including the *Guardian*, *Politico* and *Newsweek*, was born in London to a Turkish mother and British father. Her first book, *Turkish Awakening* (Faber and Faber, revised edition 2015), tells of her discovery of Turkey and its contradictions, with an account of the protests that rocked the country in 2013, while *Ottoman Odyssey: Travels through a Lost Empire* (Riverrun, 2018) explores the history and the boundaries of the Ottoman Empire. She was expelled from Turkey in 2016.

> 'Prominent family dynasties that hand down their wealth from parent to child are minor gods in Turkish society; they are few but mighty, and everyone knows them.'

in both Kurdish and Turkish, Tatlıses has acted in scores of films and hosted his own weekly chat show. In his hometown of Urfa fans flock to the İbrahim Tatlıses Museum to ogle shiny waxworks of the great man. His businesses are varied, but the most famous are his eponymous kebab chain and bus company, both of which dominate the entire Southeastern Region of Turkey, where Ibo fans abound. He has construction interests in Iraqi Kurdistan and unsuccessfully ran for parliament in the 2007 Turkish general election. Despite this rare personal failure he has political support when it counts – after the assassination attempt in 2011 then-Prime Minister Erdoğan visited Tatlıses in hospital before he was whisked off to Germany for treatment.

It might seem that Tatlıses has overcome extreme obstacles to achieve his success, and in some ways this is true – certainly in the case of assassins' bullets. However, his Kurdish background and lack of education were, in some ways, crucial to sustaining his appeal in the long term as a man with whom millions of working Turks and Kurds could identify. He is, significantly, a rare example of a celebrity who thrives on his Kurdish identity. From 1989 to 1991 public music performances and recordings in Kurdish were censored, so when Tatlıses erupted on to the radio waves again in 1991 it was a triumphant return, almost a personal celebration. He is the champion of a demographic who claim him as one of their own, but he has been very careful not to over-identify himself as a Kurd. He sings in Turkish and is also very popular in the Arab world

and Iran. His music has been the ultimate vehicle to national and regional fame.

Tatlıses is a prominent reminder to Turks that you *can* have it all. Far from discrediting his business gravitas, his popular music persona has boosted his commercial ventures. In Europe, and even more so in the USA, celebrities sell perfume and produce designer clothes. In Turkey they sell kebabs and bus tickets. Here, as nowhere else, success is not nuanced or compartmentalised, it is achievable and desirable in all incarnations and combinations.

Turks may not all be such ambitious dreamers as Tatlıses, but there is a strong family ethos that inspires many of them not only to provide for their immediate relations but to accumulate wealth for future generations. Prominent family dynasties that hand down their wealth from parent to child are minor gods in Turkish society; they are few but mighty, and everyone knows them.

Back in the 1920s two major family businesses took root: the Koç and Sabancı holding companies, which between them now seem to run most of Turkey's business. They dominate the construction, energy and finance sectors in particular; both have founded prestigious universities and run world-renowned private museums in a spirit of mild rivalry. The founding entrepreneurs of each family started from relatively humble beginnings: Hacı Ömer Sabancı worked as a penniless cotton picker in the early 1920s, while Vehbi Koç sold vegetables in 1917, later aided by his father's acquisition of a former Armenian-owned vineyard seized by the Turkish state. They both built business empires so successful that today their grandchildren are billionaires, holding top positions in their respective companies. None of these men and women or their children or, in all likelihood, their children's children will ever need to work, but their role in carrying the baton of the family business is as symbolically important as the cooperation of any Turkish family.

The Koç and Sabancı families have had a century to accumulate and consolidate their financial and social power. Families who came later to the game are not quite so fortunate, and these days few family-based companies are allowed to achieve such influence unless they have the right political connections. The Doğan family, who founded their company in 1980, were fined ₺4.8 billion in 2009 (roughly $3 billion at the time) for tax 'irregularity'. This is a standard accusation levelled by Turkish authorities at individuals or organisations that are in disgrace for something else and is a convenient way of financially hobbling an overly successful company. The secularist bent of Doğan's popular outlets such as *Hürriyet* and CNN Türk came under scrutiny after the attempted military coup of 2016 amid the government crackdown on any oppositional voices; in 2018 their media group was sold to Demirören Holding, owner of pro-government dailies, and Doğan joined the ranks of censored outlets in an increasingly darkening media landscape.

Since the beginning of the 21st century, amid economic fluctuation, Turkey's natural entrepreneurial spirit has persisted – most visitors notice this buzz as soon as they arrive in Istanbul. Everyone wants an empire of their own in some shape or form. From small kebab joints to massive banking syndicates, there is an energy and drive to business life here that is comparatively lacking further west. Turkey is a massive country of eighty-two million, more used than most to economic crises; Turks have traditionally knuckled down in tough times, but recent years have tested even their stoicism.

Since the Gezi Park protests erupted in late May 2013 the Turkish economy has been particularly unpredictable. Terrorist attacks by the so-called Islamic State and the Kurdish PKK militant group struck further blows. But it was the aftermath of the attempted military coup in July 2016 that most affected individuals and businesses – then there was the infamous collapse of the lira in 2018, attended by a huge interest-rate spike to 24 per cent (five years earlier, before the Gezi Park protests, the rate had stood at just 4.5 per cent). It is perhaps unsurprising, then, that Turks tend to hoard gold as a security measure. The tradition of storing tangible capital, to be converted into cash in an emergency, is a habit fuelled by mistrust of conventional banking after decades of economic unpredictability as a result of hyperinflation and political drama – far beyond the most recent decade of flux. This mistrust peaked in 2001 when the inflation rate rose to 70 per cent. More importantly, gold is a big part of Turkish culture – at weddings, births and circumcision ceremonies gifts are always given in the form of gold coins or jewellery and stored for future family life. I found out the importance of gold through bitter experience, turning up at a traditional Turkish wedding with a generic wedding present instead of the requisite gold coin. To my horror the bride and groom stood by the door as guests left the reception, holding a large bag to collect the coins as they wished everyone goodbye with beatific smiles. With my wretched photograph frame in hand I could not bear to

Above: A businessman rushes through the streets of Istanbul.

join the queue; instead I found myself in a glass elevator escaping to the staff car park upstairs, probably seen by all the guests queuing below me.

Many Turks are pessimistic about the future, even during times of growth, and many felt vindicated when the 2018 recession hit. Having said that, the Turkish economy has huge potential to grow, and over the past decade Turks have been altering their spending habits, giving momentum to that growth. Banks advertise their credit cards like sweets – delicious, harmless and readily available – and many

people go for the bait. The average Turk has a clutch of credit cards which they flash impressively as they open their wallet to pay for their friend's lunch – a selection of cards still suggests wealth rather than debt. In fact, so great is the proliferation of credit cards that the government has had to step in to stop banks advertising them so aggressively. In July 2013 Erdoğan delivered these words of wisdom: 'Those credit cards, don't have them. If everybody spends as much as they [the banks] want, they would not even be able to earn that income. They could never be satiated.'

Turks have been offered more and more ways to pay for previously unrealisable dreams, and until the 2018 recession almost everything was offered for sale in monthly or even quarterly instalments. At the height of the crisis in August 2018 the

Change (in %) of the origins of tourists in Istanbul and Antalya, the 8th and 10th (respectively)
most visited destinations globally by number of nights stayed.

ISTANBUL

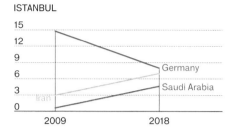

ANTALYA

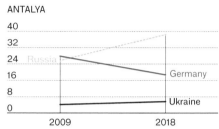

SOURCE: MASTERCARD GLOBAL DESTINATION CITIES INDEX 2019

government intervened, and the *taksit*, or instalment programmes, were heavily restricted in the amount of time allowed for repayment; certain goods – such as jewellery, food and fuel – were made off limits altogether. However, delayed payments still play a part in luring visitors to Turkey for non-traditional tourism. Since 2010 there has been a noticeable increase in Turkey in the number of men undergoing hair transplants – they generally go in pairs and can be seen wandering around major shopping streets with matching hats or post-op headbands. Online, most clinics offer credit options for treatment, with links to specific Lebanese and Swiss banks in partnership with the clinics in question. Certain companies also offer special package deals to overseas clients that include the transplant procedure with more traditional tourist trips. Medical tourism is a huge business in Turkey, attracting Arabs in particular to come for cosmetic procedures, combining their visit with a skiing holiday or a few days wandering around the Blue Mosque and Hagia Sophia. The most intriguing

cosmetic speciality in Turkey is moustache transplant surgery for men who want a more virile-looking moustache. Arabs are particular fans, probably inspired by the well-endowed upper lips of celebrities like İbrahim Tatlıses.

While the weakened lira post-2018 has enticed some tourists looking for a cheap currency-exchange rate, there have been fewer American and European tourists since the Gezi Park protests of 2013 and particularly since the ISIS attacks of 2015 and 2016. Meanwhile, there has been an inverse rise in Arab tourists. These tourists still come in their millions and head straight to historic sites and museums which celebrate Turkey's romantic Ottoman heritage.

There is a noticeably laissez-faire attitude to business here, and a thin line separates friends and business associates – nepotism abounds, an alternative way of looking at the culture of sustaining family businesses. Most annoyingly, lax payment is totally normal, although this has become less common since the days of sky-high interest rates and the corresponding profit one could make simply from sitting on cash for as long as possible. The Russian great-grandfather of a Turkish friend of mine was the tsar's pastry chef in the early 20th century; he emigrated to Turkey and set up a successful wholesale bakery which, until the 1990s, used to supply some of the main supermarkets in the country. Eventually, the family business was sold because they could not cope with the cash-flow problems caused by late payments. Their debtors were companies with multi-million-lira turnovers, but they operated in the same way as any other opportunistic enterprise.

Refreshingly, however, the style of Turkish business is very direct. If you want to trade with a Turk you ring him up (yes, almost always a he) or walk into his shop and pitch an offer. The lack of protocol can sometimes be a problem, but single traders and small companies find it liberating. It is not a coincidence that Italian companies do very well in Turkey, with their Mediterranean adaptability. They manage to win huge contracts here, for example the $2.5 billion third Bosphorus bridge project, carried out by an Italian company called Astaldi, which also built the metro system in Istanbul. In 2015 Astaldi signed a $985 million deal to build a hospital complex in Ankara.

Turks also traditionally see eye to eye with Middle Eastern companies, as is evident from the shift in business away from the EU and towards the Middle East and North Africa over the past decade – something which has been accompanied by increasing disillusionment with Europe on a geopolitical level. Turkish construction companies secure multi-billion-dollar projects in countries like Qatar and Saudi Arabia, while these countries are rumoured to invest heavily in Turkey. Rightly or wrongly, people assume that there are important political reasons for this trend, which has coincided with

HOLIDAYS IN HOSPITAL

At first sight they look like members of a strange sect that practises self-flagellation: men with white bandages wrapped around shaven heads divided into geometrical forms made up of thousands of bleeding follicles. They are, in fact, patients recovering from hair-transplant operations, one of the fastest-growing sections of the Turkish economy and part of a more general growth in medical tourism in the country: in 2018 around a million tourists visited to receive healthcare. Turkey performs more transplants (including beards and moustaches) than any other country as well as offering dental care, plastic surgery, cardiology, dermatology and genetic-consultancy services, all at very affordable prices: a hair-transplant operation can cost between $550 and $2,250 compared with $22,500–$28,000 in Europe. The government has encouraged the creation of health hubs and has boosted the national health system (which proved extremely useful during the COVID-19 pandemic, when Turkish hospitals were never overwhelmed as they were elsewhere). Despite the generally very high standards, however, there has been no shortage of unfortunate incidents, if only in cosmetic terms. A hair transplant, for example, is a demanding operation lasting several hours and carries a high risk of infection, long-term scarring or hair that grows in unnatural directions, particularly when the clinics, which operate in a climate of cut-throat competition, decide to cut costs by taking on unqualified staff or break the law by entrusting operations to assistants or nurses.

Above: Hacı Sabancı High School in Üsküdar, Istanbul.
Below: The headquarters of Yapi Kredi bank in Şişli, Istanbul; the Koç family is the majority shareholder in the bank.

the rule of President Erdoğan's party, the Justice and Development Party (AKP).

The backbone of the Turkish economy is still mass production. There are obvious practical reasons for the success of this sector in this country – relatively low wages compared to Europe, plenty of workers and space for big factories among other factors. Helped by a move towards fast fashion, Turkey continues to challenge China as the main exporter of mass-produced clothes to Europe, mainly because it is much closer, significantly reducing shipping costs and delivery times. Chinese factories operate on such low profit margins that it is only worth their while to take orders in the thousands of tonnes; Turkish companies will do smaller orders, which means that high-street chains can order a new season's worth of stock, receive it on time and order a different batch a few months later for next season. Dealing with China involves the risk of having thousands of late, outdated stock items sitting in warehouses accruing dust and storage fees, while Turkey is a relatively low-risk business partner. Yet only the biggest of Turkish companies succeed in the world of mass production – several of the independent clothes factories in central Istanbul have gone bust in the last few years because competition is so fierce, and cash-flow problems are usually fatal.

One of Turkey's most successful clothes-related markets is the replica designer industry. Foreign designer items are prohibitively expensive, especially when the lira is low, but there is a roaring trade in what are often called 'genuine fakes', or good reproductions. While the concept of genuine fakes may raise some interesting metaphysical questions, they are straightforwardly real when it comes to hard cash: from the 'Channel' perfume bottles sold in street bazaars for a few lira to the exquisite replica Mulberry handbags displayed in reputable shops for the equivalent of around $275, the Turkish passion and success in copying foreign designer brands is widely evidenced. The market value of Turkish-produced fakes is second only to the counterfeit markets of China and Hong Kong, and the subject of thousands of lawsuits brought by individual brands as well as Turkey's long-suffering Registered Brand Association.

Big brands are the gold standard of quality, dizzyingly desirable, but why pay a fortune when you could have effectively the same product for so much less? In the most chi-chi parts of Istanbul one can find authorised Prada, Louis Vuitton and even Diane von Fürstenberg outlets; far more widespread are shops with names like FAME and LÜKS selling pretty much the same products at a fraction of the price. The better the fake, the higher the price, but the discerning Turkish fashionista is still saving several hundred or even thousand lira apiece on good-quality products which are supposedly made in the same Turkish factories that produce the originals. The salesman's story is that the fakes are made after normal working hours in, say, the Prada factory with exactly the same materials and are, to all intents and purposes, the same product. More probably, a single item is bought and copied by a 'designer' who studies its details like a clever painter forging a Caravaggio.

There are a handful of highly successful Turkish designers on the international scene, such as Rifat Özbek, Barbaros Şansal and Bora Aksu, but unfortunately there does not seem to be a huge appetite within Turkey to follow in their footsteps. Designing copies for mass production is more lucrative in the short term than going to design college, but I think there are more important reasons than mere practicality behind the Turkish appetite for copying

ERDOĞAN'S PET SCHEMES:
THE AIRPORT, THE BRIDGE AND THE CANAL

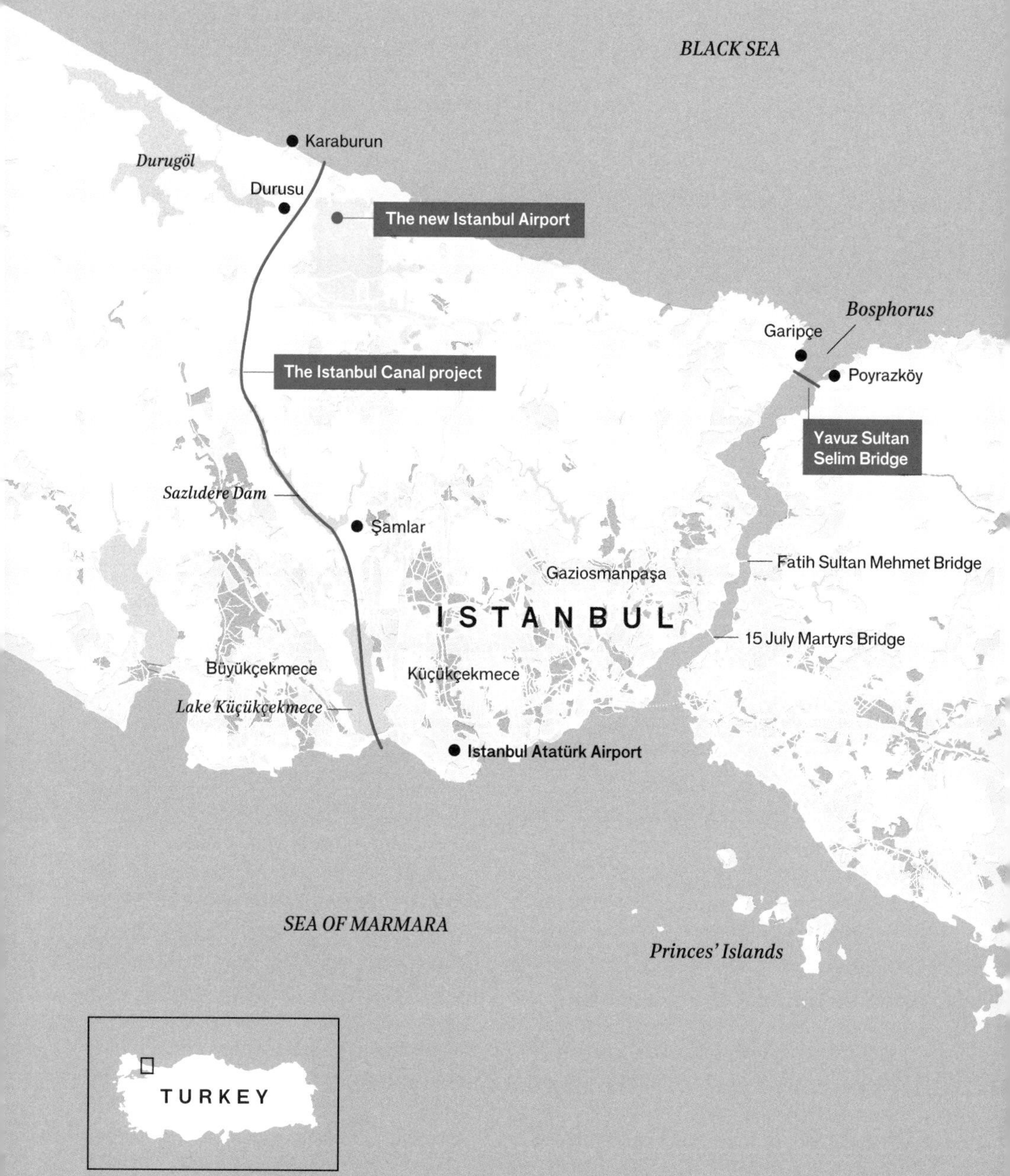
BLACK SEA
Karaburun
Durugöl
Durusu
The new Istanbul Airport
Bosphorus
Garipçe
Poyrazköy
The Istanbul Canal project
Yavuz Sultan Selim Bridge
Sazlıdere Dam
Şamlar
Gaziosmanpaşa
Fatih Sultan Mehmet Bridge
ISTANBUL
15 July Martyrs Bridge
Büyükçekmece
Küçükçekmece
Lake Küçükçekmece
Istanbul Atatürk Airport
SEA OF MARMARA
Princes' Islands
TURKEY

existing models and playing it safe. Having taught at an Istanbul university, I believe the real reason is education. In Turkish schools children learn a great deal by rote and regurgitate it for big exams in high school. Independent thinking is not encouraged, and creativity consequently suffers. For such a large country there are not as many designers or inventors as there should be, because Turkish ingenuity is largely focused on new business ideas rather than invention for its own sake. Turkey is one of Europe's biggest car producers, with massive Renault factories in Bursa and outside Istanbul, but there has been no Turkish-designed car since the demise of the Anadol marque in 1986. One still sees a few on the streets of Istanbul today, but they went down especially well in rural Turkey, where their fibreglass bodywork was eaten ravenously by roaming farm animals.

I had never quite noticed the correlation between education and industry until I had a conversation with the owner of one of Turkey's biggest construction companies. As we talked, the man who had made billions from building roads and energy plants idly picked up his coffee cup. 'Look. A Turk picks up this cup and thinks, I can make this. And he does – he makes hundreds of thousands, exactly the same. But it does not occur to him to design his own. This is Turkey's problem.' I found it both impressive and depressing that a man who had made his money by constructing things on a bigger scale than his competitors had such a clear insight into Turkey's problem with creativity. He was dazzlingly successful proof of his own theory.

While Turkey has become famous for domestic industries like the production of genuine fakes, the Turkish government has long expended efforts on promoting a more respectable and authentic business image abroad, building on the success of

'CRAZY PROJECTS'

Over the course of his long political career, President Erdoğan has changed the face of his country with a raft of projects that, at its peak in 2013, earned Turkey the title of the world's leading infrastructure investor – and nowhere can evidence of the construction boom be more obvious than in Istanbul. As well as the gigantic third airport and the third bridge over the Bosphorus, the country's economic capital now boasts countless new mosques, hospitals and residential skyscrapers that have transformed the city's skyline. Some of what Erdoğan himself describes as his 'crazy projects' have caused irreparable damage to the environment and ecosystems, swapping forests for concrete (an estimated thirteen million trees were felled for the airport alone) and draining marshland that provided a habitat for hundreds of species of animals and migratory birds. The most ambitious has yet to be built, however: a 45-kilometre canal parallel to the Bosphorus that would effectively turn the city of Istanbul into an island. The government claims it can recoup the immense investment in less than ten years thanks to the tolls that cargo ships would have to pay, with the simultaneous benefit of reducing traffic in the Bosphorus, which is free to navigate. The canal project is vehemently opposed by Ekrem İmamoğlu, the mayor of Istanbul, elected in 2019, who is leveraging growing ecological awareness among the public to denounce the project as a potential environmental and economic disaster.

In March 2020, while much of the world was scrambling to stockpile the last rolls of toilet paper from supermarket shelves, Turkish people were replenishing their stocks of a product that they saw as arguably even more essential: *kolonya*, the traditional eau-de-Cologne that is ubiquitous in Turkey. It made its way from Germany to the Ottoman Empire during the 19th century and over time has become a staple in every Turkish home as a symbol of hospitality and hygiene. Guests' hands are doused in *kolonya* when they enter a house, and it is used in shops, restaurants (at the end of the meal), long-distance buses and at the barber's – rubbing your temples with *kolonya* is even guaranteed to relieve a headache! With an alcohol content of at least 60 per cent, but more commonly around 80 per cent, it has long been used as an antiseptic and was credited for delaying – although it couldn't stop – the spread of COVID-19: everyone already had it at home and used it to disinfect their hands regularly. After the minister of health publicly championed its use against the virus, *kolonya* producers said their sales increased fivefold. There are several well-known brands, including Atelier Rebul (founded by a French expat pharmacist in Istanbul in 1895), Eyüp Sabri Tuncer from Ankara (credited with the invention of a lemon-scented *kolonya*) and Selin, the maker of Izmir's famous Altın Damlası (Gold Drop) *kolonya*. But seemingly every town in the country can boast its own original version, made by adding to the base mix of ethanol and distilled water a local product: mandarin in Bodrum, oranges in Antalya, tea in Rize and even – don't judge until you try – tobacco in Düzce.

home-grown phenomena such as its wildly popular epic TV series (known as *dizi*), an industry that has been projected to reach over $1 billion in global revenue by 2023 (for more on *dizi*, see 'Don't Call Them Soap Operas' on page 35). These have infiltrated countries from Kazakhstan to Lebanon and even Latin America; all-time popular shows such as *Magnificent Century* and *Forbidden Love*, dubbed and subtitled, fulfil a role as a kind of commercial ambassador for Turkey.

Similarly, the national airline, Turkish Airlines, is a hugely important brand that has been heavily promoted by the government, which owns a 49 per cent shareholding in the company. Launched in 1933, it now flies to more destinations than any other passenger airline in the world and has made astute sponsorship choices with football clubs and basketball players. Before COVID-19 it carried seventy-five million passengers a year and had an annual revenue of around $12 billion. Given the AKP government's celebration of Turkey's Ottoman past and its considerable support of and influence over the Turkish Airlines brand, it has been interesting to watch the airline Ottomanise its image. First, the design for a new Ottoman style of uniform for flight attendants complete with kaftan and fez was 'leaked' to the public, only to meet with general outrage. Then, red lipstick and nail varnish for female flight attendants were banned – the same outcry ensued, and the airline quickly overturned the ban. Most controversially of all, the airline announced in early 2013 that it would no longer serve alcoholic drinks on domestic services and flights to eight international destinations, apparently because of lack of demand. Until the COVID crisis struck in 2020, revenue seemed not to have been affected by any of these decisions: apart from a loss

Above: Traffic starts to build on the streets of Istanbul as rush hour approaches.

of nearly $80 million in 2016 caused by the attempted military coup, the company recorded steadily increasing profits.

Turkish aviation is perhaps the ultimate metaphor for the soaring heights of national ambition, the risk and investment the government is willing to shoulder in its quest to impress both a domestic and a global audience. Nothing embodies this attitude more than the new Istanbul airport opened in 2019, which was constructed at reckless speed and expense on a marsh north of the city, despite the concerns of environmentalists and engineers and at the cost of twenty-seven workers' lives, according to the government itself. A national fixation with 'crazy projects' such as this and the proposed Istanbul canal – projects that serve to prove that all is well, that Turkey is triumphant, come what may – seems unyielding; it remains to be seen whether that momentum can be continued into the 2020s. Meanwhile, the instincts of Turkish citizens remain unchanged: to prepare for disaster, to aim high and work hard, because no one knows what tomorrow will bring. 🐦

This article is an adapted excerpt from Alev Scott's book *Turkish Awakening*, published in 2015 (revised edition) by Faber and Faber.

Eros and Thanatos at the Restaurant

SEMA KAYGUSUZ
Translated by Ekin Oklap

AKP supporters celebrate victory in the parliamentary elections of 1 November 2015 near the party headquarters on the Golden Horn, Istanbul.

Although the Turkish feminist movement is more than a century old, women still find themselves trapped between two opposing but equally suffocating ideologies – one secular and one religious. Only recently have they begun to make their voices heard within a patriarchal system dominated by men who 'love them to death'.

91

Picture this: a restaurant in an ordinary middle-class neighbourhood of Istanbul, a large screen in the corner showing a hard-fought football match, street musicians patrolling the room and a man and a woman facing each other across a table, talking. To the observer it is obvious that this is a romantic rendezvous. The man tops up the woman's drink; the woman shares out the plates of meze as they arrive. The man talks animatedly about something or other; the woman listens attentively. Compared with the men and women scattered in raucous groups at the other tables, the couple gives off an air of solemnity. Perhaps they are on their first date. A gypsy woman selling flowers has already homed in on them, reeling out blessings – 'God bless you and your beloved', 'God bless this beautiful girl', 'God bless you both with a happy marriage and many children' – as she picks out a rose from her basket and pushes it right into the man's face. The reality is that there is no romance or relationship between the man and the woman yet, but as the first outsider to acknowledge the possibility that there might be, the flower-seller effectively takes on the role of facilitator. We might call her a 'popular facilitator' or a moderator. By instantly promising any woman she sees out on the street to the nearest man, marrying her off to him without a moment's hesitation and pressuring her to embrace motherhood, the flower-seller fulfils the role of St Valentine bestowed upon her by society – and succeeds in selling her flowers, too. The man and the woman have now fallen under the watchful eye of a well-trained Eros. Lustful, affectionate and innately free, Eros wants nothing more than to be at one with another. But, of course, he, too, must submit to a whole range of societal conventions, and this is only the start of the process of domestication dictated by this country's heterosexist norms. The evening has only just begun.

As we approach the couple's table in this neighbourhood restaurant frequented predominantly by middle-class, white-collar workers and the city's merchant classes, we observe a conversation in which the most private of exchanges perfectly reflects the dominant mindset. The man begins to recount the battles he has won; the woman is silent. The man describes the competition he faces in his professional life, while the woman, who has a professional life of her own, who earns less than he does but toils harder in unequal circumstances, is silent. The man orders fish without consulting the woman, who is silent. From time to time the man gazes misty-eyed at the woman, and the woman smiles and is silent. As she sits there she is slowly transformed into an object, reduced from an individual to a creature that exists solely to be gazed at, to be fed, to be gifted flowers, to be desired and to be taken. The itinerant musicians who have been circling the couple begin to play the requested songs. Now there are three more men at the table: a violinist, a clarinettist and a percussionist. Their function is not just to make music but to act as witnesses to a wedding of sorts.

SEMA KAYGUSUZ is a writer of Alevi descent. She has published numerous short-story collections and three novels, which have been translated into several European languages. Her collection *The Well of Trapped Words: Selected Stories* (Comma, 2015) and a novel, *Every Fire You Tend* (Tilted Axis, 2019), have been published in English. She also writes for the theatre and for the magazine *Atlas*.

'By the end of the night the man will take the woman's hand and declare, with a romantic flourish, "I would die for you."'

Their repertoire of traditional alaturka and arabesk songs serves to remind both the man and the woman of the psychological climate that will surround the relationship they are forging at this restaurant table. It is a kind of musical terrorism, with lively, upbeat melodies urging the listener to get up and dance and seeming to clear the way for Eros to do his work, while lyrics glorifying death and laced with angst and hostility simultaneously invite Thanatos into the scene. But ordinarily Thanatos will not appear where Eros is already present, and where Thanatos already rules Eros will stay away. Social norms dictate that they cannot be in the same place at the same time. They can only follow each other.

Applying a Freudian approach that situates individuals within the broader context of human civilisation, we might conclude that Eros, the embodiment of the life instinct fuelled by the pleasure principle, should not allow Thanatos, the death instinct, to come anywhere near him – at least not at the beginning. And yet the songs these musicians play contain both forces at once. Their melodies are joyful and exuberant, but the words are horrific: 'You left me, and I wish you nothing but a lifetime of misery,' they curse; 'Here comes a bullet to caress the space between your brows,' they sing, envisioning death even as the music urges the listener to get up and dance; 'She might look like she loves you now, but she'll take it back one day,' they warn; 'Damn you and your cruel heart,' they scold – and the people in the restaurant sing along in full voice, hovering over their chairs, their shoulders bobbing up and down with the beat, their fingers clicking, their hands clapping to the rhythm. They will renounce neither Eros nor Thanatos. By the end of the night the man will take the woman's hand and declare, with a romantic flourish, 'I would die for you,' and, in a slightly different socio-economic context, it can only be a matter of time before his expression of heartfelt surrender acquires the contours of a threat. From now on the man is also entitled to tell the woman 'You will die for me, too – if necessary.' The only god of love he knows is the kind that always demands a martyr. The remarkable tendency among some Turkish men to love some Turkish women to death is like a kind of folklore set to music. Machismo will thrive where it finds a suitable ecosystem.

If the woman at the table seems so ready to go along with this it is because she has yet to discover any exit strategies that might disentangle her from the oppressive patriarchal mechanisms of the society of which she is part. The mindset that governs her life tells her that where love is concerned violence is admissible. There are almost no women in positions of power she might look up to. The data from 2020 tells us that of the eleven members of the board of the national bar association, only three are female, and of the eighty local chapters of the association, only six are helmed by women, despite the fact that half of the association's members across the country are female. All the judges of the supreme court are men. Of university rectors in Turkey 175 are men, only eighteen are women. Just 17 per cent of parliament is female, and that is after an increase in recent years

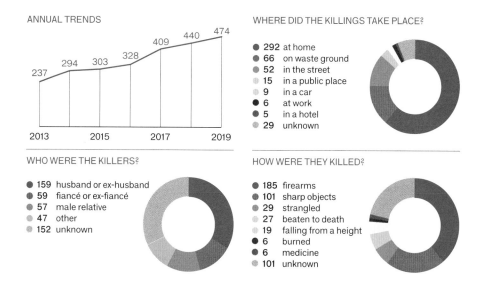

ANNUAL TRENDS

237 294 303 328 409 440 474

2013 2015 2017 2019

WHERE DID THE KILLINGS TAKE PLACE?

- 292 at home
- 66 on waste ground
- 52 in the street
- 15 in a public place
- 9 in a car
- 6 at work
- 5 in a hotel
- 29 unknown

WHO WERE THE KILLERS?

- 159 husband or ex-husband
- 59 fiancé or ex-fiancé
- 57 male relative
- 47 other
- 152 unknown

HOW WERE THEY KILLED?

- 185 firearms
- 101 sharp objects
- 29 strangled
- 27 beaten to death
- 19 falling from a height
- 6 burned
- 6 medicine
- 101 unknown

SOURCE: KADIN CİNAYETLERİNİ DURDURACAĞIZ PLATFORMU (WE WILL STOP FEMICIDE PLATFORM)

fuelled by the Kurdish political movement. Considering that the national elections of 1935 returned seventeen female MPs, it is safe to say that female representation in Turkish politics has not kept pace with the Republic of Turkey's narrative of modernisation. The situation is equally dire in the media, where, with the exception of a handful of opposition publications that take particular care to achieve a balance in gender representation, an overview of most newspaper mastheads will reveal that there are almost no women among the nation's chief and executive editors. This is a context in which women have historically had restricted access to the levers of power, and it is only in the last fifteen years that Turkish women have actively begun to express the daily aggressions they experience, be they jealous rages, bullying, intimidation, harassment, disempowerment or dispossession. Despite

its hundred-year history, the feminist movement in Turkey has only just begun to find effective ways to articulate its arguments to the public. And so the woman sitting at that restaurant table, looking into her macho lover's eyes, is not just besieged by songs with questionable lyrics, she has also absorbed the patriarchal mentality that dominates the society of which she is part, in which men have seized possession of everything there is to possess, including love. And, like many women in her position, she cannot quite see how dangerous it might be to be loved to death by a man.

Bearing all this in mind it is perhaps not altogether surprising if the woman wrestling with conflicting feelings as she sips her drink at this restaurant table should base her decisions on the patterns of love and violence jointly woven that night by Eros and Thanatos. She knows that as long as she adapts the

- **60** yes
- **20** no
- **394** unknown

WHY WERE THEY KILLED?

- **18.2%** argument
- **13.4%** jealousy
- **10%** asking for a divorce
- **6.8%** saying no
- **6.2%** honour/tradition
- **3.7%** ending a relationship
- **21.7%** other
- **20%** unknown

campaigns for an end to femicide, Kadın Cinayetlerini Durduracağız (We Will Stop Femicide), in 152 of these 474 cases the culprit was not identified; in 134 cases the woman was murdered by her husband; in twenty-five cases by her former husband; in fifty-one cases by her boyfriend; in eight cases by her former boyfriend; in twenty-nine cases by a male relative, such as an uncle, or a close female relative's husband, or by her father-in-law, or by her brother-in-law; in nineteen cases by an acquaintance; in fifteen cases by her own father; in thirteen cases by her own brother; in twenty-five cases by her own son, or by a neighbour, or by another parent at her children's school; and in three cases by a stranger. In other words, most of these women were killed by men they knew. Turkey may have been the first country to ratify the Istanbul Convention, drawn up to combat domestic violence against women and now adopted by forty-six countries across the world and by the European Union, and yet a woman in Turkey who is threatened by a man in her life cannot rely on the support of public institutions. A man can simply show up in court in a suit and tie, tell the judge that his pride and honour have been tarnished by that woman, that he has been provoked and that he would never have killed otherwise, and he will be let off with a slap on the wrist, the punishment so weak that it could never constitute any kind of serious deterrent. Today the streets are full of the ghosts of murdered women. Of the many cases of women killed by men, the murder of 38-year-old Emine Bulut has perhaps had the deepest impact on broader society. In 2019 she was murdered in Kırıkkale by her ex-husband, whom she'd divorced in 2015; he slit her throat in front of their daughter. In a video shot during the murder Emine Bulut can be heard screaming

way she dresses, her career choices, her expectations of property ownership and what she does in her private life to society's patriarchal, heteronormative, sexist mores, she will be able to lead what is considered an acceptable life. But should she become conscious one day of her own unhappiness and decide to leave the man before her in order to lead a more independent existence, things could easily change. It takes a moment for Thanatos' litany of threats to explode into fury.

Recep Tayyip Erdoğan's AKP government's increasingly oppressive interference in the lives of women has also played its part in encouraging this culture of latent male aggression. A woman is murdered in Turkey nearly every day now, often in broad daylight, and the frequency of these killings is increasing. In 2019 474 women were killed in Turkey. According to a report published by an organisation that

'I don't want to die.' Her cries still ring in our ears.

Meanwhile, politicians and mainstream media outlets engage in an endless and relentless game of labelling and hearsay concerning the murdered women: 'What was she doing out so late?' 'She shouldn't have worn such a short skirt,' 'She went out dancing on her own, she was asking for it' and other similarly outrageous statements pour down like acid rain, generating the perception that these victims are chosen specifically from among women who lead secular lifestyles. The murders of women from more conservative sections of society, on the other hand, are wilfully overlooked. But the truth is that violence affects women from every social group. There is no question that the way of life preached by Islamists is harmful to all women. In chilling speeches delivered in public spaces, on TV shows and inside mosques, inflected with demeaning rhetoric and filled with astonishing anachronisms, Islamic clerics regularly and directly threaten women's right to life, leaning on the words of the Koran and of the Hadith in the service of their final aim: to regulate everything about women's lives – from their sexuality to their marriages, from their inheritance rights to their daily existence – in such a way as to favour the interests of men. Without even needing to refer to the teachings of the Hadith, which paint women as unclean, diabolical and inferior, it is sufficient to consider just one example from the Koran, verse 4:34, which reads as follows: 'Men are in charge of women [...] But those women from whom you fear arrogance – first, advise them; then, forsake them in bed; and finally, strike them.' Ultimately, the teachings of Islam envisage only one type of woman: head covered, obedient, child bearing, meek, passive, a willing slave.

While Islamist politics seek to establish this one-size-fits-all model of the ideal Muslim woman, the Kemalist movement, having reduced the notion of modernity to a kind of regime of its own, has been busy formulating a rigid, uniform idea of femininity to rival that of the Islamists. In its path towards Westernisation, the Republic of Turkey banned the use of headscarves in public offices and conjured up a vision of a modern woman in a business suit. From 1926 to 1934 the government introduced a number of constitutional safeguards for women, ranging from equality under the law to the right to vote and to be elected for public office – today Turks still boast of having secured equal rights for women before France, Italy or Switzerland – but the truth is that this kind of modernisation has little to do with feminism; on the contrary, it portrays the gains of the women's civil-rights movement as gifts bestowed upon them by men. Meanwhile, as rates of urbanisation increased after the 1950s among the more socially conservative sectors of society previously living in the country's rural regions, a new middle class began to emerge – but when the headscarf-wearing women belonging to these new middle classes decided to leave their homes to attend university, go into parliament and work in public institutions, they were met with resistance, until eventually, in a semantic turn that caught everybody by surprise, the headscarf was paired with the notion of freedom. Today the 'freedom to wear a headscarf' is no longer in question, but Turkey has been significantly held back by this debate. Indeed, the mafia state from which we are now struggling to break free, established through what amounts to a plebiscitary dictatorship and which gets stronger by the day – run

Above: Young women chat in the garden of a mosque overlooking the Golden Horn, Istanbul.

Eros and Thanatos at the Restaurant

'The moment a woman from Turkey steps foot outside her country she is seen exclusively as a Muslim woman. All those battles she won back home will suddenly feel like defeats.'

by those elected to public office and their appointed cronies – has been bolstered over the years by the systematic aggressions of past Kemalist governments with their attempts at social engineering and their demonisation of headscarf-wearing women. In inventing the idea of what constituted a suitable woman, the state effectively also defined the characteristics of an *un*suitable woman. For the Islamists it was only a matter of time before their rhetoric of victimhood, honed like a blade over the years, found fertile political soil. Yet it still took the AKP eleven years after it came to power in 2002 to deign to lift the ban on headscarves in public offices. The headscarf debate, so rife for exploitation, simply made it easier for them to accrue the variety of political privileges they were after. Today there is no longer any issue around women who wear headscarves being represented across public institutions, but the question of their freedom remains all but taboo. The sharpest criticism of women who have decided to stop wearing headscarves and shared their experiences on social media through the #10yearschallenge hashtag has come from Islamists. These women haven't just been accused of not being true Muslims they have also been branded terrorists, charged with links to the Fethullah Gülen movement (once an ally of the AKP government but now considered a terrorist organisation following the failed 2016 coup attempt that remains shrouded in mystery; see 'Turkey's Thirty-Year Coup' on page 49). In this way, many women have been intimidated into silence.

*

Let us now set aside the diabolical triangle of homogenisation, polarisation and violence in which most women in Turkey are trapped and return to our restaurant table. Let us imagine that the woman seated at this table belongs to that fortunate minority of women who will not settle for trite courtship and are determined to make their own decisions about their future. Even though she has grown up surrounded by patriarchal family structures, she has adopted independence as her guiding principle and has been raised with love, giving her self-confidence. Perhaps she has been educated abroad or travelled for professional purposes – to Paris, say, or London, or Vienna, or Frankfurt. Yet even in the multicultural cities of Europe she would immediately have to face a human barrier of prejudices and oversimplified characterisations. She would find herself issued with an identity for which she is altogether unprepared. Despite having no religious beliefs and having managed – in her own country and within her own social sphere – to carve out for herself a relatively distinctive, individual existence, she would find that the moment she steps foot outside her country she is seen exclusively as a Muslim woman. All those battles she won back home will suddenly feel like defeats. The sight of her having a glass of wine in a restaurant will be met with astonishment. Those who know she comes from Turkey will be unable to conceal how strange they find her Westernised ways. Having never once been made to feel out of place for

The Alevis are a religious community that makes up between 15 and 25 per cent of the population of Turkey, although the figures are the subject of much debate. While they have some practices in common with Shia Islam (veneration of Ali, the Prophet Mohammed's cousin and son-in-law, and the Mourning of Muharram, for example), the Alevis are distinct both from the Shiites and, to an even greater extent, from their Sunni Muslim compatriots. With more liberal tendencies, in particular regarding the role of women (but also on alcohol), they often faced discrimination, sometimes violent, under Ottoman rule and consequently greeted Atatürk's secular project as a liberation. The republic, however, in its attempts to Turkify ethnic and religious minorities, has not always reciprocated, starting with 1938's extremely violent repression, ordered by Atatürk himself, of a revolt in Dersim in the east of the country. In the 1970s the Alevis – who are generally politically left leaning – suffered further unspeakable violence at the hands of Turkish nationalists, particularly in the pogroms in the cities of Çorum and Maraş, and again in the 1990s with the 1993 Sivas massacre in Central Anatolia, in which thirty Alevi intellectuals died in a fire started by Sunni militants. In more recent times the Erdoğan government has also opted to pit itself against the Alevis (who traditionally vote for the Kemalist CHP), and, following the failed coup of 2016, repressive measures were also extended to the Alevis in payback for the significant role they played in the Gezi Park protests.

drinking wine or not attending mosque in her own country, where 99 per cent of the population is assumed to be Muslim, she would nevertheless end up feeling uncomfortable while sipping a glass of wine in Europe, as if she were living in sin. She would be subjected to endless questions as to whether she wears a headscarf back home, whether she's ever eaten pork, whether people in her country are free to have sex before they're married. Before long, everyone she meets will seem to be channelling the Revolutionary Guards in Iran. Her European hosts will not even realise that they sound like fanatical imams. She would discover, to her disappointment, how layer upon layer of cultural nuance can so easily be erased and flattened by casual prejudice. The idea that she might be an atheist, a deist, an agnostic, a Christian (whether Syriac, Chaldean or otherwise), that she might be Jewish, that she might have little or no faith at all would not occur to them. It would never cross anyone's mind that she might be one of the twenty million Alevis in Turkey. No one would even consider that she might descend from generations of suffering, from communities first massacred and then forcibly assimilated, Turkified and Islamised, that she might have had to walk down a long road of inner revelations, appraisals and reckonings in order simply to exist in the world as a human being. To them, all she is and all she will ever be is a Muslim woman whose behaviour will be deemed disconcertingly unbefitting of the idea of the Muslim woman within the European imagination.

In this grim age where religions are too often turned into a form of mass culture and where that same mass culture creates the conditions for fascism to flourish, this obsession with reducing religious affiliation to an inescapable marker of identity

THE PASSENGER   Sema Kaygusuz

threatens the individuality of us all. Over and over again humanity has paid a heavy price for trying to classify individuals according to their faith. Yet religion is still perceived as a clear-cut form of identity inseparable from national identity. There is this simplistic assumption, for example, that, as discussed above, anyone who happens to be from Turkey must also be a Muslim – a *Sunni* Muslim to be precise – just as the institutions of the Republic of Turkey have always proclaimed as part of their project for national homogeneity and modernisation. Curiously, European society seems readier to accept the authoritarian Turkish state's homogenising drive than the various peoples of Turkey themselves have ever been. But as soon as you observe a people, a nation, from within their living culture you will discover the multitudinous layers of heritage contained within their current religious practices. Over the course of their history Turks have founded seventeen different states. They have been Confucianists and Taoists. After the 7th century they were Buddhists, Manicheans and fire-worshipping Zoroastrians. Before the Abrahamic religions took hold, they were shamanists and pantheists. For the four hundred years the Khazar Empire lasted they were Jews. Some Turkish communities who became Christians after the 9th century still live today as Orthodox Christians. Turkey's Kurdish population descends from Zoroastrians. There are still some Armenian, Syriac and Yazidi communities left, although they are small. In the west of the country live a number of Greeks. In short, it is almost impossible to look from the outside at a country as ethnically diverse as Turkey and claim to be able to define a standard model of Turkish womanhood. And any generic questions on what it is like to be a woman in a Muslim country are, by their very nature, symptomatic of an anti-secular perspective. The experience of being an Alevi in Turkey deserves its own discussion; so does that of being a Kurd, an Armenian, a Syriac Christian, a feminist, a member of the LGBTQ community. To completely ignore the very specific experiences that come with belonging to any one of these separate, independent groups and treat individuals as if they were parts of a monolithic whole is not only intellectually lazy but also hinders women from forming bonds with other women in other parts of the world on the basis of their shared experiences. If we want to find out who stands to benefit from these prejudices that tear up the global, horizontal ties that women might otherwise form, we need look no further than the workings of modern capitalism, with its insistence on extracting fossil fuels and its cultivation of war as a means of control.

But back to Turkey. In order to form a complete picture of women's lives in the country we must tell the story of the role feminism has played in the long history of Eros' struggle to overcome Thanatos and establish a social ecosystem founded on joy, peace and plenty. Indeed, up until now we have not so much discussed women themselves as the male-dominated structures within which the women of Turkey have to live their lives. It is time now to consider the distinctly female history to which the woman from the restaurant can turn, should she decide to get up and leave that table. It is time to turn to the story of a distinctly female struggle within a broader struggle to change the world.

The story begins a hundred years ago. In the period preceding the formation of the Republic of Turkey, as the movement for the Westernisation of the Ottoman state took hold, women began to appear in the public sphere in various roles, as teachers, writers, poets, painters and translators. The most frequently debated matter during the Ottoman Empire's Second Constitutional Era in the early 20th century was the question of the legal status of women. During this time more than thirty newspapers and journals were founded that were devoted specifically to this question. There was fierce debate on whether the traditional values that women were expected to embody were compatible with the needs of modern society. There was an active feminist movement, an 'indigenous feminism', as it was then referred to, before the republic was even founded. Its fundamental demands were equality and the right to vote.

The second stage of this movement was defined in large part by the outbreak of the First World War. During this period, under the rule of the Party of Union and Progress (which had come to power following a military coup), women joined not just the workforce but the army, too, within a specially created female division. In wartime women filled the gaps left behind by men. It was also around this time that they began to attend university. The Law of Family Rights, introduced in 1917, granted women living under Ottoman rule virtually every right that had been granted to women under the Swiss Civil Code. Under these new laws women gained the right to vote but could not yet themselves be elected to public office.

Following the foundation of the Republic of Turkey, the country's women's rights activists continued to follow the

Turkey is ambiguous in its attitude to its LGBTQ community. For many years it welcomed gay and transgender people fleeing intolerant states and families further east, and it was the first Muslim-majority country to permit a gay pride march (in 2003, with thirty participants; in 2014 there were ninety thousand people on the streets). Even back in the Ottoman era homosexuality was not a crime, but since then the republic has made little progress. There are no laws protecting against gender-based discrimination, and same-sex marriage is not recognised. Within a society imbued with conservative cultural values and a toxic idea of masculinity, homophobia is widespread. It might come as a surprise to learn that Erdoğan once supported LGBTQ rights. Before being elected prime minister in 2003 he declared that 'homosexuals must also receive legal protection for their rights and their freedoms'. However, over the years, and particularly following the Gezi Park protests in which the LGBTQ movement was very active, Erdoğan has performed a U-turn, stating, for example, that homosexuality is incompatible with Islamic culture. Since 2015 the authorities have prohibited gay pride events in Istanbul and other cities and cancelled many other cultural activities, while the police have met the marchers with rubber bullets, water cannon and tear gas. Yet, despite this, for many LGBTQ people from the Middle East, Turkey still remains a safe haven in which they can enjoy freedoms that would be unthinkable in their home countries.

traditions they had inherited and campaigned to establish a Women's Party – even before the Republican People's Party or the Progressive Republican Party were formed. When the state declined their request, those same feminist activists set up the Turkish Women's Society, which – up until its dissolution in 1935 – organised conferences all over the country on the subject of female emancipation. The press labelled them 'agitators'. When the leaders of the Turkish Women's Society visited Atatürk in 1934 to request full voting rights, he told them to drop these misguided demands, devote themselves to the republic and its ideals and mobilise their resources to spread the message of those ideals to women in every corner of the country. Naturally, the women were not convinced. That same year they gathered in Ankara to march on the parliament building in Ulus Square, demanding, 'We want votes!' They only dispersed once they had obtained Atatürk's promise that their request would be granted. Shortly after this march a bill to grant women the right to vote and to be elected to public office was introduced in parliament and was passed. As a result the leaders of the Turkish Women's Society, feeling that they had achieved their fundamental objective, disbanded the society, following the end of an international women's rights symposium they had organised. And soon the rights that women in Turkey had fought tooth and nail to obtain from the state were instrumentalised by those in power and used, right up until the late 1960s, as a propaganda tool and evidence of a supposed 'state-sponsored feminism'.

The 1970s saw the beginnings of a socialist women's movement. The Kemalist women's rights groups that had been most visible up to that time were soon replaced by female activist groups from the political left. The Progressive Women's Association, set up within the body of the Workers' Party, was able to get tens of thousands of women to take to the streets across the country in support of workers' rights. Thanks to the efforts of the Progressive Women's Association women became reacquainted with the concept of mass protest for the first time since the feminist movements of the late Ottoman period had first brought them out to demonstrate. Significantly, though, the female activists on the left of the political spectrum were not just fighting for their own rights but also for a future socialist utopia.

From the 1980s onwards the women's movement in Turkey entered its most active phase. As women began to forge identities of their own, female intellectuals from within the leftist movement produced numerous publications and, crucially, also began to take to the streets. Despite their differences, equality feminists, socialist feminists and radical feminists were able to work together, organising street protests, campaigns, demonstrations and a range of other initiatives. In the 1980s the main concern was sexual liberation; in the 1990s they began to think about the restrictions that women from conservative sectors of society experienced in the public sphere. In the 2000s the feminist movement in all its nuances and all its stripes was out on the streets. Kurdish women were politicised by their growing ethnic consciousness and increasingly took on active roles within the Kurdish political movement. For Kurdish women the discourse on oppressed minorities soon became inextricably connected to their gender and ethnicity. Placing particular importance on equal-gender representation within its ranks, the Kurdish political movement

THE PASSENGER   Sema Kaygusuz

Above: An Alevi woman wearing a PSAKD (an Alevi cultural organisation) vest in Istanbul's Alevi-majority Küçük Armutlu district. Residents have fought for many years to stay in this area, but its highly desirable central location means it has been targeted by the government for redevelopment.

Above: Voting at the Atatürk Library polling station, near Taksim Square, Istanbul.

– like the green movement in Europe – adopted a co-leadership model, bringing the question of unequal representation to the attention of a much wider public. Non-governmental organisations flourished, encouraging women of all classes, ethnicities and sexual orientations to become involved in politics. Countless feminist publications were born.

Turkey discovered almost overnight the universal relevance of the feminist positions adopted by this dynamic array of activist groups, each simmering with its own energy, their arguments so thoroughly modern as to translate into any language. The discovery came with an unexpected abundance of joy, a wholly new way of speaking and gatherings of unprecedented proportions. It came through the Gezi movement of 2013, which began in the wake of the violent eviction by the authorities of a sit-in against the redevelopment of Gezi Park in Istanbul. Among the environmental activists, the leftists and the anti-capitalist Muslim groups that took to the streets during the Gezi protests, women were by far the most conspicuous presence. The Gezi movement may well be remembered as the most powerful, most truly pluralistic movement in the country's history, responsible for transforming the perception of Turkish women from that of perennial victims to agents of resistance, able to speak for themselves, full of courage and endlessly diverse. Women became the Gezi protests' most powerful symbols. The woman in the red dress standing tall before a policeman's can of pepper spray, the old lady throwing rocks at the police and countless other women countering violence with dance, music and flowers quickly took centre stage. They were not fighting for equality; they were already equal. The language they used was more eloquent than is the norm in Turkish public discourse, and they invited those in power to respond in kind. Feminist groups injected an element of feminine creativity into the protests by ensuring that sexist language was banned. If the woman on the date in the restaurant had, in fact, got up and left the table, she would no doubt have been among them – and she would be unlikely ever to go on a date of that kind again. After the Gezi Park protests any events that involved the mobilisation of women – LGBTQ pride parades, 8 March International Women's Day celebrations and Take Back the Night marches – became mass movements.

On the surface it might seem that women in Turkey today have lost many of the gains they fought for over the years – death, violence and patriarchal culture do what they can to continue to oppress women – but the truth is that these women have long since learned to separate Eros from Thanatos. Today, whenever a woman falls victim to injustice or violence of any sort, countless other women will spill out on to the streets – defying prohibitions, defying the state's attempts to intimidate them – to cry, 'You will never walk alone.' They go out into public spaces and sing at the top of their lungs that 'when women come together they can shake the world'. Even when they are pushed around, even when they are arrested, even when they are dragged by their hair and kicked to the ground they do not stop resisting. Eros is in their blood now. The future they've already begun to build will be theirs in a few years' time, whatever the cost. Turkey has only just become acquainted with the power of women as a unified force. Now it is time to discover what the world looks like as dreamed by the women at the heart of the country's many communities. 🖎

Of Jinns and Light

Every summer the writer Burhan Sönmez
returns to the village in Central Anatolia
where he was born – but the only remnant
of that unspoiled rural world, with its
traditions and apolitical religious faith,
is the suppressed Kurdish language.

Burhan Sönmez

I was four years old the first time I ever saw a big town. I'd never before left my home village when we moved to a city of twenty thousand people where my father had rented a house. We loaded all our possessions on to the back of a truck and set off, my parents in the cab with the driver and all five of us kids in the back on a pile of mattresses, carpets and various tools and utensils. The winding road was rough and very dusty, and the truck moved slowly across the Central Anatolian Haymana Plain. The town we were heading for was Polatlı. My eldest brother had finished primary education in the village, and my father decided to enrol him in secondary school in the town. We were the first family from our village to move away so the children could continue their education. This was my father's vision.

The state of the roads meant the journey took three hours. Although we were covered in dust we were enjoying looking out across the plain at the distant dry-sloped hills. Everywhere in the landscape we imagined there were different characters from the tales we'd heard back home: we would see a little jinn in a deep wadi and spy a distant ditch where ogres hid from the sun during the daytime. They were as real here as they were to us in the village at night.

There was no electricity in our village then. There was no paved road from the village to the town. The village was home to around fifty families who lived by farming wheat and barley and herding sheep and cows. The nights were lit by oil lamps. Outside darkness reigned, broken only by the stars, the barking of dogs and jinns. Years later, when I was in high school, I asked my mother why we didn't see jinns or ogres any longer, and she answered

BURHAN SÖNMEZ is a lawyer specialising in human rights as well as a writer and activist of Kurdish descent. Injured by Turkish police in 1996, he received care in the UK thanks to the support of the Freedom from Torture foundation. He now divides his time between Istanbul and Cambridge, UK. He is a member of PEN International, won the EBRD Literature Prize for his novel *Istanbul Istanbul* (Telegram, 2016) and has written for several international newspapers. His most recent book to be published in English is *Labyrinth* (Other Press, 2019).

emphatically, 'Because the city is flooded with light. These creatures do not like the light, so they've abandoned us.'

As we travelled on the back of that truck I had no idea that we were leaving our way of imagining behind and entering another kind of world. But at least we were lucky enough to lead a double life that connected village and town, moving from one to the other every summer like nomads. We would spend eight months in the town then return to the village for four months in the summer to tend to our fields. This pattern of existence became widespread on the Haymana Plain, as other families rented in town so that their children, too, could be educated – and to escape the boredom of life in the village, although I didn't understand that at the time. We children loved both: the town, with its car horns, bustle and bright lights, and the village, where we could run free in the wilderness. The adults, however, who had spent their lives in the countryside, had less and less desire to go back there. And that's how in the 1960s the nomadic existence of the people of central Anatolia came to be. By the time electricity arrived in the villages in 1979 it was too late for the middle-aged farmers to rekindle their bond with their home soil; they had acquired a taste for paved roads, brightly lit shop windows and busy coffee houses – and they made enough from their wheat and barley fields to give them a comfortable enough life in the town.

When I was at university in Istanbul I was not the only member of my family there: my two elder brothers and a younger sister were studying, too. My father, a simple farmer, could afford to put four children through university in the city all at the same time. But over the decades Turkey has betrayed its agricultural

and rural heritage. Now those same fields cannot provide enough even to sustain my parents. This is how little farming is valued today.

Having lived in the UK for many years I am now trying to rediscover my old double life by spending a few weeks in the village during harvest time. I go to there to farm for my family. The population has halved since I was a child – not only the human population but the jinns and ogres have left, too. A smooth road now connects the village to the town; the journey that once took three hours now takes less than one. Houses are lit by electricity, and people rarely get together in the evening because everyone is at home watching TV.

Everyone tries to escape the village because it offers no future. There are no economic resources for younger generations, no work, and the agricultural economy is getting weaker all the time. Young people used to go to the town to continue their studies, but now education is perceived as having less value, and young people prefer to go to big cities or abroad just to make money. Almost every family has someone who is working in Europe, helping to support their families with remittances in stronger currencies. This is how we try to alleviate poverty. When you arrive in the village today you can tell immediately which families have foreign money coming in by their houses. In the past our homes were made of mud bricks with thick walls that would keep them warm in winter and cool in summer. Now those houses are being demolished and new ones built out of reinforced concrete. That is how those who work abroad invest in memory. They have no expectations of village life; they spend only a couple of weeks there during the holidays. That is how they complete the circle of their lives.

The village is now full of new-builds that are empty for eleven months of the year. When we were small, the mud-brick houses were crowded with people and jinns; the surrounding countryside was full of blackflies, foxes, rabbits and wolves. They are gone now – even the blackflies. The farmers are happy, but there's been a sharp increase in diseases such as cancer, diabetes, heart problems and deadly allergies throughout the country in recent years. People do not ask why. These increases are caused in part by urban lifestyles but mostly through exposure to new products used in farming. Every year more government-endorsed pesticides are introduced, and we do not know exactly what they contain. This is a delicate subject. Between 2011 and 2015 the Turkish Ministry of Health carried out a secret survey on the effects of pesticides and pollution on food and water supplies. The results showed that these harmful elements were responsible for the increases in these diseases – cancer in particular. Those behind the survey chose not to disclose their findings – even to other sections within the ministry itself. One academic, Bülent Şık, got hold of the information in 2018 and had the courage to publish it – and courage was needed, as he was later taken to court, tried and sentenced to fifteen months' imprisonment for 'revealing secret documents and causing public outrage'.

For eight years, as a young boy, alongside my secular studies I went to the mosque every summer for my religious education, being awarded a diploma on completion. Religion played an important role in our culture, and it had nothing to do with politics. Following the 1980 military coup religious influence increased in Turkey, promoted by the military in the hope that it would form a bulwark against the popular left-wing movements that had been so effective in preceding decades. The result was not only the increase in the political power of religion but also the changing face of everyday life. At the time I was undertaking my religious education, everyone in the village was a devout Muslim. The men regularly attended mosque, and the women would cover their heads in the traditional way with a headscarf that left some hair, including their braids, uncovered. This was how it had been for centuries. Now, after twenty years of religious pressure, there is no single woman who still wears the traditional headscarf; all cover their heads entirely in the manner of the stricter Muslim societies.

The rise of religiosity was promoted by the Turkish military and – at least initially – by NATO. The aim was to suppress progressive thinking and build a wall around the Soviet Union by creating a 'green belt' – green being the symbolic colour of Islam – that extended from the Middle East to Central Asia. The policy was designed to spread Islamist ideas from Turkey to Afghanistan, harnessing the power of religion while keeping it under control. But the situation got out of hand, and religion has become a weapon over which control has been lost both in Afghanistan and in Turkey. The Turkish Army, after successfully stifling popular left-wing movements, tried to contain the rise of Islamism as well – but it was too late. They have been defeated by their own creation.

While they kept a modern revolution at bay by trampling on

the progressive aspirations of the people, they instigated a reactionary one instead. Something similar can also be felt in the Turkish language. My early education in Polatlı was at Devrim Primary School. The word *devrim* means revolution in Turkish. The Turkish language has many loan words from other languages, including old Ottoman. Revolution is identified by two words in Ottoman Turkish, one is *inkılap*, and the other is *ihtilal*. *Inkılap* conveys the meaning of revolution by transformation, while *ihtilal* suggests revolution through revolt; *devrim*, however, includes both transformation and uprising, and that's frightening for a military junta, which is why they have erased the beautiful Turkish word *devrim* from current usage. Consequently, Devrim Primary School has been renamed Inkılap Primary School. It is the same school at which I studied, but it is also a different school.

Despite all these changes one thing remains the same: the suppression of the language of my village: Kurdish. When I was a child it was forbidden to speak Kurdish. Even using the language to communicate with friends at school was risky because you might face punishment from the teachers – although we could get away with doing so with family members or when playing out on the street. In the town the population was mostly Turkish, but there was a sizeable Kurdish population who had moved in from the surrounding villages. The two languages coexisted well enough, and there was no hostility or contempt among ordinary people. The pressure came from on high, from state officials. They were the ones who locked the Kurdish language away and banished it from schools, hospitals, courts and mosques. At one point they called Kurdish 'mountain Turkish', claiming that

there were no Kurds, only Turks who had lived isolated high up in the mountains for centuries and as a result their language had become twisted and lost its roots. It sounds like a farce, but it is, in fact, a tragedy, as Nobel laureate Harold Pinter describes in his play *Mountain Language*, which he wrote after visiting Turkey during the 1980s. And nothing has changed since Pinter wrote that play; the language of my childhood is still a 'language of the mountains'.

Is this the force that pulls me back every year? Is it so I can speak my 'mountain' mother tongue and relive my childhood memories at harvest time? When I'm there I know that I am in the same village in which I was born but also that nothing is the same. The old crowd has gone. The flies and the foxes have disappeared. The houses are now made of concrete and the newer ones surrounded by fences and barbed wire to keep trespassers out. The streets are lit, the darkness has been banished, taking the old jinns and ogres away with it. The village looks like an empty picture frame. It is like the story of the disappearance of the *Mona Lisa*. At the time that Leonardo da Vinci's masterpiece was stolen from the Louvre in Paris in 1911 it was already well known, but it did not yet have the powerful draw that it does today. The newspaper headlines and the high-profile police investigation that followed the theft meant that the painting began to attract increased attention, and queues started to form outside the Louvre for the first time as people came in droves to see the empty space where the painting had once hung. They would look at the bare wall and imagine the beauty that had once existed there. It was a place of dreams, contemplation and beauty. When I go to my village I see something similar. There used to be mud-brick houses, the howling of wolves and jinns. Maybe I fill that frame with my memories and my dreams as a way to complete the circle of my own life. 🖋

The Roots of Turkish Nationalism

Out of the ruins of the Ottoman Empire – in which Turks, Kurds, Armenians and Greeks had lived together peacefully for centuries in a multi-ethnic state – a new nationalism took hold that separated the different peoples and imposed an enforced Turkification, the principal victims of which were the Armenians.

GERHARD SCHWEIZER
Translated by Stephen Smithson

The bookstall by the entrance
to the Gedikpaşa Armenian Protestant
Church, Fatih, Istanbul.

Turks, Greeks, Armenians, Kurds – to classify Turkey's inhabitants by their ethnicity comes naturally to us today, and we all the more readily take for granted that Turks comprise an overwhelming majority of the country's population. It also seems that for centuries ethnic Turks have been quick to distance themselves from other ethnic groups on Turkish soil whenever these have sought cultural autonomy. But this behaviour and these ethnic distinctions did not really emerge until the second half of the 19th century, and only with Atatürk did the Turkish state become identified with a nationalist ideology.

To the subjects of the Ottoman Empire, ethnic distinctions appeared largely insignificant, even an entirely alien concept. It wouldn't be overstating things if one were to say that for hundreds of years the Turks thought of themselves not as Turks but merely as an ethnic group speaking Turkish, which was not *the* official language but one language among many – alongside Arabic, Persian, Kurdish, Greek and Armenian. It would not, accordingly, have occurred to the Turks to use the name Turkey to refer to the region in which they were the majority population. The Turks – along with the Greeks, Armenians, Kurds and Arabs – always referred to themselves as Ottoman, using the name of the dynasty under whose rule they lived.

Throughout the six hundred years of its existence the Ottoman Empire was a multi-ethnic state in which all men without exception were called upon to serve the state, while individual groups were allowed relative autonomy in culture and religion. That only (Sunni) Muslims could rise to high political office was the sole form of inequality practised. A distinctive feature of the empire – in contrast to the republic – is that the sultans in no way favoured Turkish-speaking subjects over other Muslims or, indeed, over the Christian Greeks and Armenians, a situation that remained stable until the mid-19th century. After the Greeks won independence in the southern part of present-day Greece in 1829 and set up a nation state along western-European lines, other Christian subjects – Bulgarians, Romanians and Armenians – started to look to them as a model, and this increase in separatist sentiment among Ottoman Christians presented a growing threat to the unity of the multi-ethnic state. It was in response to this that a form of Turkish nationalism first emerged, and the so-called Young Ottoman movement – the name of which suggested a wish to reform Ottoman structures without actually abolishing the sultanate – began to take

GERHARD SCHWEIZER is a writer and academic specialising in relations between West and East, with a profound knowledge of the Islamic world. He has written numerous books on the history and traditions of Persia, Syria and Turkey, including *Türkei verstehen: Von Atatürk bis Erdoğan* ('Understanding Turkey: From Atatürk to Erdoğan', Klett-Cotta Verlag, 2016), from which this article is taken.

'The idea that a new state should be formed, which would be populated only by Turks, unleashed a devastating series of events in Anatolia, the heart of the Ottoman Empire.'

shape in Istanbul in the 1860s. Towards the end of the 19th century, as the movement strengthened its aim of replacing the multi-ethnic state with a nation state identified only with the ethnic Turkish group, the name Young Turks (*Genc Türkler*) increasingly came to be applied.

EXTREME NATIONALISM
ALONG EUROPEAN LINES

Intellectually the Young Turks were guided largely by the conceptual framework of European nationalism. As the term Turks gradually began to acquire positive connotations, suggesting an unspoiled people in contrast to the decadence of the ruling upper class, the young reformers began to refer to regions with a majority Turk population as Türkiye – a name later adopted, with a political agenda, for the republic. The reformers were inspired mainly by the conceptual structures of European ethnic nationalism. With the rise to power of the Young Turks, a fateful process began, fraught with consequences. The idea that a new state should be formed, which would be populated only by Turks, unleashed a devastating series of events in Anatolia, the heart of the empire. Here the Young Turks wielded sufficient power to attain their goals through military means, and non-Turks – Armenians, Greeks and Kurds – who resisted Turkification could expect the gravest of consequences. The fatal fall-out of this ideology first became apparent in the early 20th century when the Armenian minority started to push for social reform and cultural autonomy, and some voices even called for an independent state.

To this day what took place next continues to weigh heavily on Turkish nationalism and Turkish history.

THE ARMENIAN MASSACRE

The far eastern part of Anatolia, close to Turkey's border with Iran, was home to more than two million Armenians at the beginning of the 20th century. But during the First World War hundreds of thousands of them were massacred in their villages and towns by Turkish soldiers; hundreds of thousands more died while fleeing or perished from hunger and exhaustion during the so-called 'death march' to the Syrian border. Armenian sources put the total number of Armenian deaths at a million or even 1.5 million, whereas the Turkish side is willing to concede only 300,000 as an official figure and denies that there was a planned annihilation of the Armenian population.

But how did such massacres come to take place?

Turkish Muslims and Armenians had coexisted in a state of relative peace until the second half of the 19th century, when relations became strained as political tensions grew and fault lines started to open up within the empire. This was a time of unprecedented exploitation of the people by provincial governors, who responded with force to any attempt to resist their arbitrary rule. Resentment at this despotism grew among Armenians who, like the Greeks, were increasingly drawn to Europe and thinking along European nationalistic

'The Young Turks were looking to found an ethnically homogenous state that would be home only to Turks; this state would have no room for minorities unless they were prepared to undergo Turkification.'

lines about the need for a state of their own. Support for the Armenian cause came primarily from Russia, whose sphere of influence bordered the Ottoman Empire in the northern Caucasus. Successive tsars saw the political weakening of the sultanate as a way to secure greater influence for themselves in the eastern Mediterranean. This in itself was sufficient reason to side with the Armenians in their bid for increased autonomy or even statehood at the expense of the Ottomans.

Naturally the sultans could only view this development as a threat, but for reasons of power politics and not religion. Abdul Hamid II, for example, was not waging a campaign against Christianity but suppressing a nationalist revolt when he sent in the troops after the Armenians staged their first open rebellion in 1894, during which uprising Ottoman officials were killed. This intervention led in 1895 to the first massacres of the Armenian population, resulting in around 200,000 deaths. But the real tragedy did not take place until later. The Young Turk revolutionaries were setting the policy agenda in Istanbul, and the Armenians could expect no mercy; it was the revolutionaries who were responsible for the 1915 massacres. Like Abdul Hamid II before them, however, they were not engaged in a fight with Christianity; they were Turkish nationalists fighting Armenian nationalists, and they were motivated by a desire to prevent the Armenians from setting up, after the looming defeat of the Ottomans in the First World War, a new state on the territory of

the disintegrating empire – and by a fear that the Armenians, as the war progressed, would support the enemy, Russia.

The Young Turks were looking to found an ethnically homogenous state that would be home only to Turks; this state would have no room for minorities unless they were prepared to renounce their culture and language and undergo Turkification. Since the Armenians would not consent to this, the logic of the Young Turks dictated that they would have to be expelled or killed. Again, the Young Turks' objectives were political, and religion could not be invoked to support them, ethnic classification being completely alien to Islam. The guiding spirit here was Europe, where nationalism was taking on a radicalised form, and the transition from nationalism to fascism was already beginning to show.

After the fall of the Young Turks at the end of the First World War, Atatürk became national leader. Having not been involved in the 1915 mass murder of Armenians, in 1920 he nevertheless led a bitter fight against the newly independent Armenian Republic, which had been established in eastern Anatolia with the support of the victorious Allied powers – Atatürk, like all Turkish nationalists, rejected the humiliating Treaty of Sèvres and the partitioning of the Ottoman Empire, which had granted the Armenians a state of their own. Under his leadership Turkish troops killed more than 200,000 Armenians. After this defeat the Armenians had to cede all Anatolian land to Turkey, and the loss of all its former Ottoman territory

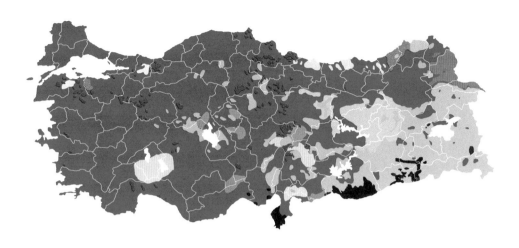

TURKIC	INDO-EUROPEAN	SEMITIC AND CAUCASIAN
■ Turkish	▨ Kurdish	■ Arabic
▨ Azeri	▨ Zaza	▨ Aramaic
▨ Turkmen	▨ Bulgarian	▨ Circassian
▨ Qarapapaq	Bosniak	▨ Laz
▨ Yörük	Greek	▨ Georgian
		Abkhaz

SOURCE: WIKIPEDIA

reduced the Armenian Republic to a region in the Caucasus.

Although Atatürk's nationalism differed in a number of ways from that of the Young Turks, he was in full agreement with them on one crucial point: the new state should be Turkish through and through. It followed, therefore, that no minority could claim a right to exist under Atatürk's rule if it insisted on retaining its ethnicity, culture and language. Even if Atatürk himself had nothing to do with the mass slaughter of Armenians during the First World War, he later rigorously prevented all discussion on the subject, taking the view that a public discussion would inevitably compromise to a considerable extent the security of the Republic of Turkey and jeopardise what had taken such a monumental effort to achieve. This stance has been maintained under his successors to the present day, and the Turkish attitude appears all the more disconcerting to Western observers when they see a refusal, even at the highest levels of government, to discuss historical truth.

SUPPRESSION OF THE 'ARMENIAN PROBLEM'

Anyone who publicly raises the subject of the mass murder of Armenians and other ethnic minorities can be sentenced to several years' imprisonment for 'denigrating Turkishness', a crime under Article 301 of the Turkish Penal Code. Silence on the subject of the massacres was first decreed several decades ago by a strictly secular nationalist government, but little has changed under the Islamically oriented leadership of Recep Tayyip Erdoğan – as will be seen.

Incidents involving such denigration began to attract the attention of the international press as early as the 1980s, particularly when the parties accused were Western tourists. On 10 June 1982 a German tour group visited the most famous of all Armenian churches in Anatolia, the Cathedral of the Holy Cross on Akdamar Island in Lake Van. While the tourists marvelled at the magnificently ornamented façades, the tour guide told them about the mass murder of Armenians in 1915. This was overheard by a German-speaking Turkish citizen, who immediately reported it to the police. The tour guide was arrested and imprisoned; only after considerable efforts by the West German government was his release secured.

For Turkish citizens with no outside agency to intervene on their behalf, however, criminal proceedings of this nature were and remain far more perilous. In February 2005 the internationally renowned novelist Orhan Pamuk caused a furore when, in an interview with the Zurich daily *Tages-Anzeiger*, he criticised not only the military for hindering the development of Turkish democracy but also the persistent silence surrounding the massacres of Armenians and Kurds. He spoke openly about the murder of more than a million Armenians in the First World War and that of more than thirty thousand Kurds since 1980. Pamuk, who had just been awarded the Friedenspreis des Deutschen Buchhandels (the Peace Prize of the German Book Trade) that autumn and would win the Nobel Prize for Literature the following year, went on trial in December 2005 under Article 301. The charge carried a severe penalty because the writer's 'offensive' comments had been made to a foreign newspaper and were thus all the more damaging to Turkey's reputation. Pamuk found himself subjected to abuse from angry demonstrators, who called him a traitor to the fatherland. Nevertheless, the trial was postponed indefinitely and later abandoned – perhaps because of the realisation that it would create too many headlines, making the damage to Turkey's international reputation even worse.

A similar sequence of events unfolded in the case of Elif Shafak, a Turkish writer born in Strasbourg in 1971 to a diplomatic family who has gone on to achieve international fame. Shafak was also charged with the same offence following the publication of her 2006 novel *The Bastard of Istanbul*, which addressed the Turkish–Armenian conflict by having a character, an Armenian woman, speak openly about the 1915 massacres. Unlike Pamuk, she had not discussed the subject directly but through a character in a novel, and it was the first time that a charge had been brought on this basis against a writer in a Turkish court. Proceedings ran from March to 21 September 2007, when they were terminated for 'lack of evidence', and Elif Shafak was acquitted. Meanwhile, *The Bastard of Istanbul* sold sixty thousand copies in Turkey in a very short time; later it went on to become an international bestseller. The book's success in Turkey suggests that the vast majority of Turks long ago ceased to object to discussion of the 'Armenian question'. (See 'An Author Recommends' by Elif Shafak on page 202.)

A courageous attempt to tackle the issue of the Armenian massacres had far graver consequences for the prominent Turkish-Armenian journalist Hrant Dink. As the founder and editor-in-chief of the Istanbul-based Armenian newspaper *Agos*, Dink had over the years become well known for his strenuous advocacy of

that had earned him the enmity of Turkish nationalists; it had also earned him several months' imprisonment in 2005 following a prosecution for denigrating Turkishness. But the greatest risk he faced was from extremist fanatics threatening to execute him as an enemy of the nation; such people have always rejected any call for self-criticism because it would involve a review of their own extreme position. On 19 January 2007 a nationalist youth shot and killed Dink in front of his office in Istanbul. The funeral turned into a powerful demonstration against fanatical nationalism when almost 100,000

Exhibits (**above left and right**) at the official memorial to the murdered Turkish-Armenian journalist Hrant Dink (**above centre**), opened in 2019 at the former headquarters of the newspaper *Agos* of which he was editor-in-chief. Dink was assassinated on 19 January 2007 right outside the building.

dialogue between Turks and Armenians still living in Turkey, always stressing that critical engagement with the legacy of the past was essential for both sides. It was his very readiness to promote dialogue

people, Turks as well as Armenians, took part in a silent protest march in the centre of Istanbul. The demonstrators carried placards with inscriptions such as 'We are all Hrant Dink', 'We are all Armenian' and

'Four out of five Armenians in Turkey are already Turkified and can be described, from a nationalist point of view, as Turks whose religion is Christian.'

'Murderer 301', in reference to the article.

However, not all signs have pointed in the same direction as this demonstration. Despite official gestures of concern at the assassination, the Erdoğan government showed itself unwilling to abolish the controversial article, nor was it able to bring itself to make the symbolic gesture of sending a representative to attend the funeral of the prominent murdered man. Furthermore, Dink's seventeen-year-old assassin was celebrated as a national hero following his arrest – there are photographs that show police officers and the arrested man holding up the Turkish national flag together. Within just two weeks of the assassination souvenir shops in Anatolia were reporting high demand for white woollen hats similar to the one worn by the killer and which had subsequently become a symbol of nationalist extremism.

Given developments such as this, it should come as no surprise that the desire to emigrate is on the increase among the few Armenians still living in Turkey. But how many of them remain and under what conditions have they been living for so long as a minority in the Republic of Turkey? The territory covered by present-day Turkey was once home to around two million Armenians. By the mid-2010s there were just 100,000, sixty thousand of whom lived in Istanbul. A sense of the advanced state of their Turkification can be obtained from the fact that around 80 per cent have at best a limited command of their original mother tongue (many speak none at all) – a consequence of the dominant position of Turkish as the language of everyday life,

while Armenian, like Kurdish, is forbidden as a language of instruction in schools. This statistic suggests that the country's only news printed in Armenian – the Armenian pages of Dink's bilingual Turkish/Armenian weekly *Agos* – can be read by just 20 per cent of Armenians living in Turkey, meaning four out of five Armenians in Turkey are already Turkified and can be described, from a nationalist point of view, as Turks whose religion is Christian.

It must be conceded that the government under the Islamic leadership of Erdoğan has in some respects shown itself more flexible towards the Armenian minority than its strictly secular predecessors. In 2005 Erdoğan let it be known that he was prepared to be conciliatory in an effort to improve Turkish–Armenian relations, making a decisive move in this direction that same year when he initiated the careful restoration of the thousand-year-old Cathedral of the Holy Cross. For almost seven hundred years this cathedral – with its (now-defunct) monastery – was the seat of the Armenian patriarch and thus the centre of Armenian culture. To this day, for Armenians scattered all over the world it remains the symbol of their history and indeed their cultural identity. After 1915 the façade of the abandoned building was used for target practice by the Turkish Army. This desecration, which continued until 2003, gave rise to worldwide protests, prompting Erdoğan to react by prohibiting any further damage to the building and the announcement of the restoration project, to which he made a personal commitment and which would be paid for by the Turkish state

THE GREY WOLVES

The grey wolf, an animal still common on the steppes of Central Asia where the Turkic tribes originally settled, is a symbol of pan-Turanian ethnic identity and ideology – a movement that (in one form) promotes the unity of all Turkic peoples. Since the late 1970s the most powerful vehicle for this ideology has been a right-wing ultra-nationalist movement founded in Turkey in 1968, the members of which go by the name of *Bozkurtlar* in Turkish, meaning the Grey Wolves. The movement was – and is – the militant arm of the Milliyetçi Hareket Partisi (MHP), or Nationalist Movement Party. Combining anti-communism, Muslim conservatism and xenophobia ('Turkey belongs to the Turks: love it or leave it' is one of their slogans), the Grey Wolves were a formidable paramilitary organisation. Between 1975 and 1980 they murdered an estimated five thousand people, notably members of the Alevi, Kurdish, Armenian and Greek minorities. Some of the most horrific episodes were the massacres of left-wing demonstrators in Taksim Square (1977) and Alevis in Maraş and Çorum (1978 and 1980). One infamous Grey Wolf was Mehmet Ali Ağca, who in 1981 made an attempt on the life of Pope John Paul II. The Grey Wolves were also behind a failed attempt to assassinate Prime Minister Turgut Özal in 1988 and the disorder in the Alevi district of Gazi in Istanbul in 1995. Towards the end of the 1990s, as the conflict with the Kurdish PKK intensified, their nationalism began to translate into electoral success, as the MHP, under the leadership of Devlet Bahçeli since 1997, has been a key ally of Erdoğan's AKP in the governing coalition.

(to the tune of $1.5 million at the exchange rates of the time), thus becoming the first Armenian monument ever to be restored in Turkey by order of the Turkish government.

But when, on 29 March 2007, completion of the work was marked in a solemn ceremony, it again became clear that fundamental problems between enabling its citizens to travel to the event by the most direct route. But this border opening was forbidden by the Turkish military command on the grounds that Turkey and Armenia did not have diplomatic relations, meaning that guests travelling from Armenia were forced to make a long detour via Georgia. More serious still was

Above left: Children at an Armenian school in the basement of the Gedikpaşa Armenian Protestant Church, Istanbul.
Above right: A chart on a wall in the school showing the Armenian alphabet.

Turkey and Armenia remained unresolved, and some highly mixed messaging surrounded the event. Armenian guests from all over the world were able to participate, and those in attendance heard Turkey's culture minister, Atilla Koç, stress during his opening address that the Erdoğan government would undertake to protect all evidence of foreign culture on Turkish soil. Erdoğan, too, had made an undertaking for the ceremony – to open the border to the neighbouring Armenian Republic, a dispute between the governments in Ankara and the Armenian capital Yerevan over whether the cathedral should serve as a place of worship or a museum. The supreme head of the Armenian Apostolic Church, Catholicos Karekin II, rejected an invitation to the ceremony after the Turkish Foreign Ministry – under pressure from the military and from political parties with a strictly secular orientation – turned down his request for permission to hold a service there. A similarly negative response

Hrant Dink was born in Malatya, Eastern Anatolia, in 1954 and moved to Istanbul with his Armenian family at the age of seven. After his parents separated, he was sent to the Armenian orphanage of Gedikpaşa, where he met his future wife Rakel. Having graduated in zoology, and despite having no journalistic experience, in 1996 he founded the first bilingual Armenian/Turkish newspaper, *Agos* ('The Furrow'), to give a voice to Turkey's Armenian community, which was the target of racism and accusations of terrorism. From the pages of the newspaper he fought for dialogue between Turks and Armenians, reaching out not just to Armenians in Turkey but also to the diaspora and to Turkish citizens. Criticising everyone in equal measure, he denounced the unjust treatment of Turkey's Armenian minority and problems within the Armenian community itself, highlighting human rights violations and the problems of democratisation, pointing out that 'after all, Turkey is reluctant to concede rights to the majority, too'. Without refraining from the use of the word genocide, which is taboo in Turkey, he was opposed to the efforts of the Armenian diaspora to have the 1915 genocide officially recognised by Western parliaments as well as its use for political ends, accusing Germany of raising it to block Turkey's accession to the EU. He believed that the Armenians of the diaspora should be able to live free from the weight of historical memory, putting the needs of the living majority first: 'Turkish–Armenian relations must be pulled out of a well 1915 metres deep.'

was received by Mesrob II Mutafyan of Constantinople, patriarch of the Armenian Church in Turkey, when he expressed the hope that a service would in future be held in the cathedral at least once a year.

Two steps forward, one step back – a pattern that characterises recent developments in Turkish–Armenian relations. In the person of Erdoğan himself we can see these contradictions expressed: on the one hand he found himself the target of vehement criticism from many nationalists for securing the restoration of the Armenians' most valued holy shrine; but on the other he responded with equal ferocity when foreign states resolved to recognise the massacre of Armenians during the First World War as an act of genocide, as the organised mass extermination of a people.

This article is an adapted excerpt from Gerhard Schweizer's book *Türkei verstehen: Von Atatürk bis Erdoğan*, published in 2016 by Klett-Cotta Verlag.

Washing Away History:

Murat, who was born and raised in Hasankeyf, outside his former home; the building is partially submerged by the rising waters of the River Tigris upstream from the Ilısu Dam.

Hasankeyf and the Ilısu Dam

ERCAN Y YILMAZ
Translated by Kate Ferguson

In the heart of the Mesopotamian basin, the cradle of the world's most ancient civilisations, the city of Hasankeyf should have been a prime candidate for UNESCO's World Heritage List – but rather than being flooded by tourists it has been submerged under the dammed waters of the River Tigris.

YELLOW AND BLUE

The day we set out on a tractor trailer to make a trip as far back in history as it is possible to go I was seven years old; our destination, on the other hand, was around twelve *thousand* years old. Everyone told me how beautiful it was, how noble. But I was about to see it for the very first time. For the first time its air would fill my lungs; for the first time my eyes would be dazzled by its many shades of yellow; for the first time my ears would ring with the elegant rustling of the leaves of its pomegranate trees; for the first time my feet would leave a faint trace on its ancient stone tracks. I was breathless – no doubt in part because of the state of the road, but what really made my breath catch in my throat was the excitement of travelling to that place. The reason for my excitement: history.

We sang and clapped along in time, the sounds of the tractor tyres and exhaust weaving with the rhythm. I held tight to the side of the trailer as I'd been told to do, and I definitely wasn't going to try standing up. Forget the lurching of the trailer, the wind alone was a threat to my small body – it wouldn't take more than a puff to send me flying. But there were no clouds in the sky that day; it was going to be a glorious Sunday. The sun, already warm, was just starting to show its face. Had it noticed my gaze locked on the mountains, it might have said, 'It is my light and my heat that turns the mountains yellow.' And, as it swelled with pride, I would be forced to screw up my eyes. The different yellows around me – of the mountains, the sun, the road, the crops, the haystacks – each shade looked so beautiful when combined with all the others. I would be reminded of this moment many years later when I saw Van Gogh's *Wheat Stacks with Reaper.* But, even as I recalled, I would struggle to find the words to describe the excitement. The reason for my struggle: memories.

My father sat up front next to my uncle. Occasionally he would look back, check I was sitting down and then turn back to face forward. It was a rough road. Bodies shaken about. My father's thick lips moved beneath his moustache. The wind had undone some of the buttons on his shirt and found its way inside, puffing it out like sail. My mother, eyes on the yellow peaks, was sitting with her sisters-in-law. The ride made her queasy; she was unable to join in the fun, and her face wore a melancholy expression. When we asked, she said, 'You know I get travel sick.' We knew just as much as she wanted us to know. She also said, 'It's so beautiful around here.' And then from her lips fell a sharp exclamation, 'Such a shame!' The reason for these words: an impending misfortune of which I was as yet unaware.

They said it would take half an hour to get there, but it didn't pass as quickly as other half-hours. The nature and logic of time had been thrown off course by the import, the thrill of our destination; the minutes just dragged. I invented games to keep myself busy. I counted the trees by the roadside, but the game soon fizzled out; I tried to count the lambs among the flocks of sheep, but that didn't last long either. Nothing I did helped time to pass.

ERCAN Y YILMAZ is a writer and lecturer in literature originally from the city of Batman in the Southeastern Anatolia Region of Turkey. He has edited various literary magazines, including *Öykü Gazetesi* and *Askıda Öykü*, and has written for national titles like *Birikim*. The author of poems, short-story collections, novels and the screenplay for a short film, he has received a number of Turkish literary awards, including the Necati Cumalı and the Yaşar Nabi Nayır.

'That day I saw the city for the first time, and whenever I saw it again I would always remember that occasion. The description of the view: beauty. Its name: Hasankeyf.'

It was as though a stone was lodged in the cogs of my heart's clock and the hands could no longer turn. I kept going, determined. It felt as though I had been fighting for hours just to make the seconds pass. I saw hollows in the hillside. I asked what they were, but my mother couldn't hear me as the noise of the tractor drowned out my words. I repeated my question, louder this time. My mother said, 'Caves. They're caves, but promise you won't go in them.' 'OK,' I said and continued to count. Twenty-seven, twenty-eight, twenty-nine, twenty-ten … I was still at an age when I couldn't yet count up to thirty. I started again. One, two, three, four … I missed out more than I actually counted. 'Mum, why can't I go in the caves?' I asked in a loud voice. She didn't hear me. I repeated my question. Even louder this time. My aunt, who was sitting next to her, answered, 'Outsiders are hiding in them.' (Outsiders, *ên derve*, is how Kurdish guerrillas are sometimes referred to.) Eyes wide with anger, my mother glared at her sister-in-law. Then she took me by the arm and drew me to her side, holding me tight to her body. 'No, no, there's no one inside them. Don't be scared, sweetheart. The caves are just full of dirt and dust, that's all.' I wondered what it was that I should have been scared of. But my mother was holding me so tight I couldn't speak. We stayed like that for a while, my mother's warmth and the shades of yellow. When everyone on the trailer turned their heads to the left, I realised there was something to see, and I ducked out from under my mother's arm to take a look. An elegant S-shaped river shone bright blue, white foam gathering around the rocks. I placed my chin in my hands and watched in wonder. Jolted by the motion of the trailer, I let myself be pulled in by the calm of the water. The name of that water: tranquillity. The name of the river: the Tigris.

'Are we nearly there yet?' I asked for what may well have been the hundredth time. My mother gave the same answer, 'Not long now.' Then she added, 'It's just behind that hill.' I fixed my eyes on the hill so I wouldn't miss the moment of revelation. Yellow again. But this time there was a beautiful ribbon of blue flowing beside it and the occasional flash of green from a bed of reeds. I tried to keep my gaze steady so I wouldn't miss anything. 'Mum, is it beautiful?' Tired of my questions, she gave a monotonous, 'It's beautiful, very beautiful.' I repeated her answer aloud, 'Beautiful, very beautiful.' She thought I was making fun of her and frowned. I turned my gaze to the river, where I saw men fishing. They looked like Van Gogh's reaper in the wheat fields near the village of Auvers-sur-Oise on the outskirts of Paris. Both there and not there. Their size indiscernible, they blended with the colours around them. The only difference was the blue in place of the yellow, the rushing water in place of the dried ears of wheat. Five fishermen. My father noticed them, too. He and my uncle would go fishing whenever they could. My father pointed the fishermen out to my uncle, who was gripping the tractor's steering wheel. He sounded the horn in greeting. The fishermen responded by raising their hands. We left the fishermen behind, but my eyes stayed on them. Two of them

THE PASSENGER   Ercan y Yılmaz

were dragging the net – one on a *kelek* (a raft made of car inner tubes and planks of wood), one swimming in the river. The others were busy retrieving the netted fish and throwing them on to the riverbank. My father had taken me fishing with him twice. The landed fish floundered on the sand, and many of them I picked up and threw back into the water. Our neighbour noticed and told my father. As I was lost in my memories of that day my mother nudged me, 'Look, there's Hasankeyf!' That day I saw the city for the first time, and whenever I saw it again I would always remember that occasion. The description of the view: beauty. Its name: Hasankeyf.

WHITE

It is difficult to describe Hasankeyf. I sat at my desk to write this piece, eager to describe it, but I had no idea where I should start. For days I would get up from my desk without having written a single word. Instead of a solution came dozens of questions. Question after question. What is Hasankeyf? Who is Hasankeyf? Is Hasankeyf a science or an emotion? Is it art or nature? Flower or insect? Amber that floats or pebble that sinks? How long has Hasankeyf stood and for what? Is Hasankeyf rebellion or oblivion? Each question leading to another. The answers, like a shy Euphrates turtle, refused to raise their heads. Through these questions to which I could find no answers I tried to reach the Hasankeyf I held inside me. The questions led me back and forth through the timeline of my life. From the enchantment of that first time I saw the city to the dejection of my last visit ... As time ran in front of my eyes like a film, these questions continued to appear like flashes of light. They were like the artist Lucio Fontana's slashes on white canvas. It was as though everything of which

Hasankeyf was made would soon come seeping through those slashes – its plants, its insects, its reptiles, its birds ...

In 1972 the ancient city of Hasankeyf was given municipal status. In 1981 it was declared a protected area. On 16 May 1990, when Batman was made a province, Hasankeyf became a district. Hasankeyf is located in Upper Mesopotamia, in the region known as the Fertile Crescent, whose ancient mounds have offered up finds that have changed our understanding of human history. It is an ancient city established on a monolithic rock on the banks of the Tigris. Other mounds in the Fertile Crescent include: Göbekli Tepe, where the remains of a 12,000-year-old temple were only recently uncovered; Karahan Tepe, considered Göbekli Tepe's 'twin' because of the many similarities between the two; Nevalı Çori, now submerged under the waters of a dam along with its 12,000-year-old artefacts; and the equally old Çemka, in the Dargeçit District of Mardin Province, discovered just a few weeks before this article was written. These mounds are all in close proximity. The Fertile Crescent is where humankind first moved to a settled existence, where agriculture was first carried out by human hands and, through its temple culture, as the place where religion and worship first emerged.

Hasankeyf is the jewel of the region, yet it is not known who founded the city nor who its first residents were. Many sources say this remains obscure 'despite research', but it is quite clear that no comprehensive research has ever been carried

Left: A photograph of the ancient city of Hasankeyf in an old tourist brochure – preserved at a restaurant in 'New Hasankeyf' – showing the city before it was flooded.

out here. According to the information we do have, the construction of Hasankeyf's citadel dates back to the 4th century CE. Strategically placed, Hasankeyf frequently changed hands between the Sasanian Empire (in modern-day Iran) and the Byzantines. It is situated on the Silk Road – which runs from China to Europe, passing through India, Iran and the Arabian Peninsula – and on the banks of the Tigris, which flows south from the Diyarbakır–Elazığ border, leaving Turkey and passing through the cities of Mosul, Tikrit, Samarra, Baghdad, Kut and Amarah before joining with the Euphrates in Basra and emptying into the Persian Gulf. Hasankeyf is thus located at the meeting point of cultures, a crossroads over which armies fought for control. The citadel was built on the orders of the Roman Emperor Constantius II as a defence against Sasanian raids after he gained control of Diyarbakır and the surrounding area. It was thanks to this citadel that, after the Battle of Samarra in CE 363, Hasankeyf remained under Roman and Byzantine rule for a long time.

The citadel is constructed out of a monolithic rock, 135 metres in height, steep slopes leading up to it on all four sides. The two paths to the citadel were guarded by four monumental gates. Neglected and uncared for, the last remaining gate was unable to withstand the elements and finally crumbled and fell in 2000. Inside the citadel are monuments dating from the Roman, Artuqid, Ayyubid and Ottoman periods, and the caves are believed to have served as dwellings for the Urartians, Assyrians and Sumerians. The cave houses above the citadel, which the locals call *Yukarı Şehir* (Upper City) and *İç Kale* (Inner Citadel), have survived to the present day. Standing high above the Tigris, the citadel resembles a medieval settlement. As well as houses and cave dwellings, in the Inner Citadel can be found the Great Palace, burial grounds, a mausoleum, the Grand Mosque, a prayer hall and a madrasa. There are around two thousand caves within the citadel alone. You can still see what remains of the system – including pipework and canals carved out of the rock – that brought water from the valley two hundred metres below to meet the needs of the inhabitants.

With the construction of the citadel, Christianity spread quickly throughout the area, and Hasankeyf became the seat of the Syriac patriarchate. In 451, at the Council of Chalcedon (Kadıköy), the head of the bishopric was awarded the title of cardinal. It was at the council that the name Cepha was used for the first time, a name believed to derive from the word for rock in Syriac (*kifo*) or Assyrian (*kipani*), so the name given to this city, home to so many different cultures, was Hesna Kepha in Syriac, or Hisni Keyfa in Arabic, which translates as rock fortress. The name took on its current form – Hasankeyf – during the Ottoman period. The Ottoman scribe Kâtip Çelebi wrote that the city was known as Ra's al Gul (Head of the Rose), while the Kurdish name is Heskîf.

The origin of the name also holds a

The Ilısu Dam is one part of the huge Southeastern Anatolia Project (GAP), initiated to bring progress to one of Turkey's least developed regions. It was originally Atatürk's idea, to help resolve the region's energy requirements by harnessing the power of the waters of the rivers Tigris and Euphrates; it comprises twenty-two dams on Turkish soil, feeding nineteen hydroelectric power plants and affecting nine provinces of the Mesopotamian basin. The GAP was planned in the 1970s, with projects for irrigation and the production of hydraulic energy, and transformed in the early 1980s into a multi-sectoral development programme that also includes seven airports. The plan for the Ilısu Dam dates back to the 1950s but was only funded in the late 1990s, with foundations being laid in 2006 and construction beginning two years later. The cost is in the region of $1.7 billion. It is Turkey's second-largest dam by capacity and the fourth-largest in terms of energy production: it should produce 4,200 gigawatts of electricity per year. Many of those affected by the construction of the dam – 110,000 if you add together the inhabitants of Hasankeyf, those evacuated by the Turkish Army in the 1990s and the three thousand nomadic families who live along the Tigris – are Kurds. The construction of the dam has been slowed over the years by the withdrawal of international partners over fears of damage to archaeological heritage sites and the natural environment. The reduction of the flow of water from the Tigris also threatens neighbouring countries downstream, Syria and Iraq, which are already afflicted by drought.

place in local folklore. There was, so the tale goes, once a shepherd named Hasan who fell in love with the sultan's daughter and she with him. When the sultan found out he was determined to put an end to their romance – it was a matter of reputation. But, try as he might, he was unable to keep them apart and prevent them from meeting. In time the couple's feelings only grew stronger, and the sultan, afraid that their love would become unstoppable, decided to put an end to it once and for all and threw the shepherd into a dungeon. Yet even this could not prevent the lovers from seeing each other. The sultan's daughter found a passage through the rocks of the city that led to the dungeon, and she would escape from the palace and visit Hasan in secret. When the sultan learned of this he imprisoned his daughter in the highest room of the palace. Afraid that even this would not be enough to put an end to their love, he decided he had no choice but to have Hasan killed. He told his men to grant Hasan one final wish before executing him. When asked what this wish might be, Hasan replied, 'Let me walk one last time through the city with my flock.' This was granted, and, under the watchful eyes of the palace guards, he was taken to his animals. As he and his sheep reached the bridge that led over the Tigris he stopped to gaze at the palace. It was at this moment that the sultan's daughter decided to take her own life and put an end to her unbearable longing. She jumped from her room high up in the palace and fell into the waters of the Tigris. As he witnessed his beloved plummeting into the river Hasan understood that they could now be together in the afterlife where no one could separate them. He threw himself into the water after his sweetheart and was heard to cry, 'Today is the day of Hasan's joy.' Those who witnessed the two

THE PASSENGER   Ercan y Yılmaz

lovers drowning described it as '*Hasan'ın keyfi*' (Hasan's joy), a phrase that over time became Hasankeyf. For the locals, this is how the city got its name.

But whether its name came from a tragic love story or from its geology, Hasankeyf is known as the cradle of civilisation. It is also referred to as 'cave city' because of the countless caves – in fact, in Kurdish the whole area is known as the region of *şikefta* (caves). According to the Turkish Ministry of Culture there are four thousand caves in Hasankeyf, but this figure comes from sources dating back to the 1970s and other estimates put it at between six and eight thousand. While the geography of the area makes it difficult to determine the exact number, no real efforts have actually been made to do so. Nor is it known when these caves were first used as dwellings. Finds uncovered in the mounds suggest that the city is twelve thousand years old, but many believe it to be even older. As the city in the Fertile Crescent with the largest number of caves, Hasankeyf offered shelter to the many ancient civilisations that ruled over Upper Mesopotamia – the Medes, the Sumerians, the Assyrians and the Babylonians. These caves, which continued to be used as homes into the 2000s, remain unchanged today.

Hasankeyf was one of the most important medieval Islamic capitals. It was in 639, during the reign of Caliph Umar, that Muslims first captured the city. Umayyad-Abbasid rule was followed by that of the Hamdanids from 906–90 and then the Marwanids from 990–1096. Hasankeyf was later ruled by the Artuqids (1102–1232),

the Ayyubids (1232–1462) and the Aq Qoyunlus (1462–82). As Aq Qoyunlu power weakened, the Ayyubids once again took the city. In 1515, after a short period of Safavid rule, Hasankeyf was brought under Ottoman control. Through all this the city enjoyed two golden ages and suffered one period of great decline. Hasankeyf's golden years were during the Artuqid and Ayyubid periods, and most of the region's artefacts and monuments were either produced during those times or survived from the Middle Ages to the present through careful preservation during those periods. After the city was pillaged in 1260 during the Mongolian invasion, one of the most barbaric raids in history, Hasankeyf never returned to its former glory.

One of Hasankeyf's most celebrated monuments is the ancient bridge. The exact date of its construction is unknown, but from the figures and reliefs that decorate it, it is generally supposed to have been Artuqid in origin. Some also believe that it may have been built on the remains of an earlier Roman structure. Four of the piers and one small arch survive. The span between the two central piers is around forty metres, and it is thought to have had a central wooden arch that could open and close. One of the longest bridges of its day, it was much admired and was mentioned by many travellers of the period in their writings, including the 13th-century Arab scholar Izz al-Din ibn Shaddad, who described it as follows: 'The bridge was built of stone. The middle, however, has a wooden section that can be drawn back when an enemy attacks the city, thus closing the bridge off. Those left inside remain on the emplacements and stay there.' Other important historical monuments include: the tomb of Zeynel Mirza Bey – who was killed while fighting against Sultan Mehmet the Conqueror in the Battle of Otlukbeli – built by his father, the Aq Qoyunlu ruler Uzun Hasan; the Artuqid-era hamam; the Zawiya (monastery) of İmam Abdullah; the Mosque of Er-Rizk and the Ayyubid-era Kızlar Mosque (or Mosque of the Maidens); the Sultan Suleyman complex; and the churches of Kısır, Shabik and Deriki.

And then there is the flora and fauna to be found around Hasankeyf, nature that will be ravaged by the waters of the Ilısu Dam.

BLACK

In the questions that run through my mind like momentary flashes against a dark background, the colours of Hasankeyf now turn from white to black, from yellow to grey, from green to brown, from blue to mud. We in Turkey are faced with a government that never lets us forget, not for one second, that these colour changes are taking place in every area of our lives. A government that defends its politics of destruction by dismissing the beauty that exists in the world. Of the destruction of history, they say, 'What of it? It's just some old pots and pans.' Of the destruction of nature, 'It's only a few trees.' And of this ancient city, they say, 'It's nothing but a few stones and some caves.' I should also remind you that this same leader, Recep Tayyip Erdoğan, said in a speech in 2006, 'Whether it's a woman or a child, we will do whatever is necessary,' encouraging the use of force, even lethal force, by the police. They are carrying out a series of massacres, both of nature and of people. The destruction is in every area of our lives. We share the same fate as Hasankeyf. Every day we witness a new massacre of nature, of history, of culture. Forests are burned down, only for hotels to spring up from the ashes like mushrooms. People are murdered, and judges spring up to acquit the murderers. Building contractors ready to pour a sea of concrete over all that is beautiful have multiplied with state support. Journalists and writers have been thrown in prison, while fundamentalists, murderers of women and child abusers are given early release for good behaviour.

Hasankeyf was the latest victim of those who dream of a concrete future for coming generations. Hasankeyf was our mirror, and, when night fell, the scream of that mirror could be heard. The westernmost of the bridge's two central piers took the form of a woman, throwing back her head to let out a scream. The ruins became the image of that scream. It was the scream of the Tigris, a scream to alert us to the approaching danger but one which, as the waters rise, will be drowned.

Hasankeyf will be submerged in the waters of the Ilısu Dam. Ilısu is a village in the Dargeçit District of Mardin Province; this is where the dam has been built. The old name of the village was Germav, which means thermal spring in Kurdish. It is just one of the thousands of place names in Turkey that were changed because the original name was Kurdish, Armenian, Georgian, Syriac or Greek. The village has now lent its current name to the dam that will swallow Hasankeyf. Most of the Ilısu residents were moved out of their homes and resettled in social housing in surrounding villages. Now, as the waters rise, Ilısu is completely underwater – and the water is steadily backing up towards the cradle of civilisation.

A study published by Istanbul University on 17 April 2009 found that Hasankeyf and the Tigris Valley met nine out of the ten criteria for inclusion on the UNESCO list of World Heritage Sites; it is believed that it meets the highest number of these criteria of any site anywhere. To be included on the list, the Great Wall of China, for example, meets five, the

'Hasankeyf, a place that bears the traces of numerous civilisations, Hasankeyf, our shared world heritage, has been destroyed in plain sight.'

Pyramids three, Angkor Wat in Cambodia two, the Taj Mahal one, the Grand Canyon in the USA four and the city of Venice and its lagoon five. Of Turkey's own heritage sites that have been included on the list of shared human heritage, Cappadocia and Ephesus each meet two, Pamukkale three and the Great Mosque of Divriği one. For Hasankeyf, however, no application was even made. Hasankeyf, a place that bears the traces of numerous civilisations, Hasankeyf, our shared world heritage, has been destroyed in plain sight without the consequences of the dam's construction being taken into consideration, and, what's more, with no environmental-impact assessment carried out and with no alternative proposals put forward. Whenever anyone spoke up they were reminded that there were also 'security' motives behind the dam's construction. Although this has never actually been stated by the authorities, it has often been suggested that these security motives include cutting off the crossing points and shelters used by Kurdish PKK guerrillas and gaining control over the water supply in the Middle East. By implying that the guerrillas' room for manoeuvre would be restricted as the rising waters of the dam filled the caves and the valley, the state tried to discourage the public from holding demonstrations

Right: A motorbike parked in one of the caves that had been inhabited by the people of Hasankeyf for many hundreds of years before they were forced to move elsewhere.

– and they were, by and large, successful. Until 2010 protests against the dam remained at a local level; in 2010, thanks to an initiative by the Turkish nature-rights association Doğa, such famous figures as Orhan Pamuk, the singers Tarkan, Teoman and Sezen Aksu and the actor Okan Bayülgen spoke out against the Ilısu Dam, and the project's international partners pulled out. The Turkish–PKK peace process that began in 2009 also had a part to play in this. During the process, work on the dam came to a virtual standstill, but after it collapsed in 2014 it all started up again – a clear sign that the dam is both a political and a military project.

Many people also believe that the destruction of such an important settlement serves another purpose: to wipe out all memory of the historical presence of Kurds in the region. Among the many powers that ruled over Hasankeyf there were several Kurdish states: the Medes, the Hurrians, the Mitannis, the Hamdanids, the Marwanids and the Ayyubids. This is believed to have played a role in the evidence being washed away before any real archaeological studies had been carried out. Dressed up as a 'regional development initiative' and a 'mega-project', the Southeastern Anatolia Project (GAP) has been designed to erase history while also serving as a tool of assimilation. The historical sites that have been destroyed, damaged or flooded because of the dam could very easily have made a significant contribution to the economy through low-investment tourism initiatives, which would also have protected the region's history and natural habitats. If the aim had

Below: A rickety ladder propped up against an abandoned house in Hasankeyf and, in the background, the construction that will form the embankment once the whole of the ancient city is flooded.
Right and page 152: Cave dwellings in Hasankeyf.
Far right: The concrete edifice that now encases the ancient city's mosque.

THE KURDISH AND TURKISH
LANGUAGES COMPARED

The desire for linguistic freedom is a key issue in Turkey, where minorities have long been oppressed through the prohibition of languages other than Turkish, and speaking Kurdish in public was banned for several decades. Thousands of Kurdish – as well as Armenian, Greek and Georgian – place names have been swapped for Turkish names. The official stance has softened in the 21st century, but the Kurds are still demanding the right to

central tool in the elimination of minorities: under the 'Citizens Speak Turkish!' campaign launched in 1928 it was the duty of citizens to check that everyone was speaking the same tongue – on pain of being ostracised. The Turkish Language Association, meanwhile, was established in 1932 to replace Ottoman Turkish with a standard language based on the dialect spoken in Istanbul, with foreign influences expunged. The same period saw the switch to the Latin alphabet from one based on the Arabic script. Kurdish, however, like English and almost all other European languages, belongs to the Indo-European family. With thirty million speakers, 14.5 million of them in Turkey, it is the most commonly spoken language in majority-Kurdish regions in Turkey, Syria, Iraq and Iran (sometimes referred to as Kurdistan), although it had no written form until the 15th century. It is not a single language, however, rather a collection of dialects, the main groups of which are Kurmanji, Sorani and Pehlewani, Kurmanji being the most widespread in Turkey.

use Kurdish as the language of education in Kurdish-majority areas of Turkey – only in Iraq, since 2005, has Kurdish, alongside Arabic, been an official language anywhere in modern times. Turkish has almost nothing in common with Kurdish. Turkish, the first language of eighty million people, is a member of the Altaic family, like other Turkic languages as well as Mongolian and possibly (very distantly) Japanese and Korean. In the Ottoman Empire the official language was a version of Turkish with marked Arabic and Persian influences, but, for Atatürk, language was a

The Partiya Karkerên Kurdistanê (Kurdistan Workers' Party, PKK) is a paramilitary group founded in 1978 by Abdullah Öcalan with the aim of creating an independent state in Kurdistan, an area straddling the borders of Turkey, Syria, Iraq and Iran. In 1980 the Turkish government prohibited the dissemination of Kurdish culture in the country, and in 1984 the PKK decided to switch to an armed struggle, and terrorist violence from both sides claimed tens of thousands of victims. With the arrest of Öcalan in 1999 the PKK scaled back its demands, calling for greater cultural and political autonomy, but it did not give up. In 2013 Öcalan announced from prison a truce with the Turkish state following the adoption of a more conciliatory stance by the Erdoğan government and lengthy talks with the secret services. The pro-Kurdish Halkların Demokratik Partisi (Peoples' Democratic Party, HDP) entered parliament in 2015 and immediately joined the opposition ranks, causing Erdoğan to lose his majority. The president reacted with an anti-Kurdish campaign to capture nationalist votes, meaning the peace was short lived, and the truce was officially suspended in July 2015. In reprisals for the Suruç attack (a bombing that killed dozens of Kurdish activists), which some believed had been carried out with the complicity of the Turkish authorities, the PKK killed three policemen. Erdoğan responded by bombing PKK bases and arresting Kurdish activists and sympathisers. The return to war has devastated the southeast of the country, particularly Diyarbakır, the (unofficial) capital of the majority-Kurdish areas of the country, and Cizre, which was besieged and razed to the ground.

been truly about regional development, the towns of Samsat, Belkıs and Halfeti would have been transformed into tourist havens, and Hasankeyf would not be about to drown in the waters of the dam. GAP, of which the Ilısu Dam is a part, was designed to erase Kurdish history under the pretext of bringing security to the region.

The origins of such strategies can be found in the assimilation policies of the 1950s. It is worth noting that the chronology of the dam progressed under nationalist governments and following military coups. Plans for the dam were first put forward in 1950, after the elections that marked the end of the country's one-party era. The first studies were carried out following the military coup of 1971. After another coup in 1980 work began on drawing up a plan, which was approved in 1982 and finally set in motion under the rule of the AKP and Recep Tayyip Erdoğan. The projects of assimilation and massacre that were launched seventy years ago are still being put into practice, perhaps more enthusiastically than ever. The destruction of cultural spaces and the murder of innocent people sheltering in basements during the 2015 curfews in Diyarbakır and Cizre can only be explained by the AKP government's all-out war and their policy to eradicate all forms of diversity.

Doğa has stated: 'According to data from Dicle University in Diyarbakır, environmental studies have only been carried out on 5 per cent of the 400-kilometre area that will be affected by the Ilısu Dam project.' They wanted to build the dam without conducting any research into the biodiversity of the majority of the Tigris or into the level of environmental destruction that would follow – and, unfortunately, they have succeeded. The only argument put forward by those in favour of the dam is that it will provide electricity – yet the Ilısu Dam will

> 'Kurdish artist Ahmet Güneştekin interred his paintbrushes in the sands of the Tigris at Hasankeyf, saying, "I am here because this is where they want to bury my tales, my legends, my stories, my epics."'

operate at 36 per cent efficiency, making it one of the least efficient hydroelectric plants.

The volume of water to be held by the dam will alter the region's climate. Oxygen levels in the water will drop, water quality will decline, mud will accumulate and many species will be left facing extinction. Those most affected will be the Euphrates soft-shell turtle, the griffon vulture, the striped hyena, the pied kingfisher, the lesser kestrel, the olive bee-eater and the Euphrates poplar. And then there are the people. Sixty thousand, twenty thousand of them children, will be directly impacted, losing their homes, villages, fields and gardens. In the new towns in which they settle they will face problems of social integration and unemployment. Just as it is impossible to keep Hasankeyf alive by transporting a few of its monuments to a new location, so it will not be possible for the people of Hasankeyf to carry on with their lives in concrete blocks after losing their gardens. Expropriation was unregulated, and the purchase values set were low. The new city was built opposite the dam that will leave Hasankeyf under the water. The houses offered to the people of Hasankeyf look out over the dam that has flooded the graves of their ancestors, the streets of their childhood, the fields and gardens of their youth. The compensation offered to those who did not want to move to the new settlement was not enough to buy a house in the city, so they are forced to rent. Those who had no choice but to move to the new settlement will face the prospect of unemployment as the amount of agricultural land shrinks.

As he interred his paintbrushes in the sands of the Tigris at Hasankeyf, Kurdish artist Ahmet Güneştekin said, 'I am here because this is where they want to bury my tales, my legends, my stories, my epics. This is the site of the history that gave life to my person, my art, my culture. Here lie the traces of civilisation ... Now they want to bury Hasankeyf. If Hasankeyf is to go under, then let my brushes, the tools of my soul, go under, too. Let them be buried together.' And the artist laid his brushes to rest in the conscience of those who wish to flood Hasankeyf.

Hasankeyf is now nothing but concrete. All its yellows, greens and blues have been turned grey by the concrete. Hasankeyf is now black, because in these lands the grief for this heritage, for these thousands of years of history, will last for ever.

GREY

We all have special places in the towns and cities in which we grow up. It is those that we miss the most. For me it is the streets of Batman where I would sell yoghurt – and Hasankeyf. Every time I'd go back to visit my family I'd wander those streets and pay a visit to Hasankeyf. This time it was different. I wanted to go to Hasankeyf but was afraid of the devastation I would find. After some hesitation I decided not to go. While walking the streets of Batman I met a young journalist. We follow each other on social media, but this was the first time we had met in person. He told me,

THE PASSENGER   Ercan y Yılmaz

'There's still hope for Hasankeyf.' He said that a group of writers, musicians and artists were working on a video. 'There's still hope!' he repeated. There was still hope. There always is. The Zeynel Bey tomb was disassembled and relocated, as was the Artuqid-era hamam, the İmam Abdullah shrine and the main gate of the Hasankeyf citadel. The monuments were damaged during the process. Yet there was still hope for the ancient city of Hasankeyf, with its caves, its hundreds of living creatures and its breathtaking natural environment. I wanted to be taken in by his rallying cry. We exchanged numbers and parted. Some time later he called me. He wanted to interview me about the short-story magazine *Öykü Gazetesi* that we had just closed down and my book that was about to be published. The site of the interview: Hasankeyf. 'And we'll do a short video about Hasankeyf, too,' he added. I remembered his rallying cry, 'There's still hope!' Despite my initial hesitation I accepted. 'When?' I asked. 'Today,' he replied. And so we found ourselves on the road to Hasankeyf. Along the way he told me what they planned to do for the city, but all I could think about was what I would find when we got there.

I parked the car at the entrance to Hasankeyf. We got out. Immediately we were surrounded by a group of children. The history of the site, memorised by rote, fell from their lips. One spoke in English, another in Turkish. Another said, 'We can do it in Arabic or Kurdish, too, if you want.' We thanked them. We set up the camera at a spot that took in the bridge, the citadel and the Tigris, a spot that should have shown Hasankeyf's yellows, blues and greens in all their glory. But now all we could see were the grey shades of concrete. A muddy river, citadel walls plastered in concrete, an ancient bridge covered over in preparation for its underwater burial ... In

sadness we watched as the historic stone bridge of Hasankeyf, legs weighed down by concrete, surrendered itself to the blue waters of the Tigris. The claim that the bridge's piers would be protected from the negative effects of the water was clearly false. One of the reasons for the withdrawal of the project's European backers in 2011 was that there was no plan to preserve anything that would be submerged when the waters rose. For show, they proposed using vacuum chambers, easing one of the concerns of the new backers. There were alternative plans that could have saved the whole of Hasankeyf. But Hasankeyf's death warrant had already been signed.

I remembered the day I first saw this landscape at the age of seven, the day we crossed the river on *keleks*, the day we went rafting with a photography group, the day we celebrated a friend's marriage here. And I remembered all those nights when, unable to sleep, I would escape here to take refuge in the sound of the Tigris. A succession of memories of happy times usually mark the end of something. This time that which was facing its imminent demise was the 12,000-year-old city.

As we were shooting our video, looking at the ugly concrete blocks that rose from the Tigris, we held on to the smallest glimmer of hope. In November 2019 the city's historical bazaar was emptied. In December 2019 that beautiful winding road of our childhood that led to Hasankeyf was closed to traffic. The dam was beginning to fill. February 2020. The waters rose. The water arrived at the cradle of civilisation like a barbarian horde destroying everything its path. This ancient tale does not have a happy ending.

Hasankeyf has drowned in the waters of the Tigris, the same waters that gave it its voice. Hasankeyf is under the water. 🐦

'I Rap Istanbul': From Kreuzberg to Turkey and Back

Turkish rap first emerged in the Kreuzberg district of Berlin and reached Istanbul in the 1990s, where it remained a niche genre for many years. When it exploded into the mainstream in the 2010s the time was ripe for it to become the Gezi generation's lead instrument for protest and the reclamation of their physical and cultural spaces.

BEGÜM KOVULMAZ
Translated by Ekin Oklap

Şamil Oymak, aka 'Şam', during a performance at Nayah in Kadıköy, Istanbul.

It would be impossible to hazard a guess as to how many verses have been dedicated to Istanbul over the course of its considerable history, but of the many poems written and recited in honour of this capital of three empires, perhaps the best known and best loved of all belongs to one of the most venerated names in Turkish poetry, Orhan Veli Kanık: 'I listen to Istanbul, my eyes closed.' Orhan Veli was an innovator who rejected traditional poetics; in the 1940s he began to introduce scenes from daily life and colloquial language into his poetry, and in 1947 – three years before his death from a brain haemorrhage at the age of thirty-six – he wrote the free-verse poem 'I Listen to Istanbul' on his way back from a trip to Ankara. In the poem's six stanzas, each of which begins and ends with the line 'I listen to Istanbul, my eyes closed', the poet closes his eyes to upend the traditional hierarchy of the five senses; he floats above his city, over the Bosphorus, over street markets and pavements in the evening, describing all that his senses perceive, and as the moon rises in the night, he meets up with a lover who is, perhaps, the city itself.

Today most of the things Orhan Veli heard when he closed his eyes and listened are no more: the sound of a light breeze and the rustle of leaves swaying on a branch are drowned out by the constant thrum of traffic that seeps into every corner of the city; the soft, gentle sound of a water-carrier's bells, of a fishing net being reeled in, of bare feet dipping in the sea have been displaced by the noise of construction sites, the rattle of suitcase wheels, by calls to prayer, sirens and car horns. Yet to this day the idea of closing their eyes and listening to their city resonates powerfully with the people of Istanbul – evidence that there must be some synaesthetic quality to the city, something about it that lends itself to being experienced through sound rather than sight. In time the phrase 'I listen to Istanbul' has become a slogan, a theme, co-opted and used in a variety of ways – the Ministry of Education's 'I Read Istanbul' project to encourage reading, the municipal authorities' decision to name the city's marathon 'I Run Istanbul' – for commercial purposes or to raise public awareness. 'Listening to Istanbul' has become the city's catchphrase.

According to Seamus Heaney, a person's poetic sensibility is inextricably tied to their surroundings – to a sense of home, to the place they lean on for support when they reach out into the world, the emotional scaffolding that feeds their poetic imagination, the place they turn to when in need of a firm footing. In hip-hop, too, sense of place has always been valued; it is the element that sets it apart from other

BEGÜM KOVULMAZ graduated in English literature from the University of Istanbul and earned a doctorate in cinema and television from Bilgi University. Since 2000 she has worked for Turkish publishing houses as a translator and editor as well as writing about art and culture. She is a passionate rap fan.

'Istanbul in 2000 as chronicled by Ceza and his fellow rapper Dr Fuchs is a city "difficult and crowded, smothered in concrete, filthy and cruel", but it is also their city.'

youth movements and subcultures. Ever since its inception, rap has always been the voice of the self; rap artists are their own subjects, the centres of their own universes, and their surroundings are a kind of lens through which they develop their own way of looking at the world outside. It is one of rap's unwritten rules that as a genre it should paint a comprehensive character study of the place and the community from which it comes and always acknowledge the sources that inspire and inform it.

So it is not altogether surprising that the first popular (although not *pop*-ular) Turkish rap song written in Istanbul by rappers from Istanbul should have taken the city itself as its subject and based itself upon the Orhan Veli line that has etched itself so indelibly into the public consciousness. 'İstanbul', the fourth song on the album *Meclis-i Âlâ İstanbul* ('The High Council of Istanbul') released in 2000 by the group Nefret (Hate), was quite possibly the first ever Turkish rap song to be a nationwide hit, and its accompanying video was one of the first rap videos to be broadcast on mainstream television channels in Turkey. The song highlights the devastation wreaked on city life by the forces of rural–urban migration and globalisation, and its chorus ends with the hook 'I listen to Istanbul, my eyes closed'. In the third verse, rapper Ceza pays explicit homage to the great poet with the lines 'What I want today, Orhan Veli described / When he closed his eyes back in the day'. Istanbul in the year 2000 as chronicled by Ceza and his fellow rapper Dr Fuchs is a city 'difficult and crowded,

smothered in concrete, filthy and cruel', but it is also their city. The self-declared 'rulers of Istanbul / and kings of Turkish rap' lambast those who abuse their city – the city they love 'in all its pleasures and troubles'.

But what is surprising is how the song is constructed. It begins with the sounds of a synthesiser accompanied by an acoustic *bağlama*, the lute-like instrument which is the bedrock of Turkish folk music, which was played live in the studio during the recording. This ostinato is soon joined by a beat, by guest DJ Mahmut's scratching (including several scratch solos), by stringed instruments that recreate the sounds of traditional Turkish music and by violins that accentuate the beat and mimic the popular arabesk genre. In the chorus, an operatic female voice sings the city's name like a cantor in a Byzantine choir. Putting its melodic elements firmly in the foreground, the track successfully draws on the various musical traditions of multicultural Turkey to create an intersection of melancholy, rage and solemnity.

Ceza and Fuchs's Istanbul may be troubled and ruthless, but 'it is ours and always will be'. Besides displaying rap music's characteristic tendency to lay claim to its place of origin, the song also employs a series of nationalist and chauvinistic slogans. The roots of these particular inclinations, however, lie in the music of the first ever practitioners of popular Turkish rap: in 1995, five years before Nefret released 'İstanbul', a German group named Cartel burst 'like

Top: Çağrı Sinci during a performance at Nayah, Kadıköy, Istanbul.
Centre: Ceza performing in Bahçeşehir, Istanbul.
Bottom: The rapper Kamufle at a show in Kadıköy.

a rap-bomb' into the Turkish national consciousness.

Turkish rap can trace its roots to one area of one German city. The inhabitants of Kreuzberg in Berlin were mostly working-class Turks who had moved to the country in the 1960s under Germany's *Gastarbeiter* (guest worker) programme, a political scheme designed to attract cheap labour. The first immigrants to arrive under this programme had mostly lived in dormitories, but soon they started taking advantage of family-reunification laws to bring their relatives over and began to settle in the cheaper run-down neighbourhoods closest to the Berlin Wall – Kreuzberg in particular. The German government had conceived of the *Gastarbeiter* scheme as a temporary measure, so the children of that first wave of immigrants grew up without ever integrating into German culture or ever having seen the country from which their parents had come.

Born in the 1970s in New York's South Bronx, by the early 1980s rap music had already found its way to Germany, where it was played in clubs and on the radio. But it was through American films such as *Style Wars* (1983) and *Beat Street* (1984) that young Germans really became acquainted with hip-hop culture. The birth of Turkish rap was a slightly more organic process, a result of the interactions between US Cold War soldiers stationed along the Berlin Wall in the late 1980s and the second-generation Turks who lived there. The voice of the oppressed African-American minority in the USA resonated with Germany's young immigrants. Many members of early German rap groups like Advanced Chemistry and Absolute Beginners had foreign origins – African (particularly Ghanaian), Haitian, Italian – and the children of the Turks who now found themselves squeezed between the Berlin Wall and the city's more middle-class areas saw in hip-hop a space in which to negotiate the construction of an identity of their own, defined in their own terms, independent of the prescriptions of the state, of German and Turkish social mores and of parental expectations.

In the 1990s, after the fall of the Berlin Wall, Germany began implementing *Ausländerpolitik*, a new immigration policy that encouraged guest workers to return to their countries of origin. As xenophobia grew, Turkish-German youths found in rap an increasingly important political tool to fight back against racism and right-wing ideologies. In May 1993 the home of a family of Turkish immigrants in Solingen was targeted in an arson attack, and five people – including three children – were killed. Two years later the rap group Cartel was formed, and their debut video – which was screened frequently on the main music channels of that era – began with news clips about the Solingen attack. During their first ever gig, Cartel's Kurdish, German and Cuban members did something that had never been done before: they rapped in Turkish. That same year they released their eponymous Turkish-language rap album whose songs invited Turkish-immigrant youths in Germany to stand together against racism and injustice and to take pride in their identity. The album did well in Germany, but more surprising was the huge commercial success it achieved in Turkey. In the USA rap duo Luniz had knocked Michael Jackson off the top of the R&B charts with their 1995 album *Operation Stackola* (which featured the hit single 'I Got 5 on It'); in Turkey Cartel did the same with their hit 'Cartel'. That same year Cartel became the first and only rap group to perform at İnönü Stadium, a venue that had previously hosted the likes of

Madonna, Michael Jackson and Metallica. Cartel brought together the sounds of traditional Turkish folk and pop music with rap beats, and their stance against neo-Nazism appealed to Turkey's nationalist camp. Their lyrics about 'crazy Turkish hellraisers' from the song 'Cartel' chimed with the nation's self-image. Cartel's ability to put a modern spin on old nationalist slogans and present them in a fresh context proved immensely popular, and the mainstream media was quick to embrace them.

Nefret's Ceza and Dr Fuchs were respectively eighteen and seventeen years old when Cartel took the country by storm, and it would have been impossible for them not to have been affected by the style and preoccupations of the first popular outfit to rap in Turkish. Aside from the nationalist clichés featured in the lyrics to 'İstanbul', even the accents in which they sung and the poses they struck in their videos bore the clear signs of the influence of the niche *Almancı* (Turkish-German) subculture. Nevertheless, if the form and content of Cartel's song followed in the footsteps of N.W.A.'s ghetto anthem 'Straight Outta Compton', with its emphasis on the gangsta ethos and on identity, Nefret's hit 'İstanbul' could be likened in its efforts to address social issues to an angrier version of Grandmaster Flash's 1982 urban-realist record 'The Message'.

Ceza and Dr Fuchs formed Nefret in 1998, and, although they've provided a number of explanations for the name they chose, I'd like to think that they were inspired in their choice by Mathieu Kassovitz's timeless and universal 1995 film *La Haine* ('Hate' in English), released in Turkey in 1996. Portraying twenty-four hours in the aimless yet extraordinarily harsh lives of three young immigrants from different ethnic backgrounds all living in the same Parisian *banlieue*, this

ARABESK

As its name suggests, this music has Arab origins – deriving as it does from the music of belly dance – and is permeated with Eastern sounds. And precisely for this reason it was not popular with the elite of the newborn Republic of Turkey, who were doing their utmost to ensure that the population looked to the West in music – by funding jazz, tango and classical music schools – as well as in other areas, from the introduction of the Latin alphabet to the replacement of the Ottoman fez with the top hat. But not even the 1948 ban on listening to Arabic music could overcome the people's passion, and they got around the prohibition by tuning in to Radio Cairo and listening to one of the first arabesk artists, Haydar Tatlıyay. Inevitably, love was the subject of many of the songs, expressed in sighs and sobs against a backdrop of stringed instruments, but the word that most of all characterises the genre is *gurbet*, nostalgia for the homeland. Arabesk became the soundtrack of the 1950s and '60s migration from the towns and villages of Anatolia to the urban centres of Istanbul, Izmir and Ankara. Orhan Gencebay, regarded as the founder of the scene, as well as such performers as Müslüm Gürses and İbrahim Tatlıses, came from the east of the country and sang of this nostalgia for their rural roots. However, while arabesk's fatalistic tone and its overwhelming success annoyed many intellectuals, who regarded it as unsophisticated, by this point even politicians had embraced it, not least former prime minister and president Turgut Özal, who fraternised with arabesk musicians and used their songs in his election campaigns.

cult classic caught the outcast youths of Europe on the cusp of a global cultural transformation influenced by American hip-hop and cinema. Young people in Turkey, whose socio-cultural development had been severely curtailed by the 1980 military coup, were in a similar situation; in the decade following the coup, even as a current of liberal internationalism was sweeping through the country, the military government – eager to punish the nation's rebellious university students – went so far as to ban all pop music from the country's one and only TV channel, state broadcaster TRT. But in the 1990s Turkish society – now firmly in the orbit of global capitalism – became acquainted with private TV and radio channels, fast food, magazines and shopping malls, and its younger generations managed to more or less catch up with their peers in the MTV generation. If the 1980s were dominated by the hybrid arabesk genre – itself an expression of the search for identity and belonging among rural–urban migrants – the 1990s which opened the country up to the world, saw the rise of Turkish pop music and its home-grown stars. Meanwhile, the 1970s craze for Anatolian rock had prepared the country's middle-class university students for the global rise of alternative rock, and now local bands like Mavi Sakal (Bluebeard), Kramp, Whisky and Pentagram were touring regularly and putting out their best work. Rock was widely accepted as the music of rebellious youth, while its nemesis, electronic music,

had established itself in the country's nightlife in the 1970s under the label of 'disco music' and had been a fixture in movies from that era. At the time, rap was still in its infancy, and in Turkey it was virtually unknown. Its territory went no further than the battery-operated stereos of a small group of youths from the satellite town of Ataköy in Istanbul's Bakırköy area, who spent their days rollerblading and skateboarding, creating graffiti and tagging, and their nights throwing breakdance parties at the huge open-air chessboard known as the Satranç.

The 1999 release of the compilation album *Yeraltı Operasyonu* ('Operation Underground') was a turning point. Released by the independent label Kod Müzik and produced by hip-hop artist Tunç 'Turbo' Dindaş, it was instrumental in bringing rap and the early stars of the Turkish scene to the fore. Soon the Hammer Müzik label – whose shop had been a haven for rock and metal lovers since it first opened its doors inside Kadıköy alternative-culture mecca and shopping arcade Akmar Pasaji in 1991 – began offering the artists featured in *Yeraltı Operasyonu* recording contracts, and over the next ten years the course of Turkish rap was determined by a handful among the thirty or so rap albums that Hammer Müzik released between 2000 and 2004. Nefret's *Meclis-i Âlâ İstanbul* was the first of these. When Dr Fuchs left to do his eighteen months' compulsory military service, Ceza began to work on a solo album, releasing his debut, *Med-Cezir* ('Tide') in 2002, the same year the conservative AKP first won a general election. The year 2004 saw the release of Sagopa Kajmer's ground-breaking two-and-a-half-hour double album *Bir Pesimistin Gözyaşları* ('Tears of a Pessimist'), considered by fans to be a kind of encyclopaedia of rap, and whose melancholy beats and elegiac lyrics left a lasting impression on Turkish rap culture. Self-centred to the point of narcissism, rap is by its very nature a competitive form, and Turkey soon had a whole host of aspiring popular poets from which to choose.

I first discovered that Ceza had pressed three thousand copies of *Med-Cezir* from an entry in Ekşi Sözlük (Sour Dictionary – a website that since 1999 has served as the chronological online database of the collective consciousness of Turkish youth); in 2002, the year of its release, actually paying for a new CD was hardly common practice, but I went straight to Hammer Müzik to buy myself a copy and wrote about it on Ekşi Sözlük. The spread of MP3s, soon to transform the global music industry, was already under way in the late 1990s with the passage from physical to digital media, but I was not going to wait for Ceza's album to be leaked online. Although I had always been a fan of rock and punk and a proud member of the grunge tribe, I had also loved Snoop's 1993 album *Doggystyle*, and the recurring, predictable nature of rap beats gave me a sense of security that I enjoyed. In rap music, my favourite instrument – the human voice – was always to the fore, and a good beat was both an MC's playground and a means to make the listener more receptive to the story the lyrics told. I knew that a song was never just a song because I knew that, while listening to something like 'Serial Killa' – the most gangsta track on *Doggystyle* – would not necessarily make me want to go out and shoot someone, it could certainly pump me up to do better in my maths test. Even a gangsta rap track could be an aesthetic realm in which physical violence and aggression acquired symbolic overtones; gangsta rap could provide a different perspective on the world and on your own experiences, express your unvoiced feelings, offer a new point of view or a way out, help settle your emotions. Still, anyone could come up with one good song, but a whole album was something else. I was curious about *Med-Cezir*, which opened with the squawking of seagulls and the sound of waves and the lines 'A wanderer who wants to be a poet / A jaded soul with no will to live left ...' Ceza – his furious tenor ringing loud as a bell – announced the existence of Istanbul Style and the Bosphorus Underground, neither of which I'd heard of before. He was a technically accomplished MC, his diction clear and his delivery rapid. The beats in his work were gentle and understated, but Ceza's voice provided its own flowing rhythm anyway. 'The Hannibal Lecter of mics' was in control, Istanbul was his city, Üsküdar was his neighbourhood, he even had a posse, and he was as defiant as his name (which means Punishment) suggested: 'All you rookie MCs, grab your diapers and come to me / I'll fuck you on the Bosphorus Bridge where both Asia and Europe can see'. He was angry, he was melancholy, he was rebellious, he was funny and he was sincere. There were no love songs on *Med-Cezir*; clearly Ceza's 'rheostat' heart beat for rap alone. Two years later his new album *Rapstar* – which sold more than 100,000 copies – confirmed that he was here to stay, and over the next decade he released a new album every two years, so despite the still-marginal role that rap occupied within the Turkish music industry, at a time when it wasn't even considered music, Ceza brought hip-hop culture to the mainstream, and it is difficult to imagine the history of Turkish

Çağrı Sinci
'Lobotomi'
2017

Kayra
'Kafamda Cehennem'
2019

Ceza
'Med Cezir'
2002

Otonom Piyade
'Varyete'
2017

İstanbul Trip
'Kural ne Bilmiyorum'
2019

You can find these, along with many others, on a playlist put together by the author at: open.spotify.com/user/iperborea

Above: 90BPM perform at Babylon in the Şişli district of Istanbul.
Right: Kamufle during a show in Kadıköy.

THE PASSENGER   Begüm Kovulmaz

Top left: A Ceza fan during a performance in Bahçeşehir.
Centre left: Çağrı Sinci in his home district of Kadıköy.
Bottom left: Kayra during a show at Babylon.
Below: Kamufle performing at Babylon.

rap without him. He has been accused of selling out for performing duets with pop singers and starring in television adverts, but before him it wasn't possible even to imagine what a rapper who'd emerged from the cultural underground might be able to achieve in the world of Turkish music. I can also understand his political naivety; I, too, belonged to that very specific generation born around the time of the 12 September coup, raised in the sanitised 1980s with politics kept strictly separate from day-to-day life, our childhoods analogue, our later years digital. In the course of his rap career, now spanning more than twenty years, Ceza has never

been in the news for anything other than his music and the occasional (and rather restrained) diss. All eyes are still upon him, but he maintains his poker face; he has always performed live every few weeks, so he keeps his hand in.

The rise of Turkish rap in the early 2000s slowed towards the end of the decade: the music industry, radio stations, television channels and the press all slammed their doors shut on the genre. But the success of arabesk music in the 1980s had shown how a banned or otherwise marginalised form could transcend the places and streets and spaces it came from and take centre stage. Although some artists – like Ceza, Sagopa, Fuat, Mode XL from Ankara or Yener Çevik and Anıl Piyancı from Izmir – were fairly well established by then, Turkish rap retreated into the new underground: the internet. Hiphop artists and their young urban listeners began to organise online, finding each other on social media and other web-based platforms. The evolution and democratisation of digital-recording equipment allowed amateur musicians to produce their own music at home, instantly share their creations and reach their core audience without going through intermediaries, thus gaining more and more listeners among younger people.

It became clear during the Gezi Park protests that rap was now effectively the soundtrack for the younger generation and that as well as encouraging a sense of local identity it could also be a means with which to vocalise local issues. The actions had first began in 2012, bringing together NGOs, trade associations, neighbourhood organisations and private individuals to take a stand against the plans – announced that same year – to bulldoze Gezi Park and turn the Taksim area, Istanbul's beating heart, into a construction site and a rentier's paradise. On 5 January 2013 the group Tahribad-ı İsyan (Revolt Against Destruction) performed in Taksim Square to protest against the redevelopment. The group had been founded in 2008 by high-school students Slang and Zen-G; that year their part of town – Istanbul's historic Roma quarter of Sulukule – had been earmarked for one of the government's hugely unpopular urban-gentrification projects, and indeed the duo's first song was written to protest about the destruction of that neighbourhood. Along with Fuat Ergin they were featured in Halil Altındere's video installation *Harikalar Diyarı* ('Wonderland') for the 2013 Istanbul Biennial, which was later acquired for the permanent collection at MoMa in New York. Slang and Zen-G had first started making music at the Sulukule Children's Centre for Music and the Arts, set up by local volunteers around the time their local area was being razed to the ground, and while they are both now working on solo projects they have also taken over the running of the arts centre and plan to include kids from the centre in their own shows and stage shows alongside them.

As the soundtrack of the Gezi protests, rap artists such as Şiirbaz, Hidra, İnfaz, Joker, tracks like Kdr and Kafi's 'Çare Var' ('There Is a Way', which includes the lines 'When Uncle Sam took off from Incirli to bomb Baghdad / The very Muslim Mr Recep Tayyip just turned a blind eye') or Şanışer and Alef High's 'Guerrilla Warfare II' ('We're out on the streets, a hundred thousand strong; the police, the people, the sound of sirens; 480 hours standing up to fascism – Gezi resists!'). Indigo's 2014 track 'Gönüllü Ordusu' ('Volunteer Army') named and celebrated each of the seven protesters who died during the demonstrations: 'I used to think the cop who fired the shot was a victim too / Fuck it! I don't care

how sorry he is / He sold his soul when he put on that uniform / Paid soldiers, the lot of you, but Gezi is a volunteer army'. Hip-hop was becoming a kind of barometer of the public mood and mindset; rappers were accruing social capital and beginning to grasp and openly embrace the idea that theirs might be the only true voice of the 'New Turkey'. Rap music has been a subject for analytical study ever since it first began to spread through a globalising world, and theorist Mark Fisher once charged it with 'a kind of super-identification with capital at its most pitilessly predatory' (the neoliberal ideology he termed 'capitalist realism' in his 2009 book of the same name), but what happened during the Gezi protests demonstrates that hip-hop can also be a battleground for localised resistance against the global dominance of that same neoliberal order.

There is some consensus that the latest, largest and, indeed, still growing surge in the popularity of Turkish rap is connected to a 2017 album released not in the capital of three empires but in Ankara, the capital of the Republic of Turkey. Yet there were signs before this that hinted at the boom that was soon to come. In Otonom Piyade's 2017 album *Hal ve Gidiş Sıfır* ('Zero for Conduct'), rappers Saian and K"st cut straight to the chase: 'The system's at home, in the classroom, in the sky, and it's totalitarian'. The hard sound of their protest album is a call to arms from start to finish: 'I'm gonna write my song in blood again, find a language that rhymes revolt with rebellion'. Theorists like Mark Fisher and music critics like Simon Reynolds have emphasised popular rap's proclivity for nihilistic materialism and argued that it could never exist outside the capitalist sphere of influence Frederic Jameson termed the 'global and totalizing space of the new world system', but as

'BEBEK' ('BABY') BY ÇAĞRI SİNCİ

Happy birthday, baby.

250 households in the
neighbourhood you were born in,
Only the shabbiest buses go
there, just one every hour.
Bus stops with no billboards,
the streets in ruins,
They sniff glue in parks with
swings unfit to swing on.

Expensive cars drive by in the dark
With visiting criminals, it's all for commerce.
So what if it's betrayal, they don't care,
The world swears allegiance to whoever's
got the money and the power.

The house you were born
in is cold and damp,
Your parents came to the big
city to find some work,
Your father's a textile worker now,
makes a thousand lira tops,
And always so serious, life's
seeped right into his face.

Your mother's unemployed and uninformed,
She's had eight children – easier said
than done – and the first one died,
She's always praying, her prayer
beads always at hand,
One thing's for sure, she's
given up on this world.

You'll grow up, you'll watch those ads on TV,
And soon you'll want what you see there.
When you finally understand you'll
need some way to escape,
By then you'll be so high you'll
stay right where you are.

You'll be bored at school and
bored at the mosque

You'll dread the big city and
hide out in your hood
Until one day you'll tell the world
'Goddamn your justice!'
One day you'll tell the world
'Goddamn your justice!'

Your mother's girlhood dreams
tucked away in her trousseau,
No matter where you end up,
remember your hood!

The city centre's a fifty-minute bus ride away,
And when you go to see it, it'll hurt your head.
You'll be ashamed of your
shoes and even your hair,
You'll be ashamed of your handmade
sweater, colours fading.

Now let's get to the point, if
you think you're ready,
You'll put up with your life, with
your endless sorrows,
But you're the wretched of the earth,
remember: you can drown in your dreams
Or you can get ready for a glorious fight.

For us life is not just a sad song you sing,
One day we'll come to terms
with that shit they call fate.
There's a tightness in our
chests, our path is dark,
Our light is our anger – but let's
cut to the chase now.

When you grow up, baby, there'll
be two choices for you:
You'll either rot on the streets
(no skills required)
Or you'll teach yourself, be proud,
and know your rights,
And revolution will rise over the city
from your grey suburban slum.

Lyrics reproduced courtesy of the artist

Richard Shusterman asked in his 1992 work *Pragmatic Aesthetics*, 'why should rap's profitable connection with some of [the] features [of this all-embracing system] void the power of its social critique?' As Çağrı Sinci – a rapper from Izmir's Karşıyaka neighbourhood – sung in 'Dönek Dünya' ('Fickle World'), 'You won't understand us with your sociological theories, / We have no banks to lean on, only empty benches to sit on'.

But the spark that truly triggered the latest explosion of Turkish rap and carried it even further than the mainstream was a record from the nation's capital, which opened with the line 'Ankara's cold cuts right through my soul'. Born in 1990, Ezhel released his debut Anatolian urban core/hip-hop/reggae-dub/trap album *Müptezhel* (a word which, with the h removed, means dopehead) in 2017. Like Orhan Veli, Ezhel destroyed the usual hierarchy of the five senses and stuffed the capital right into his listener's mouths and noses: 'I can taste my city on my tongue again; soot, rust, filth, coal, plastic, trash cans, tyres, exhaust pipes, drugs.' He described the things that happened at night in the city's hidden recesses, told stories about the alternative existences that populated the country's bureaucratic capital ('This city is a nightclub and we have no cash'), and suggested different ways of living ('Your kids are unemployed; fuck it, who needs jobs with bosses like you, / I'll be my own boss, my hoodie's my suit'). Ezhel, whose interest in music began with reggae, had a kind of heightened energy and talent reminiscent of an archetypal trickster figure and quickly gained an enormous following – although his earliest supporters and champions were hip-hop's core audience and people from his home town of Ankara. A year after the release of his album Ezhel was arrested on a charge of advocating drug use, and shortly thereafter the rappers Khontkar and Young Bego also suffered the same fate. In its endless witch-hunt to root out dissent the regime had normalised the use of legal proceedings as a form of intimidation and oppression, and now they had turned their attention to rappers – some of whom continue to face similar charges today. The AKP government could see the music's influence on those younger generations it had so much trouble connecting with and had even tried to harness it by commissioning a rap track for its 2015 general election campaign. But when Ezhel was targeted and arrested on trumped-up charges the public reaction was unanimous and unexpectedly vehement, and, in a deeply draconian context in which no form of political dissent ever went unpunished, the 26-year-old suddenly became a symbol of freedom of expression. Social media was up in arms, the #freeezhel hashtag appeared all over the internet and on the streets, and at his hearing a month later he was acquitted. He'd already begun the year at the top of the streaming charts; by the end of 2018 he was the year's most streamed artist, and his song 'Geceler' ('Nights') was the year's most popular.

2019 in Turkey was the 'year of rap', but there had been a number of political and economic developments previously that had paved the way for this. Istanbul had always been a popular travel destination, but after the Gezi protests, after the night of 15 July 2016 and the series of suicide bombings that had preceded it (in Sultanahmet, in Taksim, at Atatürk Airport) and in the light of the government's growing penchant for kidnapping foreigners, the city had become isolated from the rest of the world. Meanwhile, a precipitous fall in the value of the Turkish lira was keeping the usually more mobile sectors of society imprisoned within

Rap is not the first Turkish-German genre to have done the rounds in Germany; back in the 1960s some DIY record labels did everything they could to satisfy the immigrants' desire for their own music. At the time, *Gastarbeiter* could not even set up a business without a German partner, but, thanks to the support of a politician, Yılmaz Asöcal was able to obtain special permission to found the Türküola label. It was unthinkable at the time that he would be able to get his albums into record stores, so Asöcal had to make do with door-to-door distribution to small Turkish establishments, particularly food shops. Way under the radar of the music industry, a scene developed around often amateur musicians who, in their own way, told stories of the traumas of leaving their country, expressing heart-rending nostalgia for the motherland or repressed rage at the arrogance of the factory foreman, as was the case with former Ford worker Metin Türköz, who made thirteen albums. Some homespun recordings became massive hits, selling in the hundreds of thousands, like *Beyaz Atlı* by Yüksel Özkasap, a singer, known as the 'Nightingale of Cologne', with more than five hundred songs to her name. As well as singing about the Turkish-German experience, these groups experimented with linguistic hybrids, combined Anatolian pop with Western psychedelia (like Grup Doğuş in their 1975 debut) and created new genres like the 1980s disko folk of the wildly successful group Derdiyoklar İkilisi. These musical experiments are now achieving cult status, as evidenced by the 2013 collection *Songs of Gastarbeiter*.

national borders. But, at the same time, this withdrawal from the outside world was opening up performance spaces and the national consciousness to local rap and alternative/indie musicians. With the mainstream media almost entirely taken over by government-friendly investors and therefore stripped of any credibility it may once have had, society as a whole – starting with its younger members – was increasingly turning to social media. Hip-hop artists, who had long been uploading their music, were able to grow the live-streaming channels through which they connected directly with their audiences and found that they had no need for the mainstream media after all. Turkish *dizi* (multi-episode TV series) are still the nation's favourite television entertainment, and soon writing songs especially for these shows became a new way for rappers to appeal to sections of society they might previously have been unable to reach (for more on *dizi*, see 'Don't Call Them Soap Operas' on page 35). These shows became vehicles for songs like Gazapizm's 'Heyecanı Yok' ('The Thrill Is Gone'), Allame's 'Kısır Döngü' ('Vicious Circle') and Eypio's 'Gömün Beni Çukura' ('Bury Me') to be broadcast throughout the country. Ever since official charts began assigning greater weight to streaming, rap has exploded in Turkey. Arabesk rap and alaturka rap remain popular, and more recent styles, such as trap, are also growing, pioneered by the likes of Ceg, Khontkar and Şehinşah.

Şanışer's 2019 track 'Susamam' ('I Cannot Remain Silent') – a collaboration with seventeen other artists – is a lengthy public-service announcement and protest song tackling a number of topics that have recently been on the nation's news agenda, such as the environment, the justice system, women's rights, animal rights, suicide and road traffic. The night the track

> 'It remains to be seen which ideologies Turkish rappers will speak up for in future and how they will deal with such problems as hyper-masculinity and the unchallenged use of the N-word in their lyrics.'

was released even opposition MPs started sharing it on Twitter, while the leader of the government's coalition partner accused the artists who'd participated in the project of 'emboldening would-be coup organisers in the name of rap'.

The other track that was released that night and led to the 2019 declaration of the year of rap in Turkey was Ezhel's 'Olay' ('Incidents'), a song whose narrative force was magnified by its video – composed of a collage of silent news footage from Turkey's recent history. As soon as it was posted the video racked up millions of views; within a few hours YouTube had removed it from its trending lists because it contained 'inappropriate content', and the video still comes with a warning notice today. In one sequence, in which the visuals match up with the lyrics, a camera focuses on a yellow street sign pointing towards Kreuzberg just as Ezhel sings 'the whole world's my hood, my ghetto'. Now Kreuzberg is again as central to Turkish rap as it once was. It is as if the authorities' crusade against rap and hip-hop culture and rap musicians' yearning for greater contact with the rest of the world have initiated a sort of counter-remigration towards the birthplace of Turkish rap: Germany – specifically Kreuzberg. In 'Angela Merkel', Xir – a member of the rap

collective Istanbul Trip – sings: 'We've got no Schengen visa / So you come over to Karaköy instead'. If Xir's song was an expression of that yearning for the outside world, then the collaboration of Turkey's three most popular rappers – Ceza, Ezhel and Ben Fero – with Kreuzberg-based Killa Hakan on the 2019 track 'Fight Kulüp' ('Fight Club') was a declaration of intent. In the video the three Turkish artists 'represent' Kreuzberg with as much pride and sense of belonging as if it were their own. Ezhel and Ceza weren't born in Kreuzberg, Ben Fero wasn't raised there, but claiming ownership of a neighbourhood is another way of claiming ownership of a particular culture, and Kreuzberg is certainly one of the places that has always defined these artists, their home from home. It remains to be seen which ideologies Turkish rappers will speak up for in future and how they will deal with such problems as hyper-masculinity and the unchallenged use of the N-word in their lyrics, but they are certainly equipped with the creativity and the poetic spirit – what T.S. Eliot termed auditory imagination – to invent the new language that Mark Fisher argued is necessary to cope with the capitalist condition. To Orhan Veli's list in 'I Listen to Istanbul' of 'curses, music, folk songs, insults' they have already added rap, which today can be heard blasting out of car windows right across the country. The Turkish representatives of the rap ecosystem are ready to claim not just Kreuzberg but every single neighbourhood of the global capitalist metropolis as their own. 🐦

Left: Young Ceza fans at one of his shows.

The Sharp End of the Pencil: Satire in the Age of Erdoğan

Amid protest and censorship, satire is one of the few remaining channels for taking the government in Turkey to task, and cartoonists are continuing their battle against attempts to squash the right to freedom of expression.

VALENTINA MARCELLA
Translated by Alan Thawley

Tuncay Akgün, cartoonist and editor-in-chief of the magazine *LeMan*, sitting in the magazine's own themed café in the Beyoğlu district of Istanbul.

In a photograph showing him leaning forward to sign an album of his drawings, his long beard and hair almost white by that point, he resembles a modern-day Leonardo da Vinci. His name is Nuri Kurtcebe, and he is one of the leading artists in the world of Turkish satire. Born in 1949, he was one of the first Turkish illustrators to experiment with comic-strip stories in the 1970s, helping to popularise a genre that was unknown in the country at the time. As well as his comic strips, Kurtcebe is known for his satirical political cartoons, in which he has captured the state of the nation in some of Turkey's leading newspapers and satirical magazines, winning himself fans from across the generations as well as garnering numerous awards in a career that spans fifty years.

As much for his popularity as for the fact that he is no longer in the first flush of youth, the news of his arrest on 4 July 2018 quickly spread throughout the country. Kurtcebe had been accused of insulting President Recep Tayyip Erdoğan in some cartoons published between 2015 and 2017. Hours after his arrest it was still unclear, even to his lawyer, exactly which cartoons had caused the insult – but the punishment was as clear as day: one year, two months and fifteen days' imprisonment.

After two days in detention Kurtcebe was released on probation.

His was just one of the most recent examples of the persecution of satirists: the new millennium has seen a series of denunciations, trials and other key events that have repeatedly highlighted an aversion to satirical language on the part of the Justice and Development Party (AKP), which has been in power since 2002.

EARLY WARNINGS

In the early 2000s relations between Turkey and Europe were at the heart of the political debate, and membership of the EU was looking likely thanks to the start of the accession process. Both in Turkey and in Europe the newly elected AKP was seen by many as the party of hope: hope for a democracy that did not deny religious identity, that recognised minorities and would take Turkey into the EU. And yet it was precisely in this climate of optimism that Erdoğan began to target cartoonists, revealing a hitherto unsuspected sensitivity to criticism that would become increasingly apparent in other fields as well.

It was in 2003 that Erdoğan (who was prime minister at the time) took Sefer Selvi to court. Selvi is younger than Kurtcebe but equally well known. Erdoğan was seeking compensation of 10,000 Turkish liras

VALENTINA MARCELLA is a scholar of contemporary Turkey with an interest in the relationship between repression, dissent and popular culture, mainly through the lens of political satire. Since 2004 she has regularly visited Turkey for study and work, and she lived in Istanbul between 2011 and 2016. She has a PhD in history and was previously a researcher at Istanbul's Kadir Has University. Since 2016 she has taught Turkish at the University of Naples 'L'Orientale'. She is a co-founder of the online magazine *Kaleydoskop – Turchia, cultura e società*.

(roughly $7,000 at the exchange rate at the time) for a cartoon that caused him 'pain, torment and distress'. The cartoon in question portrayed him as a horse being ridden by one of his advisers. The following year it was the turn of Musa Kart, another renowned artist, noted, like Selvi, for the directness of his political commentary. His offending cartoon showed Erdoğan as a cat tangled in a ball of wool, referencing various policies in which the prime minister was tied up, and on that pretext the artist and *Cumhuriyet*, the newspaper he worked for, were dragged into court to face a claim for ₺5,000 (*c.* $3,500). Erdoğan also targeted a small newspaper that had reprinted the cartoon. While the cases against Selvi and Kart-*Cumhuriyet* were thrown out at later stages of their respective proceedings, in this case the judge immediately ruled in favour of the newspaper, pointing out that public figures should be able to accept criticism as well as praise. Although this ruling became famous in Turkey, subsequent events reveal how little Erdoğan took on board.

PANDORA'S BOX

While Selvi's cartoon can claim to have been the first to be censored in the AKP era, Kart's effort holds the distinction of having opened a Pandora's box of intolerance: the persecution of the cartoonist and his newspaper inspired a host of initiatives to express solidarity, and this provoked further reaction.

Like Kurtcebe, Selvi and Kart have mainly drawn cartoons for newspapers in recent years, but weekly humorous magazines, which have historically been very popular in Turkey, have performed an equally important role in satirical protest. One of these was *Penguen* – a magazine first published in the year the AKP came to power – which tackled countless sensitive

issues with a consistently ironic and perceptive approach. In 2005, in response to the Kart-*Cumhuriyet* verdict, *Penguen* created a cover adorned with various animals, all of them bearing, like Kart's cat, Erdoğan's face. This act of solidarity saw the magazine being taken to court on a charge of defamation, a process that ended with the cartoonists being found not guilty and a rejection of Erdoğan's request for ₺40,000 (*c.* $30,000) in damages.

In the meantime, the Kart affair, which by then had become the Kart-*Penguen* affair, was causing even more of a stir, leading to a protest from the Cartoonists' Association and ultimately resonating with artists working in other genres as well.

Michael Dickinson, a British artist who moved to Istanbul in the 1980s, creates satirical collages that usually take aim at British and American politics. Although he had previously avoided commenting on the Turkish political scene, Dickinson decided to join the chorus of protest and created two collages that express a defiance of despotism and solidarity with the cartoonists of Turkey. Both works superimposed Erdoğan's face on the body of a dog and poked fun at the much-vaunted friendship between the Turkish leader and George W. Bush. The publication of these two works signalled the beginning of a legal odyssey that ended in 2013 with Dickinson's deportation. A cartoon by Selvi in his honour shows Erdoğan crossing the British artist's name off his cartoonists' blacklist with a satisfied expression.

While the blacklist cartoon seems to take us full circle – Selvi, Kart, *Penguen*, Dickinson and Selvi again – its protagonists were not the only ones facing their day in court during that time. *LeMan* is a weekly humorous magazine that, since its launch in 1991, has always stood out for its ability to connect current affairs with broader political and social issues and taking a stance that is unfailingly critical and caustic. It was set up by a group of cartoonists previously involved in another humorous magazine, *Limon*, who were determined to preserve their independence. *Limon* belonged to a publishing group, and disputes between the owners and the editorial staff led to the closure of *Limon* and the creation of *LeMan* in the immediate aftermath.

LeMan's independent stance led its cartoonists to one trial in 2006 and another in 2008, the first for a cartoon in which Erdoğan was shown as a tick and the second for a photomontage of him giving the finger. The first court decision went against Erdoğan, thus denying him the ₺25,000 (*c.* $16,500) he was after, although he was awarded compensation to the tune of ₺4,000 (*c.* $3,000) for the photomontage.

This first victory for Erdoğan vs. the cartoonists was a sign of the changing times. When the prospect of EU membership began to look as if it was slipping away following a halt in negotiations in 2006, the Turkish government began to look elsewhere in pursuit of a bigger role in the Middle East. This repositioning was accompanied by an accentuation of its conservative side: from the loosening of restrictions on headscarf-wearing in universities in 2008 to a call in 2013 for families to have at least three children, by way of a series of bans on alcohol and an intensive campaign against abortion, it became increasingly clear that the AKP was no longer the same party that had initially also been trusted by a section of secular society and was now speaking only to its core electorate.

This shift was accompanied by a new attitude towards journalism. Since 2008 in particular, dozens of unaligned journalists have been arrested, accused of terrorist propaganda or involvement in attempted coups. For fear of retaliation the mainstream media began to put out superficial news that toed the government line with little to separate it from the media outlets already close to the administration thanks to the politicised cronyism that had existed in Turkey since the 1980s. Discontent grew, demonstrations spread and, in tandem, police presence and police violence increased. And then, in late May 2013, the various groups who up to that point had for the most part protested separately (feminists, LGBTQ activists, environmentalists, trade unionists, students and many others) joined forces in the mass protests of what would later be remembered as the long summer of Gezi.

STRENGTH IN NUMBERS

The protests that took place throughout the summer of 2013, triggered initially following plans to redevelop Gezi Park in Istanbul, quickly became an expression of people's unhappiness with the government, but without the satirical component they employed they would not have been so effective and memorable. Irony, self-deprecation and satire became fundamental to the protests, not just during the succession of initiatives that took place in the park (demonstrations, sit-ins, occupations and forums) but also in the rest of the country and on the web. Through slogans, drawings, writing, photomontages, videos and stencils, the authorities, as embodied above all by the police and Erdoğan, were challenged in surprisingly creative ways, so much so

Right: An amorous couple in the *LeMan* café.

THE PASSENGER Valentina Marcella

that the demonstrators were described as possessing *orantısız zeka* – 'disproportionate intelligence'.

This amateur satire combined with the work of professionals to create a dialogue. The magazines showed their support for the protestors on the streets in their cartoons but also in a number of symbolic initiatives. The team at *LeMan*, for example, supplemented the magazine's title with the strapline *kronik çapulcunuz* – 'your inveterate looter' – following the demonstrators' ironic appropriation of the term *çapulcu* (looter), which was first used by Erdoğan in an attempt to smear the demonstrators and belittle the protest. The team at *Penguen*, on the other hand, expressed themselves visually, transforming the magazine's mascot – a penguin trying to fly with strap-on wings – into a demonstrator. With its face covered by a bandana, it prepares to throw a bunch of flowers like the figure in the famous Banksy artwork that provided its inspiration. From being the magazine's mascot, the Gezi Park penguin quickly became an icon for the demonstrators, who created different reinterpretations, notably a purple version for Istanbul's gay pride parade that year.

Further emphasising the interrelation between satire in the magazines and satire on the streets, there was no shortage of out-and-out tributes to the demonstrators' creativity and sense of humour from the professionals. *Penguen* added a section to the magazine for a number of issues in which photographs illustrating 'the disproportionate intelligence of the streets'

were reprinted, while *LeMan* posited that satire from the streets had 'outclassed the satirical magazines'.

The other two leading satirical journals of that period, *Gırgır* and *Uykusuz*, also joined in with the chorus of compliments. *Gırgır*, the oldest of them all, founded in the early 1970s by a group of humorists including Kurtcebe, published an editorial encouraging the demonstrators to persist with their 'disproportionate intelligence' because 'the more subtle your humour, the more you make your adversaries boil with rage'. *Uykusuz*, meanwhile, was the youngest of the magazines, having been created in 2007 when six *Penguen* cartoonists defected, growing rapidly to build a team of more than twenty. 'History has been written by you,' one of them exclaimed in its pages, 'what could I add to that? You have written on the web, on the streets, on banners and even on my front door! This week I've been the one reading you.'

In this great wave of protests and mutual influence between amateurs and professionals, the government never took direct action against satire, a response that differed both from the desire for control it had demonstrated in previous years and from its repressive response to the protests on other fronts. Even though writing, cartoons and other forms of satirical expression were swept away in brutal police interventions at the protest sites, this happened during broader clearance operations rather than as a targeted objective. In the field of professional satire, no cases were brought against any individual cartoons.

THE END OF AN EXCEPTIONAL EXPERIENCE

When the Gezi Park protests died down towards the end of the summer of 2013 without securing the government

Left: *LeMan* cartoonist Güneri İçoğlu.

Ekrem İmamoğlu

Born in 1970 in Cevizli, Akçaabat, in Trabzon Province in the Black Sea Region, İmamoğlu is a businessman and politician who became mayor of Istanbul in 2019. After working in the family business and serving as chairman of the sports company Trabzonspor, in 2008 he became leader of the youth section of the main opposition party, the Republican People's Party (CHP). In 2014 he was elected mayor of Beylikdüzü, on the outskirts of Istanbul. During his term his popularity grew through his cultural initiatives and policies to support young people and women as well as his work to raise awareness of environmental issues. In 2019 he became the CHP candidate for the local elections in Istanbul, presenting himself as the new voice of the opposition, in coalition with the nationalist party İYİ. The campaign he ran, based on unity and positivity – his slogan was 'Everything will be all right', and the defining image was of him using his fingers to form a heart shape – contrasted sharply with that run by his opponent, Binali Yıldırım, the outgoing mayor and former

prime minister. Yıldırım took advantage of support from Erdoğan himself, who warned his supporters that 'if we lose Istanbul, we lose Turkey'. İmamoğlu emerged as the surprise winner, by just twenty thousand votes, but, at the government's request, the elections were declared void by the Supreme Electoral Council for alleged irregularities and called again. At the second attempt İmamoğlu was confirmed as the winner, this time by a margin of almost 800,000 votes: after twenty-five years of AKP administration Istanbul had fallen to the opposition. With the municipality's coffers empty and no state funding, İmamoğlu's first challenges have included the search for foreign finance – such as the package of $120 million received from Deutsche Bank for the construction of a new metro line – and the attempt to block the Istanbul Canal project, the government's mega-infrastructure plan that would open up a second maritime channel linking the Black Sea to the Sea of Marmara, a scheme that has been vehemently opposed by environmentalists.

Selahattin Demirtaş, aka 'Selo'

Born in 1973 in Elazığ, Eastern Anatolia, to a Zaza-speaking Kurdish family, Demirtaş was joint leader of the Peoples' Democratic Party (HDP) from 2014 to 2018 as well as a candidate for the Turkish presidency. A lawyer by training, having graduated from the University of Ankara he worked on human rights in Diyarbakır, one of the most important cities in the Kurdish-majority Southeastern Anatolia Region of Turkey. In 2006 he was placed on probation for five years after stating on television that the PKK leader Abdullah Öcalan should have a role in the peace process between the Kurds and Turkey. He entered politics in 2007 as part of a pro-Kurdish party that was deemed unconstitutional two years later. In 2012 he was elected co-leader of the latest incarnation of the Kurdish political movement, the HDP, which, under his guidance, opened up to the Turkish left and all of the country's minorities, promoting rights not only for Kurds but also for women and the LGBTQ community. In the 2015 elections the HDP achieved the best ever result for a Kurdish-majority party, taking it beyond the 10 per cent electoral threshold

and into parliament. In November of that same year protests in Diyarbakır – which began as a call to set up a humanitarian corridor to Kobane, a Kurdish stronghold in Syria – and the chaotic situation in the country caused by a series of attacks attributed to ISIS led to an abrupt suspension of the peace process between the Turkish state and Kurdish forces. On 4 November 2016 Demirtaş, along with ten HDP MPs, was arrested, accused of spreading terrorist propaganda in favour of the PKK; this led to his resignation as party co-leader in February 2018. Although he was unable to campaign, he managed to pull more than 8 per cent of the votes in the presidential elections that year. From prison, where he remains, even though the European Court of Human Rights has ruled that he must be released, Demirtaş has published two collections of short stories (one, *Dawn*, published in English by Hogarth in 2019), a novel and poetry plus paintings and cartoons for the satirical newspaper *LeMan*. He has been described as the Kurdish Obama, thanks to his skills as an orator and his youthful good looks, and is known affectionately by his supporters as 'Selo'.

'The world of satire did not give in to the climate of censorship, and both individual artists and satirical magazines kept to their political line.'

resignations they had called for so loudly, it did not take long for the cartoonists to experience personally the revitalised witch-hunt.

The 18th Didim Peace Festival, in Aydın Province, had planned to put on an exhibition of cartoons in early September themed around the Gezi Park protests. The local AKP authorities, having learned about the event through street advertising, prevented it from opening on the pretext that the cartoons were offensive to Erdoğan. The illustrations were confiscated and an investigation launched into five people connected with the exhibition, not just organisers but even a representative of the advertising company responsible for putting up the posters.

But the world of satire did not give in to the climate of censorship, and both individual artists and satirical magazines kept to their political line. Like clockwork, new attacks were launched by the authorities, marking the opening of a new front in the fight against satirical protest. Thus far Erdoğan's intolerance had mainly been directed at cartoons depicting him as an animal, revealing more about his touchiness than his unwillingness to accept political criticism. But from late 2013 other types of cartoon also ended up in the firing line. On top of that, as the Didim episode had shown, following Gezi other figures in the AKP now joined Erdoğan in his fight against satire.

In November 2013 the governor of Adana, Hüseyin Avni Coş, filed simultaneous complaints against *Gırgır* and *Uykusuz* for two front-cover cartoons poking fun at an incident in which he had been involved. Panicked by a group demonstrating against him during a ceremony to commemorate the death of the founder of the republic, Mustafa Kemal Atatürk, the governor had taken against one of them in particular, calling him *gavat* – a pimp – except that he then refuted the evidence and even categorically denied ever having used the term.

In April 2014 the mayor of Bingöl, Yücel Barakazi, had *LeMan* withdrawn from sale and reported its writers for a cover in which he was portrayed at the head of the sequence of hominids used to represent the evolution of the species: in this version one of his ancestors kicks a woman out of the way. The cartoon was a response to the mayor's decision to exclude women from high-level institutional posts on the grounds that it 'went against religion and tradition'.

In August of the same year *Penguen* published a cover that had them dragged into the courts, this time by someone who was not even an AKP member but simply a supporter of the party. He had been upset not by the main thrust of the cartoon nor the joke on which it was based but a minor detail in the posture of a figure who was allegedly making an offensive gesture while talking to Erdoğan.

This intensifying of the censorship mirrored the government's attitude

Right: Blow-ups of cartoons on the walls of the *LeMan* café.

WE ARE FREE

One of the best-known exiled Turkish journalists, Can Dündar, was editor-in-chief of the Turkish opposition newspaper *Cumhuriyet* when, in May 2015, it published photographs and videos of a Turkish intelligence-service lorry passing arms to ISIS in Syria. Infuriated, Erdoğan promised that the journalist responsible for the piece would 'pay dearly'. Annoying the government was nothing new for Dündar – he had previously been fired from the newspaper *Milliyet* for his articles on the Gezi Park protests – but this time the scoop saw him arrested on the charge of spying and revealing state secrets. As if that were not enough, on the day of his sentencing, while he was awaiting the verdict (five years in prison), he was shot at – but not hit – by a man who shouted 'traitor to the motherland' before being blocked by Dündar's wife Dilek. In June 2016 Dündar moved to Germany. In October a warrant for his arrest was issued in absentia in Turkey. Dilek, whose passport had been taken away, only managed to rejoin him three years later. But even in Germany, where two-thirds of the Turkish population of around three million supports Erdoğan, Dündar lives under police protection. In Berlin he founded an online radio station, Özgürüz (We Are Free), which is banned in Turkey. His book *We Are Arrested: A Journalist's Notes from a Turkish Prison* was published in English by Biteback Publishing in 2016. He has received the International Press Freedom Award from the Committee for the Protection of Journalists (CPJ), whose website publishes news, interviews and statistics on the conditions journalists work under in Turkey and elsewhere.

'Reactions in Turkey to the *Charlie Hebdo* massacre eliminated any doubts about the views of certain AKP figures on the right to engage in satire.'

towards other means of expression: 2014 was also the year in which a series of laws were passed making it easier to control information and take down unwanted content from the web. While this and a number of other episodes painted an ever gloomier picture for freedom of expression, in January 2015 reactions in Turkey to the *Charlie Hebdo* massacre eliminated any doubts about the views of certain AKP figures on the right to employ satire while also highlighting the divisions within a Turkish society ever more polarised between supporters and opponents of Erdoğan.

THE CHARLIE HEBDO MASSACRE: A WATERSHED

When the tragic news arrived from Paris on 7 January 2015, initiatives were organised in Turkey to express solidarity with the team at *Charlie Hebdo*, the victims' families and the French people as a whole. Some of those who took part were atheists, but it was comprised mostly of secular Muslims strongly opposed to the exploitation of religion for political or terrorist ends. A section of the press joined in with the demonstrations of solidarity: *Cumhuriyet* in particular lost no time in announcing its decision to publish extracts from the first post-attack edition of *Charlie Hebdo*, four pages in total. Cartoonists also paid tribute to their French colleagues in various ways. Straight after the attack *Penguen*, *LeMan* and *Uykusuz* were all published with the same cover, the words 'JE SUIS CHARLIE' in a speech bubble against a black background. *LeMan* also published a special edition devoted to *Charlie Hebdo*'s writers and cartoonists, which included photographs of the victims during a stay in Istanbul in 2002 when the French editorial team visited the Turkish magazine for a joint publication.

In contrast to these initiatives, however, there was also condemnation from other quarters. Although not openly siding with the terrorists, the most conservative section of society opted to focus on the presumed causes of the attack, in other words the cartoonists' work, deeming the images of Mohammed blasphemous and, consequently, offensive. Furthermore, when the editors of *Cumhuriyet* announced their intention to include some *Charlie Hebdo* material they received thousands of threats. Rather than helping to calm the frayed tempers, some government-supporting newspapers initiated an out-and-out media witch-hunt against the secular journal.

The declarations of individual AKP figures helped to legitimise this open warfare. The mayor of Ankara at the time, İbrahim Melih Gökçek, was the first to rail against *Cumhuriyet*, describing its ties to the French magazine as a provocation and accusing it of being part of an international plot to brand Muslims as violent. He was echoed by the prime minister of the day, Ahmet Davutoğlu, who declared that the *Cumhuriyet* affair had nothing to do with freedom of expression, that in Turkey it is not permitted to insult the Prophet and that publishing an offensive cartoon was tantamount to openly inciting attack. Along similar lines, Erdoğan thundered,

'Where do you think you are living? Sacred values cannot be insulted in this way.' Even though the editorial team at *Cumhuriyet* had, at the time they announced that they would be reprinting a number of *Charlie Hebdo* cartoons, clarified that the selection would take into account the country's religious sensibilities – thus implying that any caricatures of the Prophet would not be included – the police still took it upon themselves to burst into the newspaper's headquarters as the issue was being printed. When no cartoons relating to Mohammed were found, the newspaper was distributed as normal. Once on sale, however, its detractors spotted the fact that two journalists had decided to replace their profile photos in the magazine with the now-famous first *Charlie Hebdo* cover following the attack, in which a regretful Mohammed is holding a sign reading 'JE SUIS CHARLIE'. It took just a few hours for an investigation to be launched.

IN A STATE OF EMERGENCY

The period following the Paris attack was a time of real tension in Turkey, during which the government made its authoritarian stripe increasingly clear. A total of twenty-three journalists were in prison in early July 2015, and Reporters Without Borders ranked the country a lowly 149th out of 180 for freedom of expression.

The state of emergency that was declared the day after the attempted coup of 15 July 2016 – and which remained in place until July 2018 – only exacerbated the situation, as simply being part of the opposition had become reason enough to be investigated, arrested and taken to court on accusations of varying levels of involvement in terrorist activities and with terrorist organisations. In all, 317 journalists were arrested in the space of two years and more than 2,500 lost their

ACADEMICS FOR PEACE

In January 2016, 1,128 academic staff at Turkish universities signed a declaration entitled 'We Will Not Be Complicit in this Crime' following the suspension of the peace process between the state and the PKK. The document, which criticised the state's armed intervention, immediately attracted Erdoğan's anger. He accused the academics of 'treachery' – which simply encouraged more people to add their names to the plea, bringing the total to 2,212. None of these Academics for Peace could have imagined the consequences. Before long, staff at private universities, whose funding is controlled by the government, began to be dismissed. Following the attempted coup of July 2016 more than 7,800 academics were purged – including hundreds of the Academics for Peace. Their dismissals also included a ban on working for public institutions and the private media, the withdrawal of their passports and, in some cases, confiscation of their assets. In late 2017 court cases began against 742 of the signatories, who were accused of engaging in 'propaganda for a terrorist organisation'. In most cases the accused pleaded guilty in exchange for suspended sentences in order to avoid prison – an effective way of silencing them. One of the academics who chose instead to appeal was Füsun Üstel of Galatasaray University, who served three months of her fifteen-month sentence (later reduced to eleven) before a court ordered her release.

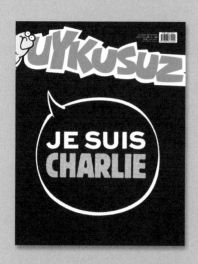

THE PASSENGER Valentina Marcella

'In the space of two years 317 journalists were arrested and more than 2,500 lost their jobs; fifty-four newspapers, twenty magazines, twenty-four radio stations, seventeen TV networks and six press agencies were closed.'

jobs. A total of fifty-four newspapers, twenty magazines, twenty-four radio stations, seventeen TV networks and six press agencies were closed, while 85 per cent of the mainstream media came under the control of companies with ties to the government. The country slipped a further eight places in the Reporters Without Borders ranking. In the process, Turkey said goodbye to many of its most respected journalists, such as Can Dündar, sentenced to ninety-two days in prison and currently in exile in Germany, or Aslı Erdoğan, who spent 136 days behind bars and, like Dündar, took refuge in Berlin.

Cartoonists were not spared this wave of repression. As well as new court cases triggered by individual illustrations or multiple drawings – as in the case of Kurtcebe – some of them had to put up with systematic persecution. The most glaring case was that of Kart. After spending nine months on remand accused of providing support to terrorist organisations, he, alongside sixteen *Cumhuriyet* colleagues, ended up in court in a trial that many feel was aimed not just at the newspaper but at the freedom of the press and freedom of expression more generally.

In this hostile climate, along with the newspapers that closed or were forced to close, *Gırgır* and *Penguen* also fell by the wayside. *Gırgır*'s story came to an end in February 2017 when it was closed by its owners following the publication of a highly controversial cartoon on a religious theme. Three months later *Penguen* went the same way, its closure decided by the

editorial team itself. In a farewell message to the readership, the reasons it gave included limits on the freedom of expression. 'We want to put our beloved magazine out the way we like it,' they wrote, 'and if we cannot keep to the level of quality we have set ourselves we would rather not do it at all.' So, although they did not shut up shop through the direct intervention of the government, both *Gırgır* and *Penguen* felt the effects of the general climate of intimidation.

THE COURAGE OF THOSE LOOKING TO THE FUTURE

The silencing of dissent did not end with the state of emergency, and, two years on, cartoonists continue to skate on thin ice. Despite the numerous challenges they must face in the name of press freedom, satirical or otherwise, some continue to resist and are even making brave new decisions. In December 2019 *LeMan*'s editorial team welcomed a new member, a pretty extraordinary new signing to say the least: Selahattin Demirtaş, former co-leader of the People's Democratic Party (HDP) and, since November 2016, an inmate of Edirne maximum-security prison. Although he is not a cartoonist and cannot meet the team in person, Demirtaş has chosen cartoons (as well as other forms of expression, such as writing and painting) to communicate with the outside world. In the face of all this adversity the collaboration between *LeMan* and Demirtaş sends out a powerful message of unity, courage and resistance. ✒

Ultras United: How the Gezi Park Protests Brought the Fans Together

The 2013 protest movement was so widespread that it even achieved the miracle of bridging the chasms between football's big three in Istanbul – Galatasaray, Fenerbahçe and Beşiktaş – which are among the most deeply held rivalries in world football.

STEPHEN WOOD

Scarves in the colours of the three giants of Turkish football – Beşiktaş, Galatasaray and Fenerbahçe – at a secondhand-clothing market in Kadıköy, Istanbul.

Flares illuminated the clouds of smoke that rolled down the streets. Lines of policemen in riot gear threatened civilians with clubs, water cannon and rubber bullets. Anti-autocratic fervour had gripped the city, and the government's response was a crackdown that only proved the protesters' point. The police had used so much tear gas that its effects could be felt across the Golden Horn in the conservative districts of the old Ottoman city, but the ultras of Istanbul were at the centre of it all, begging for more.

Turkey went through a shock early in the summer of 2013, when scenes like these played out all over the country and, particularly, in its largest city. People had not expected such brutality in response to a peaceful environmental protest, nor could they have imagined how many around the country would take to the streets to protest the government's reaction. The Gezi Park movement was full of surprises; the ultras were one of them. Although their presence in the thick of the violence and their gleeful taunting of the police were nothing new, something was happening that most Turks had never believed possible: supporters of Galatasaray, Fenerbahçe and Beşiktaş were coming together.

In some countries it's not uncommon to see fans of rival teams put their differences aside and show solidarity in times of national crisis. Turkey was never one of those countries. Until the protests swept the nation, supporters of the Süper Lig's three most successful clubs were about as likely to find common ground as conservative leader Recep Tayyip Erdoğan would be to appear at an LGBTQ pride parade.

UltrAslan, the premier ultras group supporting Galatasaray, is known across Europe as one of the most fearsome football-supporters' outfits in the world. They became world famous for the 'Welcome to Hell' banners with which they greeted visitors to the old Ali Sami Yen Stadium, and their satanic imagery and ubiquitous flares make visiting the home of Turkey's most successful club a rather frightening experience.

The club, born out of the first European-style high school in Turkey, calls the western side of the Bosphorus home. The area around the school, known as Galatasaray, Beyoğlu or Pera, is the closest thing Istanbul has to a true centre, a stretch of old monuments and expensive shops sloping up from the Galata Tower to Taksim Square and, next to it, Gezi Park. Gala – also known as the Lions or the Conquerors of Europe – now play further inland in an arena with a capacity of more than fifty-two thousand, but their yellow-and-gold banners and shirts appear all over the European side of the city on match days. A tourist visiting Istanbul could easily surmise that Galatasaray was *the* force in the city's footballing world.

Fans of Fenerbahçe would have something to say about that. Hailing from the Asian side of the Bosphorus, the Yellow Canaries have won the league nineteen times to Gala's twenty-two, but their fan base is every bit as fervent. Their detractors accuse Fenerbahçe fans of being new-money statists, pointing to the fact that Erdoğan himself identifies as a supporter. While there are right-wing Fenerbahçe

STEPHEN WOOD is a writer and journalist based in New York who covers politics, sport and any combination of the two. His articles have appeared in *Jacobin*, *Paste* and *McSweeney's*. He also writes regularly for sports magazines.

supporters' groups (the same can be said of Galatasaray), there are vocally left-wing ones as well. Outside Left and Vamos Bien, which touts its opposition to 'industrialised' football, joined in during Gezi.

For most fans, however, the Gala–Fener divide is far and away the most important. The rivalry between the two clubs is as intense as any in sport. Most of the country has taken a side, and the Intercontinental Derby is always tense, if not worse. When the two teams contested the final of the Turkish Cup in 2016 the referee dished out a total of seven yellow cards and one red. For large portions of Süper Lig history, away fans have been banned from attending on derby day, and for good reason.

'Even for the firmest believers of the idea that a football match can only be better with the participation of both sides' fans, it is getting harder to object to the sports authorities' decision to keep the derbies open to one side only,' said a writer for the *Hürriyet Daily News* in 2012 when things were at their worst. 'The fracas that forced the wheelchair-basketball match between Galatasaray and Beşiktaş to be called off is the most recent example.'

Things had come to a head, horrifyingly, only two weeks before Gezi Park. Allegedly incensed by Fenerbahçe's fans' racist taunting of a Galatasaray player, a Lions' ultra stabbed a young Fenerbahçe supporter to death while waiting for a bus. Burak Yıldırım was not the first fan to lose his life to this rivalry, nor would he be the only young supporter Fenerbahçe would lose that summer.

Financially and in terms of historical success, Beşiktaş is the third of Istanbul's big three. Its ultras, however, are far and away the most politically and socially active. Situated downhill from Taksim and its tourist attractions, bumping up against

> 'Beşiktaş ultras have also been heard to chant "We are all Armenian" – no small thing in a country where discussion of its history regarding the treatment of its minorities is still largely taboo.'

the strait that divides east and west, the neighbourhood that gives Beşiktaş its name is vibrant and, traditionally, working class. More than the other big-three clubs, the Black Eagles identify with the area from which they arose, and many locals respond by giving their hearts and souls to the club.

That spirit drives Çarşı, Beşiktaş's famous ultras. The group, who frequently replace the A in their name with the anarchy symbol, claim to be 'against everything' but are, in fact, known for their support of far-left politics and a particularly radical brand of inclusivity. Çarşı were quick to claim 'We are all black!' after opposing fans hurled racist taunts at a black Beşiktaş player. They have also been heard to chant 'We are all Armenian' – no small thing in a country where discussion of its history regarding the treatment of its minorities is still largely taboo. No cause is too big or too small – Çarşı were equally supportive of Pluto after its demotion to the minor-planet catalogue, chanting, 'We are all Pluto!' Members of the far left, which long ago ceased to be a force in Turkish politics, find a place to express themselves among these ultras. Çarşı are quick to take up the causes of labour, the environment and anyone else they feel needs a protector, and as a result they are no strangers to dissent. Not only had they come up with a chant about tear gas ('Sık Bakalım') well before Gezi, they also knew how to mitigate its effects.

The Gezi Park protests began on 28 May 2013 with a simple environmental demonstration. A small group camped out in Gezi Park, a shady area adjacent to Taksim Square, in an attempt to stop it from being bulldozed and turned into an Ottoman-themed mall. The simple construction project was rife with symbolism, particularly because it came at a time when many feared the centre-right government was slipping into authoritarianism. After the police used pepper spray on the environmentalists and burned their tents, protesters flocked to the park and the adjacent square. Several days and nights of clashes between protesters and police followed. Every time the police tried to clear demonstrators out of the area, their numbers grew, and by June protesters were coming out in their tens of thousands in Istanbul, Ankara and other Turkish cities.

Soon Gezi Park was a movement, uniting all those who felt that the Erdoğan was becoming a dictator. That turned out to be a lot of people. Although Turkey's environmentalists, Kurds, feminists, leftists, LGBTQ community and others had all publicly expressed their grievances before, they had never come together in this way, nor had so many other Turks sympathised with them. Taksim Square took on a festival atmosphere. There were communal

Page 191: Fenerbahçe fans gather at the entrance to the team's home ground at the Şükrü Saracoğlu Stadium ahead of a local derby against Başakşehir.
Left: A Fenerbahçe fan near the stadium holding a huge club flag with a picture of Mustafa Kemal Atatürk at its centre.

BAŞAKŞEHIR

Unloved by the majority of supporters of the three main Istanbul football clubs – Galatasaray, Fenerbahçe and Beşiktaş – and wary of attending their matches for fear of being booed, Erdoğan decided to throw in his lot with İstanbul Başakşehir, an outsider team with no history and few fans. The club is an oddity within the Turkish football scene, which is characterised by an extremely strong bond between the historic clubs, often with over a century of history behind them, and their fans. None of this is true of Başakşehir, which was only founded in 1990 (under the name of İstanbul BB, which it kept until 2014) and owned at first by the municipality and now by the Ministry of Youth and Sports. Even though the team regularly finishes near the top of the Süper Lig (the highest division) – and actually won the championship for the first time in 2020 – its players are well used to taking to the field in front of a crowd of just a few thousand. To make things even more absurd, for years the home of İstanbul

Fenerbahçe fans **(above left)**
and Galatasaray fans **(above)**
arrive at the Şükrü Saracoğlu
Stadium to watch a game.

BB was the Atatürk Olympic Stadium,
which has a capacity of 76,000. Then
in 2014 came the change of name and
the move to the Fatih Terim Stadium in
the satellite town of Başakşehir, which
has been a stronghold of the AKP since
Erdoğan initiated its development when
he was mayor of Istanbul. The links with
the party are proven and extend from
the contract for the stadium – which was
awarded to the same holding company
involved in the revamp of Taksim Square
and the construction of the city's third
airport – to the sponsors and the seats in
the stands, which just happen to be in the
party's colours of orange and blue. The
inauguration of the stadium further sealed
the partnership, with Erdoğan taking
part in a friendly match and even scoring
a hat-trick, after which Başakşehir
permanently withdrew the number-12
shirt he had worn in his honour.

From national hero to traitor to the motherland is one way to describe the journey of Hakan Şükür, the 'Bull of the Bosphorus', perhaps the greatest Turkish footballer of all time: 112 caps for the national team, eight champions' titles, winner of the Europe-wide UEFA Cup with Galatasaray and member of the Turkey team that finished third in the 2002 World Cup. His fame survived his retirement, enabling him to enter parliament with the AKP thanks to his excellent relations both with Erdoğan and the influential cleric Fethullah Gülen, both of whom attended his wedding, as officiant and witness respectively. But when he controversially left the party a few years later, everything changed. The climate around him became increasingly hostile, forcing him to flee to the USA. Following the attempted coup of 2016 Şükür has been regarded as no better than a terrorist, accused of being a supporter of Gülen and even pursued thousands of miles away from Turkey: the bar he used to run was closed after threats were received, and it now seems that the former striker works as an Uber driver. Stones have been thrown at his wife's shop, his children have been insulted in the street, his accounts blocked in Turkey and his father imprisoned for a year after Erdoğan decided to make life hell for a high-profile Turk who dared to criticise him. The same fate befell another star of Turkish sport, who also lives in the USA and is the subject of an arrest warrant: Enes Kanter, who plays basketball for the Boston Celtics, even had his Turkish passport withdrawn during a visit to Indonesia. Unlike Şükür, however, Kanter is known to be a supporter of Gülen.

prayers, pop-up libraries, even concerts staged in this public space, but there was also the constant threat of police brutality.

As if drawn by the peculiar blend of festivity and danger that characterises so many Turkish match days, Çarşı quickly joined the demonstrations. They hoisted their banners and spray-painted their anarchist symbols, but they also brought a wealth of police-defying experience to a movement that badly needed it – as many of those who demonstrated during Gezi were new to confrontations with the authorities. In their accounts they often credit the ultras with keeping protesters safe, breaking up fights and instructing others on how to evade and take shelter from the police.

Just hours after Çarşı had appeared on the scene, Fenerbahçe and Galatasaray's ultras arrived. There was a feeling among all the left-leaning ultras that their involvement in this movement was pre-ordained. Videos from all over Istanbul appeared on social media, depicting marching lines of gold-and-red Galatasaray jerseys, blue-and-yellow Fenerbahçe kits and the black-and-white of Beşiktaş.

Then came the scenes that Turks had never imagined possible. One could have been forgiven for expecting violence when these groups met in the midst of a riot, but there was none. Instead there was solidarity. Images coming from Istanbul showed burly Galatasaray supporters locking arms with women in Beşiktaş colours. Gala and Fener supporters posed with Çarşı banners. Ultras from all three sides embraced draped in the Turkish flag and chanted, 'Shoulder to shoulder against fascism!' Just weeks before a young man had lost his life for wearing a Fenerbahçe shirt. Now there was only Istanbul United.

Çarşı's name and slogans became synonymous with the movement. The 'Sık

'Veterans of Gezi are divided: some say they failed to create a political movement, while others point to the park and say, "We won."'

Bakalım' chant could be heard wherever there was tear gas. They even had their meme turned back on them, as Twitter users proclaimed, 'We are all Çarşı!' Suddenly, every big-three supporter *could* be Çarşı. Fenerbahçe fans choked a bridge between Europe and Asia with their flags as they marched towards Taksim. When ultrAslan announced it did not want to be involved in the unrest, other Galatasaray fans carried on anyway. They sang the name of their star striker, Didier Drogba, whose mildly supportive comments they took as proof that their club resisted Erdoğan.

As far as anyone can tell, these demonstrations of unity arose organically. Some described them as inevitable. Although various supporters' groups made their presences known to varying degrees, hundreds of individual supporters of each club took part in the protests, often making a point to embrace those wearing their rival's colours. These individual acts were, in a way, the most profound.

Ultras tend to take on some kind of political affiliation, so perhaps it was inevitable that each club's leftists would find one another in the fray. But there had been millions of fans for whom club football was a blessedly separate from politics, and now *they* had taken to the streets.

Something had changed. The following September fans stormed the field and hurled chairs at police during the dying minutes of the first Beşiktaş–Galatasaray game since Gezi. Political statements were supposed to be banned from all matches, but Fenerbahçe's supporters solemnly sang about Ali İsmail Korkmaz, a nineteen-year-old Fenerbahçe fan beaten to death by the police during a Gezi Park protest in Eskişehir.

Of the thirty-five members of Çarşı arrested that summer, several faced life in prison on terrorism charges, although they were eventually acquitted. Recep Tayyip Erdoğan remained in power; he remains in power today. Gezi Park, too, remains. Anti-Erdoğan graffiti still pops up here and there, but by and large the city has moved on. Like the Occupy movement before it, the Gezi Park movement may have been too sprawling in its idealism to bring about lasting political change. In the years since the protests Erdoğan has consolidated power and gone after the press, bringing his nation closer to the authoritarian state the protesters feared. Veterans of Gezi are divided: some say they failed to create a political movement, while others point to the park and say, 'We won.'

If there is any cause for the ultras of Gezi to take heart, perhaps it is a similar symbolic victory. Turkey did not enter a new golden age that summer, nor did Gezi usher in an era of good feelings between the three warring clans. That era lasted only an instant, but the images it produced will live on as proof that Istanbul's ultras *can* agree on something. 🐦

Page 197: A member of the Beşiktaş ultras group Çarşı.
Left: Galatasaray fans at the exit from the metro tunnel leading to the Türk Telekom Arena, the club's new stadium in the Seyrantepe neighbourhood of the Sarıyer district of Istanbul.

A Sign of the Times

KALEYDOSKOP

Translated by Alan Thawley

With almost a thousand kilometres of coastline bridging the Aegean and the Mediterranean, Muğla Province in southwestern Turkey boasts one of the most extraordinary coastal landscapes anywhere – but is also among those that have been hardest hit by a combination of mass tourism and energy production. This growth in tourist numbers has been so meteoric that it led to the expansion of Dalaman international airport in 2014, raising its annual capacity to ten million passengers. Coupled with the exploitation of natural resources, the surge in tourism has led to a construction boom that is degrading the landscape. Where once there were rocks there are shop windows, and vineyards have been replaced by quarries ...

Overlooking a wide expanse of azure water, Ölüdeniz, the 'Land of Light' to the Lycians, or 'Dead Sea' in Turkish, is one of the busiest resorts in the area. If you head there from the port city of Fethiye, it is a fifteen-kilometre journey along a winding road that offers the promise of the sea below the sheer cliffs. Your arrival is announced by a procession of structures flanking both sides of the road: the façades of makeshift facilities, a collection of mini-markets, saunas, massage parlours, Chinese, Mexican and Ottoman restaurants, bureaux de change and trinket shops, with water slides in the background and bars that all offer the same non-stop happy hours with live sports and British pints. A ghost town for five months of the year, full of graceless buildings with no pretence of authenticity, it has no purpose other than the rapid consumption imposed by high-turnover tourism offering people a week in the sun.

The ultimate destination is the beach, a great strip of sand alongside the Blue Lagoon. Thanks to the powerful currents that keep the seawater clear and picture-postcard blue, Ölüdeniz was voted Turkey's best beach in 2006. But the attractions lie elsewhere: dozens of hang-gliders constantly pass over the beach, and many agencies offer flying lessons. Boats of all kinds are moored by the shore, from improbably huge Viking tourist ships to motorboats for small groups, which serve as taxis for daily excursions to nearby beaches.

Chief among these is Kelebekler Vadisi (Butterfly Valley), where, between May and June, forty different species of butterfly can be found, although they are becoming increasingly rare. The canyon is difficult to access by land, with its sheer rock walls, dense woods, natural waterfalls and sheltered beach, and until the 2000s it remained a paradise enjoyed exclusively by the few who risked the dangerous descent or had the means to approach by sea. Once the preserve of young hippies escaping the big cities, the valley is today a destination for organised day trips on motorboats (to the soundtrack of ear-splitting music) that moor right up to the shore. Although the terrain does not allow for large structures to be built, Kelebek now has more in the

loggerhead turtles come to the area to lay their eggs, but, disorientated by strobe lights and trance music, they began to desert the beach until a few local activists built cages, cordoned off the laying area and raised awareness of the phenomenon among the tourists.

Once a Greek area that was resettled by ethnic Turks between 1915 and 1918 during a period of widespread suppression of Christian minorities in Anatolia, the stretch of coastline known as Faralya was largely overlooked for many years and only rediscovered and reappraised as a tourist destination in the mid-1980s. Since the 2000s it has undergone transformations that have undermined the natural balance of the area.

Moving inland from the coast, Muğla Province has been the theatre of other environmental battles. Since 2014 production of electricity from lignite combustion has been increased at the area's three power plants, which were built in the 1980s. Extraction from the two mines that extend over 44,000 hectares has devastated the agriculture of the entire area; land, olive groves and vineyards were subject to compulsory purchase, the villages were emptied and the incidence of tumours has since skyrocketed.

In nearby Antalya Province, a few kilometres to the east, local people ran a dogged campaign against the construction of the fifth hydroelectric power plant on the River Alakır. In 2007, after an eight-year battle, they managed to have the valley, with its hundreds of endemic species, declared a protected area for nature. Here, too, though, the goals of energy independence and tourist exploitation increase the chances of drastically altering the face of the landscape through granting land concessions, construction contracts, building amnesties and land privatisations.

way of organised facilities, and in 2019 the valley's status was changed from a protected natural site to a 'sensitive' site, meaning work could begin on the construction of a surfaced road.

The same is true of the nearby Kabak Valley, a little further to the east, which is wider and has a road that runs six hundred metres above the sea. The very first campsites began to spring up there in the early 1990s. Located on the first stretch of the Lycian Way – a 540-kilometre coastal path dotted with remains from the Lycian, Roman and Byzantine eras – Kabak Valley was once accessible only on foot or by mule. Over time an unpaved road was laid here, too, and in 2018 work began on the construction of a second, surfaced access road parallel to the path through the rocks. Following a 2018 planning amnesty, when prefabs and improvised constructions were thrown up overnight, it now has more than thirty campsites and other structures. In high season, between July and August, the valley can accommodate up to five thousand people, causing an unsustainable environmental impact on the fragile balance of the 200-metre long beach, which had remained largely unexplored until 1987. Thanks to its isolation,

An Author Recommends

A film, a book and a song to understand Turkey, chosen by:

ELIF SHAFAK

Elif Shafak is an award-winning British-Turkish author, who writes in both Turkish and English. The most widely read female author in Turkey, she has published seventeen books, eleven of which are novels, and her work has been translated into fifty languages. In 2019 her most recent novel *10 Minutes 38 Seconds in this Strange World* was shortlisted for the Booker Prize and chosen as Blackwell's Book of the Year. Her 2010 novel, *The Forty Rules of Love*, was chosen by the BBC as one of the 100 Novels that Shaped Our World. Shafak holds a PhD in political science and has taught at universities in Turkey, the USA and the UK, including St Anne's College, Oxford, where she is an honorary fellow.
www.elifshafak.com

THE FILM

**CROSSING THE BRIDGE:
THE SOUND OF ISTANBUL**
Fatih Akin, 2005

I adore this documentary by the very talented film director Fatih Akin. *Crossing the Bridge* is moving, charming. It is a sociological – and, to a certain extent, political – work of art about a massively complicated metropolis: Istanbul. Music is at the heart of everything here, so the question is, can you tell the story of a city as complicated and elusive as Istanbul through its songs, ballads, melodies and musicians, both professional and amateur? This fascinating film shows that you can. Istanbul is a city of old and new, ambitions and ruins, dreams and scars, constant migrations and displacements, newcomers, locals, natives and then expats, exiles and those who have to leave ... and the music of the city reflects all these. It is also brilliant that the film is narrated by Alexander Hacke, a remarkable musician known for his work with Einstürzende Neubauten, the German industrial-rock band. He leads you through the city, and I like the fact that an 'outsider with a genuine interest and clear love for the city' is our guide here. There are many wonderful artists covered in this documentary, but, if I may, I'd like to highlight in particular the Kurdish singer Aynur – she is wonderful – and there is a song performed in the middle of the Bosphorus by the psychedelic band Baba Zula which is breathtaking. As one of the characters in the documentary notes, Istanbul is a remarkable city of sounds, and even if you lock your door and close your windows you will still hear its melodies.

THE BOOK

BEYOND THE WALLS: SELECTED POEMS
Nâzim Hikmet
Carcanet/Anvil Press Poetry, 2002

One of my favourite poets in the Turkish language is Nâzim Hikmet. I was a high-school student when I read him for the first time. Something shifted in me, but, to be honest, I didn't quite know what to make of him. He puzzled me. His writing was unlike anything I had read before. The experience was almost like seeing a breathtaking landscape for the first time and not being able to process it all at once. Then, a year or two later when I'd started university, I picked him up again, and this time I read everything I could find by him and about him. I developed this amazing obsession with him, his poems, his life. What I most like about him is the way he brings together contrasts and merges them in harmony. There is anger in his writing, there is fight, resistance, rebellion, revolution. He cares about freedom, human dignity, equality, justice; at the same time there is enormous care, tenderness, gentleness, compassion, friendship and love. Nâzim is that rare kind of human being who can talk about important ideals while appreciating the morning breeze, the blossom, the softness of silk between your fingers, the drop of rain on a leaf, the smile of a stranger you will never see again. The way he weaves seemingly mundane details in with bigger questions is remarkable. His voice is timeless. This is the man who said, 'The most beautiful sea hasn't been crossed yet. The most beautiful child hasn't grown up yet. Our most beautiful days we haven't seen yet. And the most beautiful words I wanted to tell you ... I haven't said yet.' Anyone who wants to understand Turkey's soul – past and present and future – should read Nâzim Hikmet. Not silently, but boldly and out loud, listening to the rhythm, the energy, the flow ...

THE SONG

SUSAMAM
Şanışer feat. Fuat Ergin, Ados, Hayki, Server Uraz, Beta, Tahribad-ı İsyan, Sokrat St, Ozbi, Deniz Tekin, Sehabe, Yeis Sensura, Aspova, Defkhan, Aga B, Mirac, Mert Şenel and Kamufle, 2019

I wonder if I might cheat a little in this section and, instead of recommending an album, recommend a recent song? The piece is called 'Susamam', which in Turkish means 'I Cannot Remain Silent'. It is a very powerful and courageous work of art, about fifteen minutes long, that brings together a number of young musicians – eighteen in all – most of them involved in rap, so if you want to learn something about some of the most talented musicians working in Turkey today then this is the video to watch, this is the song to listen to. It goes without saying that in a country where there is no freedom of speech, rappers have been repeatedly targeted by the authorities – yet it is amazing to see them coming together, writing such powerful lyrics and speaking up and speaking out. It is one of the most political songs made in recent years, and it touches upon various issues of fundamental importance – from human rights to freedom of speech, from cultural degeneration to the demise of kindness and civility, from women's rights to the climate emergency. There is a line in the song that runs: 'If you were to be arrested one night unfairly, unjustly (in Turkey), you would not be able to find a journalist to cover your story because they are all locked up behind bars.' The rhythm, the lyrics but also the friendship, the camaraderie and the chutzpah that clearly went into this song are all fascinating. As soon as it was posted online, millions of people watched it and shared it. In a nutshell, it is an important song that shows that even under the darkest of circumstances art is, and has always been, about resistance.

The Playlist

**AÇIK RADYO
AND KALEYDOSKOP**
Translated by Alan Thawley

You can listen
to this playlist at:
open.spotify.com/user/iperborea

Açık Radyo (Open Radio in English) is an independent radio station founded in Istanbul in 1995 that broadcasts on 94.9 FM as well as streaming over the internet. The brainchild of Ömer Madra, an intellectual who cut his teeth in the political climate of 1970s Turkish activism, along with more than ninety other shareholders drawn from Turkish left-wing cultural circles, Açık Radyo grew out of a desire to give a platform to independent news and the country's many vibrant socio-cultural initiatives. The station, which is funded mainly by donations from its listeners, remains a fundamental point of reference for independent news and journalism, and the numerous programmes produced by volunteers over the years have provided an outlet for the feminist and environmental movements, Kurdish and Armenian literature, LGBTQ issues and the various struggles for rights that have run through Turkey's history. But, while the microphones of Açık Radyo have broadcast a quarter of a century of history that has been marked by many periods of darkness, struggle and resistance, it champions music, too.

This playlist, put together by Açık Radyo, comprises a selection of names that have left their mark on the Turkish music scene from the mid-1990s to the present. At the time the station was founded Turkey was at a cultural crossroads. While the privatisation of television and radio contributed to a cultural expansion, much of what was produced was mediocre – but this was also a period in which many important musicians began to reach a wider listenership. The playlist demonstrates a continuity of musical tradition, with the names of artists who distinguished themselves during that cultural explosion and are still relevant today (Neşet Ertaş, Sezen Aksu, Fikret Kızılok) alongside those from more recent generations (Ayyuka, Nekropsi, Lalalar), while not forgetting to pay due tribute to some of their illustrious and innovative predecessors, a group of original artists, both popular and pioneering. In putting the list together the decision was taken to range across different genres, from folk to psychedelia to jazz. The result is a short list, undoubtedly incomplete, but eclectic – and *açık*.

1

Ahmet Kaya
*Hadi Bize
Gidelim*
2001

2

Sezen
Aksu
Kutlama
2008

3

Neşet
Ertaş
Gönül Dağı
1990

4

Fikret
Kızılok
Yeter Ki
1993

5

Nazan Öncel
*Sokarım
Politikana*
1999

6

Lalalar
*Hata Benim
Göbek Adım*
2019

7

ZeN
*Burda Bizden
Başkası Yok Ki*
1999

8

Ayyuka
Maslak Halayı
2019

9

Nekropsi
Erciyes Şokta
2006

10

Ezhel
Olay
2019

11

İslandman
Ağıt
2016

12

Ayşe Tütüncü
Panayır
2005

13

Yaşar Kurt
Anne
2003

Explore Further

NON-FICTION

Ahmet Altan
I Will Never See the World Again
Granta Books, 2019 (UK)
Other Press, 2019 (USA)

Taner Akçam
*Killing Orders: Talat Pasha's Telegrams
and the Armenian Genocide*
Palgrave Macmillan, 2018

Hrant Dink
Two Close Peoples Two Distant Neighbours
Hrant Dink Foundation and the
Gomidas Institute, 2014

Can Dündar
*We Are Arrested: A Journalist's
Notes from a Turkish Prison*
Biteback Publishing, 2016

Nedim Gürsel
Deep Anatolia
IAU International, 2019

Bettany Hughes
Istanbul: A Tale of Three Cities
Weidenfeld and Nicholson, 2017 (UK)
Da Capo Press, 2017 (USA)

Orhan Pamuk
Istanbul: Memories of a City
Faber and Faber, 2006

Alev Scott
*Turkish Awakening: Behind the
Scenes of Modern Turkey*
Faber and Faber, 2015

Norman Stone
Turkey: A Short History
Thames and Hudson, 2012

Ece Temelkuran
The Insane and the Melancholy
Zed Books, 2016

FICTION

Elliot Ackerman
Red Dress in Black and White
Knopf, 2020

Selahattin Demirtaş
Dawn
Hogarth, 2018

Aslı Erdoğan
The Stone Building and Other Places
City Lights, 2018

Hakan Günday
More: A Novel
Arcade Publishing, 2016

Sema Kaygusuz
The Well of Trapped Words: Selected Stories
Comma Press, 2015

Orhan Pamuk
A Strangeness in My Mind
Faber and Faber, 2016 (UK)
Vintage, 2016 (USA)

Elif Shafak
10 Minutes 38 Seconds in this Strange World
Viking, 2019 (UK)
Bloomsbury, 2019 (USA)

Burhan Sönmez
Labyrinth
Other Press, 2019

Hasan Ali Toptaş
Reckless
Bloomsbury, 2016

FILM

Fatih Akin
Head-On (Gegen die Wand)
2004

Nuri Bilge Ceylan
Winter Sleep (Kış Uykusu)
2014

Nuri Bilge Ceylan
The Wild Pear Tree (Ahlat Ağacı)
2018

Metin Erksan
Dry Summer (Susuz Yaz)
1963

Deniz Gamze Ergüven
Mustang
2015

Reha Erdem
Kosmos
2009

Şerif Gören and Yılmaz Güney
Yol
1982

Semih Kaplanoğlu
Egg (Yumurta), Milk (Süt), Honey (Bal)
2007, 2008, 2010

Ferzan Özpetek
Hamam: The Turkish Bath (Hamam)
1997

Yavuz Turgul
The Bandit (Eşkıya)
1996

Graphic design and art direction: Tomo Tomo and Pietro Buffa

Photography: Nicola Zolin
The photographic content was curated by Prospekt Photographers.

Illustrations: Edoardo Massa
Infographics and cartography: Pietro Buffa

Managing editor (English-language edition): Simon Smith

Thanks to: Açık Radyo, Tuncay Akgün, Giulia Ansaldo, Nicolò Bagnolini, Martina Barlassina, Marco Cacioppo, Bruno Cianci, Ebru Değirmenci, Carlotta De Sanctis, Selçuk Erdem, Andrea Gessner, Ersin Karabulut, Paolo Lodigiani, Valentina Marcella, Lea Nocera, Çağrı Sinci, Burhan Sönmez, Sevi Sönmez, Nicola Verderame

The opinions expressed in this publication are those of the authors and do not purport to reflect the views and opinions of the publishers.

http://europaeditions.com/thepassenger
http://europaeditions.co.uk/thepassenger
#ThePassengerMag

The Passenger – Turkey
© Iperborea S.r.l., Milan, and Europa Editions 2021

Translators: Kate Ferguson (Turkish), Ekin Oklap (Turkish), Stephen Smithson (German), Alan Thawley (Italian)
All translations © Iperborea S.r.l., Milan, and Europa Editions, 2021 except 'I Rap Istanbul', 'Eros and Thanatos at the Restaurant' © Ekin Oklap, 2021

ISBN: 9781787702424

Printed on Munken Pure thanks to the support of Arctic Paper

Printed by ELCOGRAF S.p.A., Verona, Italy

The Big Dig
© Elif Batuman, 2015. Used by permission of the Wylie Agency (UK) Ltd. First published in *The New Yorker*, 24 August 2015

Don't Call Them Soap Operas is a chapter from *New Kings of the World* by Fatima Bhutto, published in 2019 by Columbia Global Reports. © Fatima Bhutto, 2019

Turkey's Thirty-Year Coup
© Dexter Filkins, 2016. First published in *The New Yorker*, 10 October 2016

Business à la Turca is an adapted and updated chapter from *Turkish Awakening* by Alev Scott, published in 2015 by Faber and Faber. © Alev Scott, 2020. Used by permission of Alev Scott c/o Georgina Capel Associates Ltd, 29 Wardour Street, London, W1D 6PS, and Faber and Faber Ltd

Eros and Thanatos at the Restaurant
© Sema Kaygusuz, 2020

Of Jinns and Light
© Burhan Sönmez, 2020

The Roots of Turkish Nationalism is an adapted chapter from *Türkei verstehen: Von Atatürk bis Erdoğan* by Gerhard Schweizer, published in 2016 by Klett-Cotta Verlag. © J.G. Cotta'sche Buchhandlung Nachfolger GmbH, 2016

Washing Away History: Hasankeyf and the Ilısu Dam
© Ercan y Yılmaz, 2020

'I Rap Istanbul': From Kreuzberg to Turkey and Back
© Begüm Kovulmaz, 2020

The Sharp End of the Pencil: Satire in the Age of Erdoğan
© Valentina Marcella, 2020

Ultras United
© Stephen Wood, 2017. First published in *These Football Times* under the title 'How Gezi Park Brought Together the Ultras of Galatasaray, Fenerbahçe and Beşiktaş' on 28 March 2017

An Author Recommends
© 2020 Aleph Libros Ltd. The right of Elif Shafak to be identified as the author of this work has been asserted by her in accordance with the Copyright Designs and Patents Act 1988